WILD FLOWERS
OF BRITAIN AND NORTHERN EUROPE

WILD FLOWERS
OF BRITAIN AND NORTHERN EUROPE

MARILYN JONES

Illustrated by
Wendy Bramall

Consultant
Richard Mabey

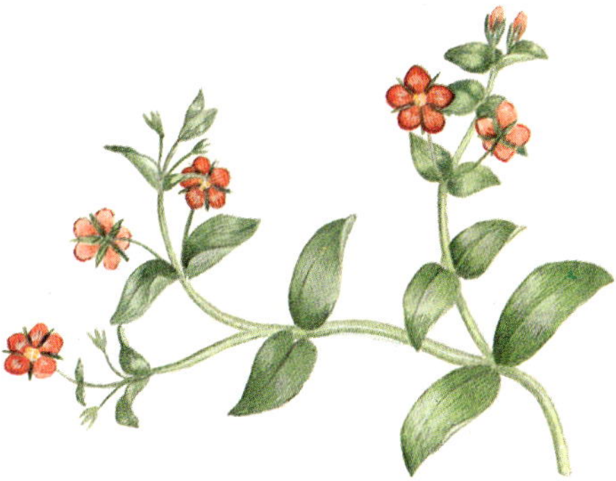

Kingfisher Books

First published in 1980.
This edition published in 1985 by Kingfisher Books Limited
Elsley Court, 20 – 22 Great Titchfield Street, London W1P 7AD
A Grisewood & Dempsey Company

BRITISH LIBRARY CATALOGUING IN PUBLICATION DATA
Jones, Marilyn
Wild flowers. – (Kingfisher guides)
1. Wild flowers–Europe–Identification
I. Title
582.13'094 QK281
ISBN 0 86272 057 5

Designed and edited by Eric Inglefield
Colour separations by Newsele Litho, Milan, London
Printed and bound in Italy by Vallardi Industrie
Grafiche, Milan

CONTENTS

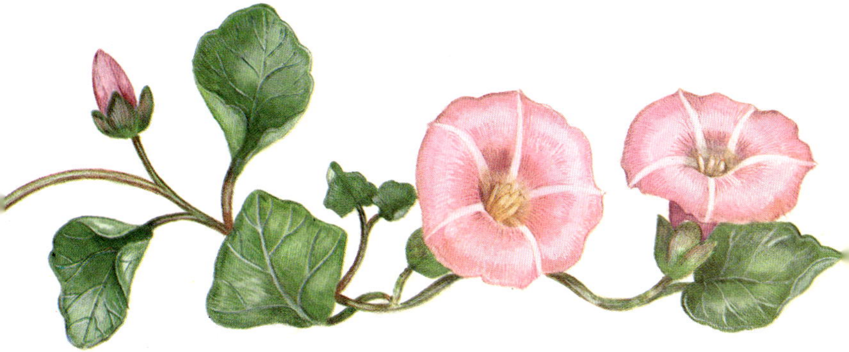

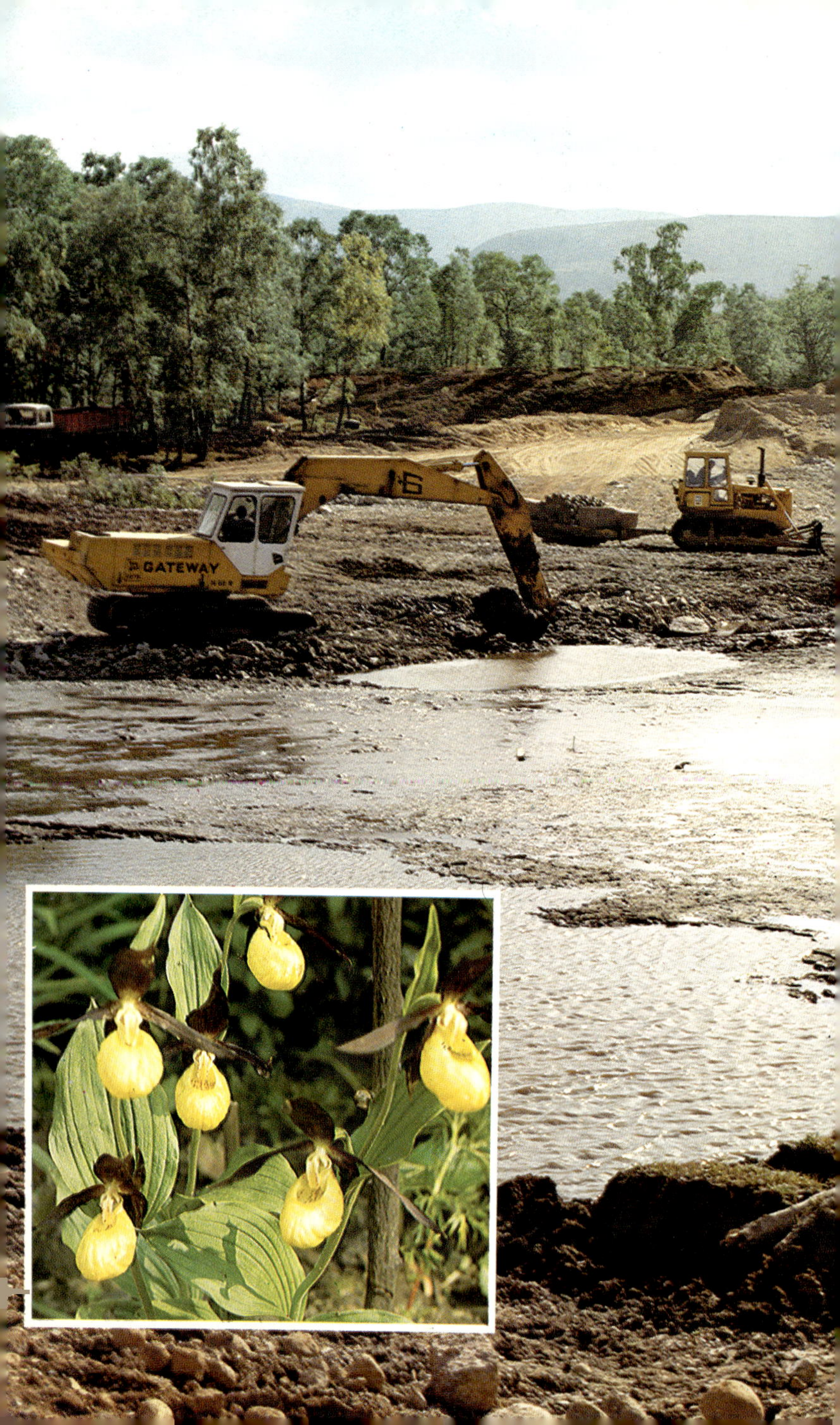
GATEWAY

INTRODUCTION

In the past, wild plants had many uses. In addition to those valued for their medicinal or supposedly magical properties many plants had common household uses. They served as sources of food, flavouring and dyes. Today, wild flowers are valued primarily for their beauty, although an awareness of the usefulness of any common species has grown in recent years. The plants included in this book are all widely distributed throughout the British Isles and northern Europe. Most of them grow in easily accessible places, such as the coast, along hedgerows and roadsides, and picnic areas, and are, by and large, those which the reader is most likely to find. Many of the plants will be familiar as garden weeds, but even these have their uses – Chickweed is delicious in sandwiches!

A few seed suppliers stock a limited range of wild flower seeds, such as Cowslip, that are suitable for garden planting, and these should be used in preference to collecting from the wild. They should not be planted outside the garden as they may compete with and possibly destroy the existing natural vegetation.

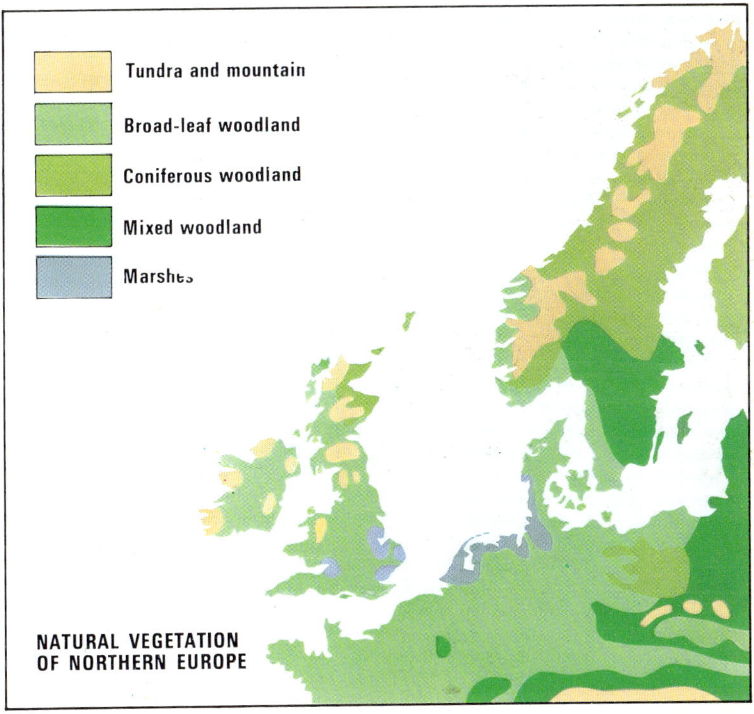

◀ *The survival of many plants, including the rare Lady's Slipper Orchid, is today being threatened by the destruction of their habitats. To help to solve this problem, nature reserves have been set up in many areas.*

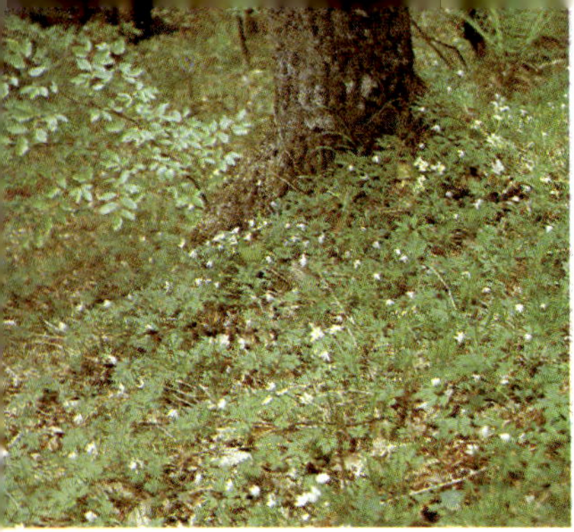

Deciduous woodland with Primroses (yellow) and Wood Anemones (white).

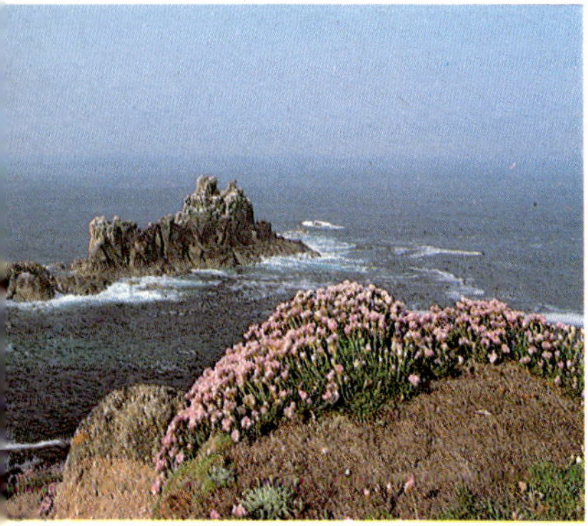

Coastal areas offer a good habitat for cushion plants such as Thrift.

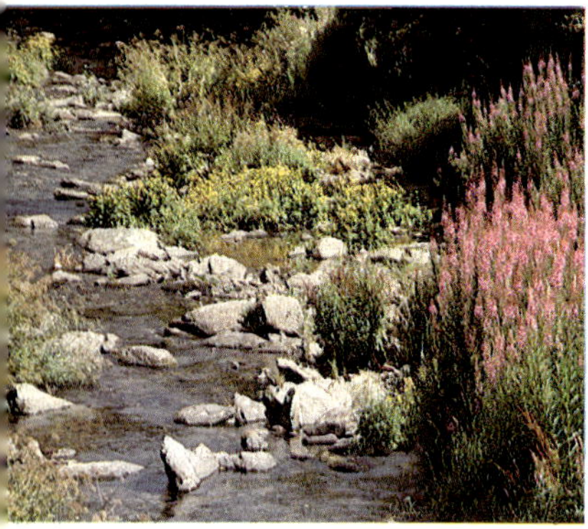

Freshwater habitats support a wide variety of water-loving plants.

Climate and Vegetation

The temperate climate of northern Europe has a considerable influence on the vegetation, and in the absence of interference by man most of the lowlands would be covered by woodland. In the far north and on mountains, pine or birch woods or a naturally treeless zone often persist, whereas most natural vegetation of the lowlands has been replaced by agriculture.

Major Habitats

A well-grown *hedgerow* is similar to a strip of woodland and supports many woodland plants. Banks, roadside verges and ditches along the hedge add to the variety of this habitat and the number of species growing there.

Deciduous woodland consists of trees which lose their leaves in winter, and lower-growing, shade-tolerant herbs and shrubs.

Mountains, upland **moors** and the dricr lowland **heath** have relatively few species. Moor and heathland both occur on acid soils and are often carpeted with heather and species of heath.

Freshwater habitats include wet places such as marshes and bogs, as well as the open water of streams, ponds, lakes and ditches.

Coastal habitats are inhospitable to many plants due to the combination of salt spray, poor soils and exposed position.

Grassland may support a variety of low-growing herbs as well as grasses. Older permanent grassland, especially on chalk or limestone, is usually richer in species than newer grassland.

Waste- and farmland may support a wide variety of weeds.

Parts of a Flowering Plant

The flower is the reproductive part of the plant and, in the case of insect-pollinated flowers, is often highly coloured. The simpler kinds of flower consist of the male and female reproductive organs, surrounded by an outer ring of coloured petals in turn surrounded by an outer ring of green sepals. Flowers are very important when identifying a plant. The shape and number of parts are usually constant for each species, although the colour may vary.

Leaves are the factories in which the plant manufactures its food from sunlight, water and carbon dioxide. They may be undivided or divided into separate leaflets, and the margins may be variously indented.

The stem, which bears the flowers and leaves, may stand upright, climb by twisting round a support, or creep along the ground.

Roots are the invisible part of the plant that anchors it in the soil and absorbs water and minerals. In some species part of the root is used for food storage. Root systems are far more extensive than is often realized; when a plant is uprooted most of the very fine roots are broken off and never seen.

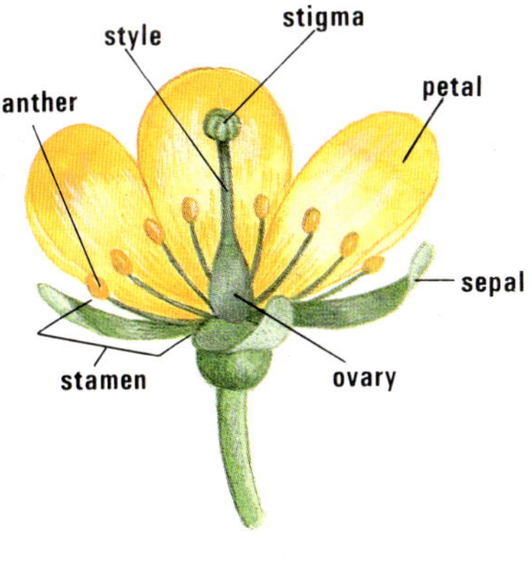

SECTION THROUGH A TYPICAL FLOWER

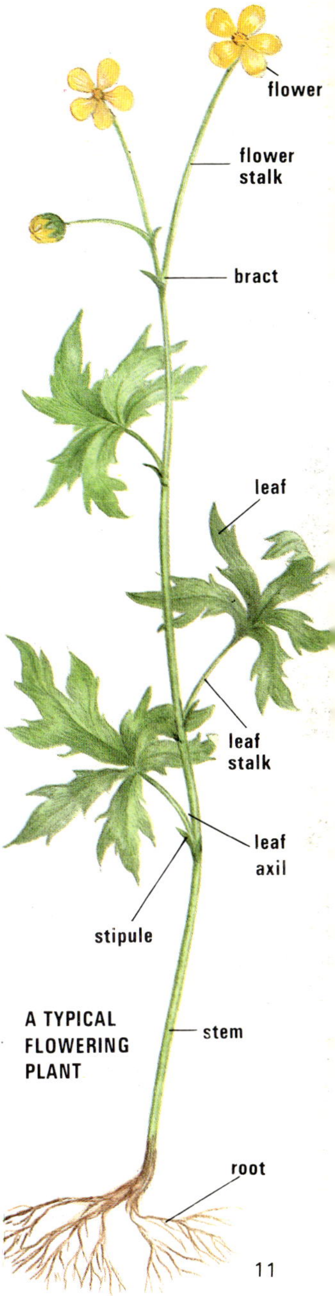

A TYPICAL FLOWERING PLANT

Reproduction in Flowering Plants

On fine summer days insects can be seen visiting flowers, attracted by the scent and colour. They are in search of food in the form of nectar and pollen. Bees and butterflies with their long tongues usually feed from long-throated flowers. Beetles and flies, with their short tongues, are restricted to short flowers. Some flowers have dark streaks known as *insect guide lines*, which lead the insect towards the male and female organs at the flower centre. Pollen can be likened to the sperm of a male animal, and some is carried inadvertently on insects' bodies from the anthers of one flower to the female stigma of another. This is called *cross-pollination* and usually causes a high seed-set. If a flower is not cross-pollinated then it is usually capable of *self-pollination*, when pollen from the anthers is shed on the stigma of the same flower. Some flowers are wind-pollinated. They do not need to be showy and are usually small and greenish, as in the Common Nettle. Other pollinators, in the tropics, are humming birds and even bats.

When the pollen reaches the stigma, each grain produces a tube which grows down the style to fertilize the *ovules*, or eggs, in the ovary. Once fertilized, the eggs ripen into seeds and the ovary forms a *fruit*. For most people the word fruit means the juicy, edible kind, but there are also dry fruits. The seeds must then be dispersed from the parent plant in order to avoid over-crowding and to colonize new areas.

Fleshy fruits are eaten by birds and other animals. The seeds are excreted unharmed and germinate where they are dropped. *Dry fruits* bearing hooks (*burs*) catch on clothing and the fur of animals and can be transported long distances. The *capsule* is a common type of dry fruit which splits to release the seeds, though some dry fruits, such as nuts, need to rot before the seed can germinate. Dispersal can also be by wind, as in the *plumed fruits* of dandelion clocks.

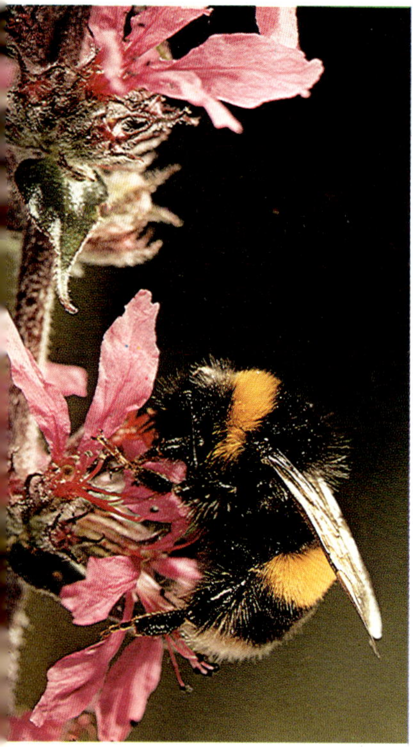

The Bumble-bee is one of the many kinds of insect which pollinate flowering plants. The pollen sticks to the bee's fur and is later gathered by the bee into 'pollen baskets' on the hind legs.

Conservation

Prehistoric people in northern Europe began to clear huge tracts of natural forest to make way for their crops and animals. They created a variety of man-made habitats, such as hedgerows, grazing land, coppice woodland, ditches and ponds. Such habitats add variety to the landscape and support a wide range of plant species. However, modern farming methods are destroying many of these habitats. Hedges are being destroyed to make way for larger fields, and marshes and water-meadows are being drained, making the species which can only grow there particularly vulnerable. Added to modern farming practice is the spread of a rising population and its housing. These are the main factors causing impoverishment of the countryside. The creation of nature reserves is important to preserve as many kinds of habitat as possible in which natural life can flourish.

Photographing wild flowers is preferable to picking, and on no account should they be uprooted. In fact it is illegal to uproot certain plants in some countries.

Naming and Classifying Plants

Apart from common names, each type of plant has a scientific Latin name. Latin has been internationally agreed upon to avoid the confusion of common names in many languages. The Latin name is in two parts: the *genus* (plural: *genera*), which can be likened to a surname, followed by the *species*, a kind of forename; for example, *Ranunculus acris* (Meadow Buttercup) and *Ranunculus repens* (Creeping Buttercup) are different species in the same genus. Just as similar species are grouped into genera, so similar genera are grouped into *families*.

How to Use this Book

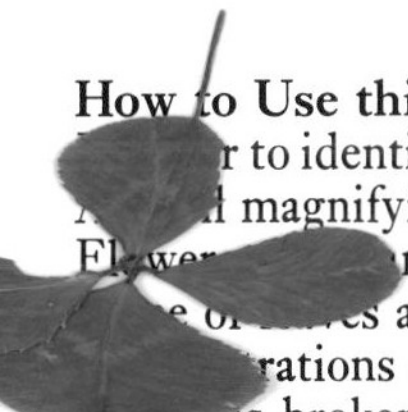

[illegible] to identify a plant, examine it carefully, making notes if necessary. [illegible] magnifying glass or hand lens and a ruler are useful at this stage. El[illegible] and structure, the arrangement of flowers and leaves, the [illegible]e of [illegible]es and any fruits, and the habitat should be compared with [illegible]ations and descriptions in this book. The description of each [illegible] is broken into sub-headings for ease of reference, with an introduction including habit, height and habitat. Difficult groups of very closely related species are represented by a single species. There is also a description for each family. All measurements are averages, and the illustrations are not all drawn to the same scale but are usually smaller than life-size.

Finally, although this book can include only a very small number of the flowering plants in Britain and northern Europe, those included are common enough to be found easily.

DICOTYLEDONS

The families up to page 107 are *dicotyledons*. They differ from the *monocotyledons* (page 108 onwards) in usually having net-veined leaves, flower-parts in fours or fives and a double seed leaf.

BUTTERCUP FAMILY
Ranunculaceae

The structure of certain flowers in the Buttercup family is often regarded as primitive, as in all the examples of the family shown here. There are many stamens. The sepals are sometimes petal-like, as in the Wood Anemone. Many species are acrid-tasting and poisonous to livestock.

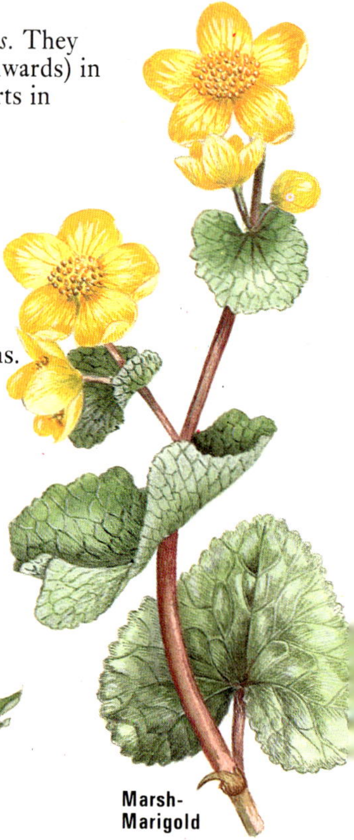

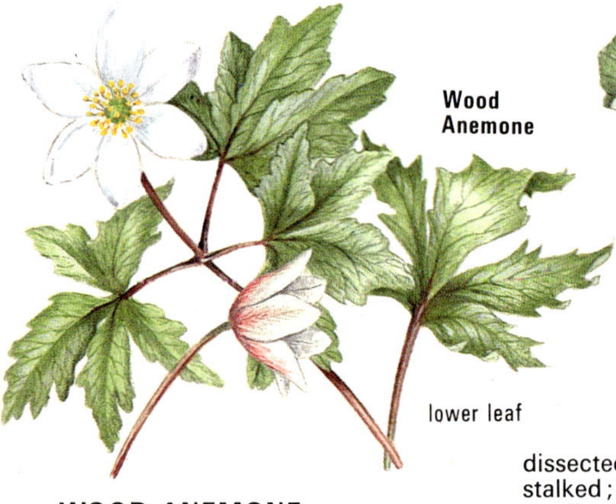

WOOD ANEMONE
Anemone nemorosa

A rather delicate, hairless plant of broad-leaved woodland, hedgebank and upland meadow, it grows 6-30 cm high. Like many woodland plants the Wood Anemone makes use of the sunlight of early spring for flowering before the trees come into leaf.
Flower: white or pink-tinged, 2-4 cm across, no petals but 6-7 petal-like sepals; stamens many.
Flower arrangement: solitary, terminal.
Flowering time: March-May.
Leaf: 1 or 2 long-stalked basal leaves of 3 segments, each segment deeply dissected, coarsely toothed, shortly stalked; upper leaves in whorl of 3, smaller with flattened stalks.
Fruit: many downy achenes in nodding heads.

MARSH-MARIGOLD
Caltha palustris

Although this stout plant has flowers that look like large Buttercups, its broad, shining, heart-shaped leaves and hollow flower stalks betray its true identity. It grows in marshy ground, often near streams, and may either be erect, to a height of 15-30 cm, or creeping.
Flower: bright golden yellow, 1·5-5 cm across; petal-like sepals, 5 or more; stamens many.

Flowerarrangement: few-flowered cyme.
Flowering time: March-July.
Leaf: broadly heart-shaped, teeth blunt or pointed; basal leaves long-stalked, upper often kidney-shaped, stalkless.
Fruit: head of 5-15 follicles, erect or curved back.

MEADOW BUTTERCUP

Ranunculus acris

Commonly found in meadows and pasture, this Buttercup grows up to 100 cm high. The stem is much branched and erect above. The very similar, common Creeping Buttercup (*Ranunculus repens*) has a creeping, rooting stem, furrowed flower stalk and stalked middle leaf segment.
Flower: glossy, bright yellow, 1·5-2·5 cm across; petals 5; sepals lying against petals; stamens many; flower stalk not furrowed.
Flower arrangement: irregular cyme.
Flowering time: April-October.
Leaf: more or less hairy; lower leaf with long stalk, palmate with 2-7 deeply toothed segments, middle segment not stalked; uppermost leaves stalkless, deeply cut.
Fruit: achenes many, hairless, each with short hook, in a round head.

LESSER CELANDINE

Ranunculus ficaria

One of the early spring flowers, Lesser Celandine has more petals than a Buttercup and glossy, heart-shaped leaves. It grows 5-30 cm high on hedgebanks, in woods and stream-sides. The roots form tubers.
Flower: bright golden yellow, whitening with age at petal-base, opening only on fine days, 1·5-5 cm across; petals 8-12, more or less pointed; sepals 3; stamens many.
Flower arrangement: solitary.
Flowering time: March-May.
Leaf: broadly heart-shaped, dark green, hairless; basal leaves long-stalked, in a rosette.
Fruit: achenes, many, downy.
Uses: the tubers look like piles and were used in their treatment in the belief that like cures like. Farmers also used Celandine, as they did Buttercups, to charm more milk from cows.

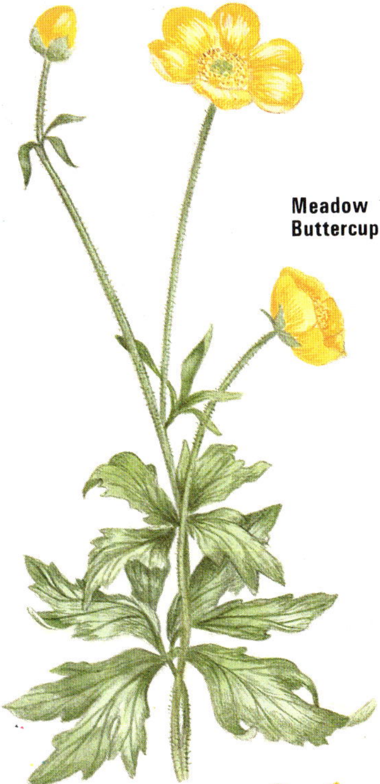

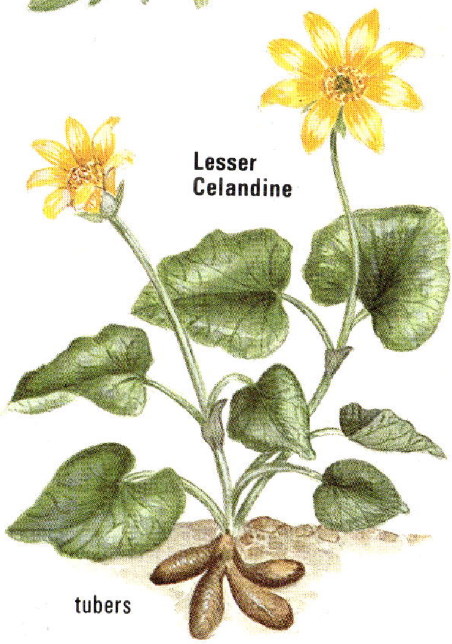

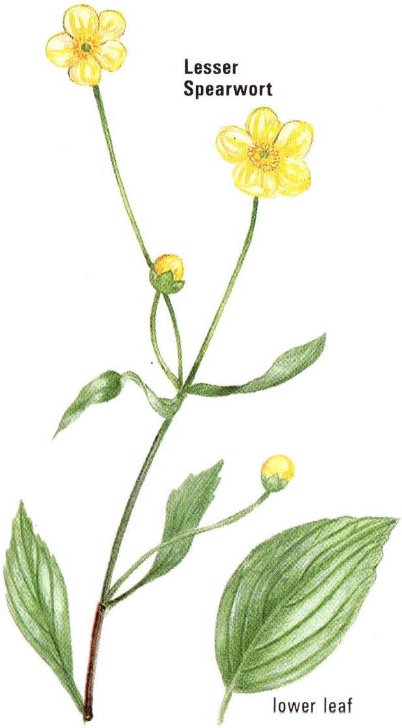

LESSER SPEARWORT

Ranunculus flammula

This is a Buttercup of wet places easily distinguished by its undissected leaves and pale, rather than golden, yellow flowers. Erect or creeping, with a hollow stem, and usually hairless, it grows between 8 and 80 cm high. Irritant poisons are present in larger amounts than in other Buttercups.

Flower: pale yellow, glossy, 8-20 mm across, petals 5; sepals 5; stamens many; flower stalk grooved.

Flower arrangement: solitary or in a cyme.

Flowering time: May-September.

Leaf: lower leaves circular, stalked; upper leaves stalkless, smaller, pointed, parallel-veined, with or without teeth.

Fruit: achenes, hairless, in a round head.

THREAD-LEAVED WATER-CROWFOOT

Ranunculus trichophyllus

This Water-crowfoot has small, white flowers and grows in ponds, slow streams and ditches. There are no floating leaves, and the needle-like segments of the submerged leaves do not lie flat. Several other species of Water-crowfoot grow in N. Europe, some of which have entire, floating leaves in addition to submerged.

Flower: white, petal-base yellow, 8-10 mm across; petals 5, not touching at edges; stamens 5-15.

Flower arrangement: solitary, opening above surface of water.

Flowering time: May-June.

Leaf: all submerged, finely dissected, bristle-like, not lying in one plane, 2-4 cm, shortly stalked.

Fruit: achenes; stalk usually less than 4 cm.

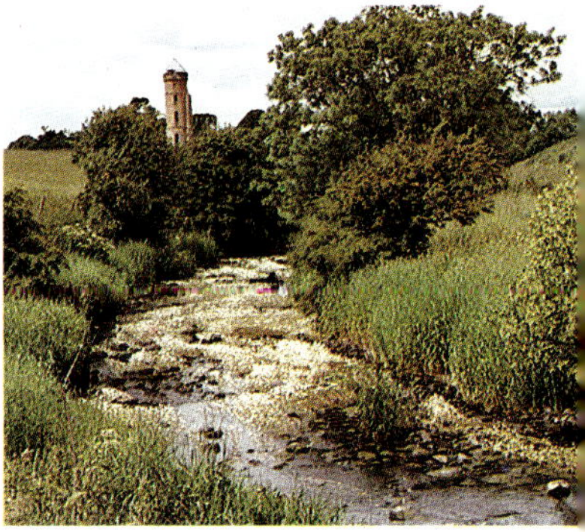

A bright mass of flowering Water-crowfoot.

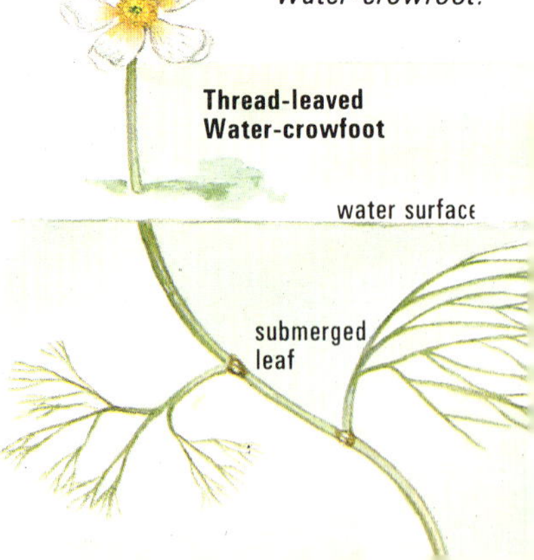

WATER-LILY FAMILY
Nymphaeaceae

Water-lilies grow in fresh water, the flowers and most of the leaves floating on the surface, with their roots in the mud. The leaves may cover large areas of water. As with the Buttercup family, the Water-lilies are considered to have a primitive flower structure.

YELLOW WATER-LILY
Nuphar lutea

Growing in freshwater lakes, ponds and slow streams, the Yellow Water-lily is more widely distributed than the White. The floating leaves are oval compared with the almost circular White Water-lily leaves.

Flower: bright yellow, cup-shaped, smelling of alcohol, 4-6 cm across, rising clear of the water; sepals 4-6, large, petal-like, rounded; stamens many; stigma flat with 15-20 radiating ridges.

Flower arrangement: solitary.

Flowering time: June-August.

Leaf: floating, oval, 12-40 × 9-30 cm, entire with a deep cleft where stalk joins; veins forked, not joined at leaf margin; submerged leaves thin, lettuce-like.

Fruit: bottle-shaped, ripening above water.

Uses: Water-lilies, not surprisingly, were held to have cooling properties. Gerard's *Herbal* of 1633 states, 'the root of the Yellow cureth hot diseases of the kidnies and bladder.'

WHITE WATER-LILY
Nymphaea alba

The White Water-lily grows in standing or slow-flowing water up to a depth of 3 m. It is more tolerant of polluted water than many other water plants. The large, floating flowers are scented.

Flower: white, 10-20 cm across, floating; 20-25 pointed petals; sepals 4; stamens many; stigma flat with 15-20 radiating ridges.

Flower arrangement: solitary, on long stalks arising from root.

Flowering time: June-September.

Leaf: floating, more or less circular, 10-30 cm, entire with deep cleft where stalk joins, veins joined around edge of leaf.

Fruit: flask-shaped, sometimes spherical, ripening underwater; seeds float, aiding dispersal.

Uses: the roots were sometimes eaten in parts of N. Europe, and Elizabethans ate seed and root to promote chastity.

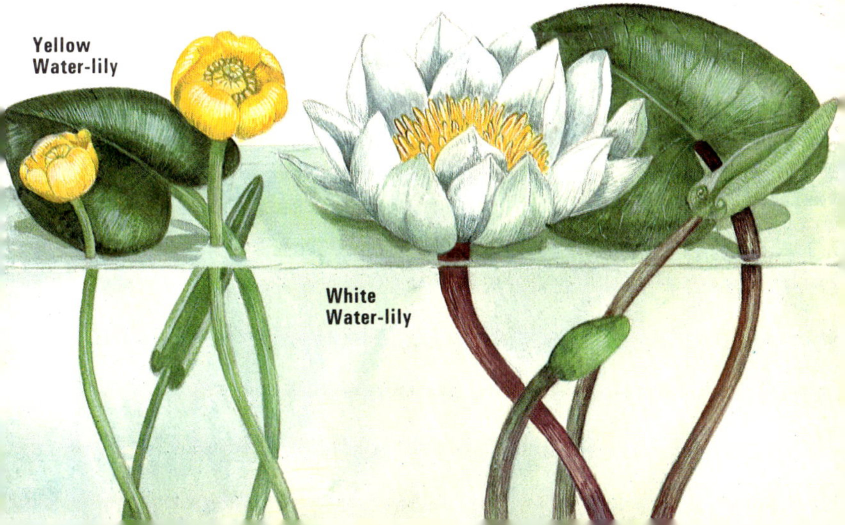

POPPY FAMILY
Papaveraceae

Several species of Poppy are weeds of cultivated fields, especially fields of grain. They are now more common at field edges and on waste land than among crops, due to the use of herbicides and the removal of weed seed from crop seed before sowing.

GREATER CELANDINE
Chelidonium majus

There seems little resemblance between this plant, with its small, yellow flowers, and its flamboyant relatives, the Poppies. Despite the common name, it is not related to Lesser Celandine. It has surprising bright-orange sap and grows 30-90 cm high on hedgebanks and walls, usually near buildings.

Flower: bright yellow, 2-2·5 cm across; petals 4; stamens many.
Flower arrangement: umbel of 2-6 flowers.
Flowering time: May-August.
Leaf: pinnate, leaflets 5-7, glaucous, blunt-toothed.
Fruit: a capsule 3-5 cm, straight, opening from below by 2 valves.
Uses: an escape from herbalists' gardens where it grew for many centuries. The bitter, orange sap was used to treat poor eyesight.

LONG-HEADED POPPY
Papaver dubium

The flowers are smaller and more orange than those of the Common Poppy. The stem is stiffly hairy. The plant grows 20-60 cm high, in waste places and as a weed of cultivation.

Flower: orange-pink, sometimes with a dark spot at petal-base; 3-7 cm across; petals circular, overlapping at base; stamens many, purple; stigma disc flat with 7-9 radiating ridges.
Flower arrangement: solitary.
Flowering time: June-July.
Leaf: greyish green, shortly hairy; basal leaves deeply lobed, end lobe not enlarged.
Fruit: long, narrow capsule, 1·5-2 × 0·5-0·75 cm, tapered at base, hairless, often ribbed.

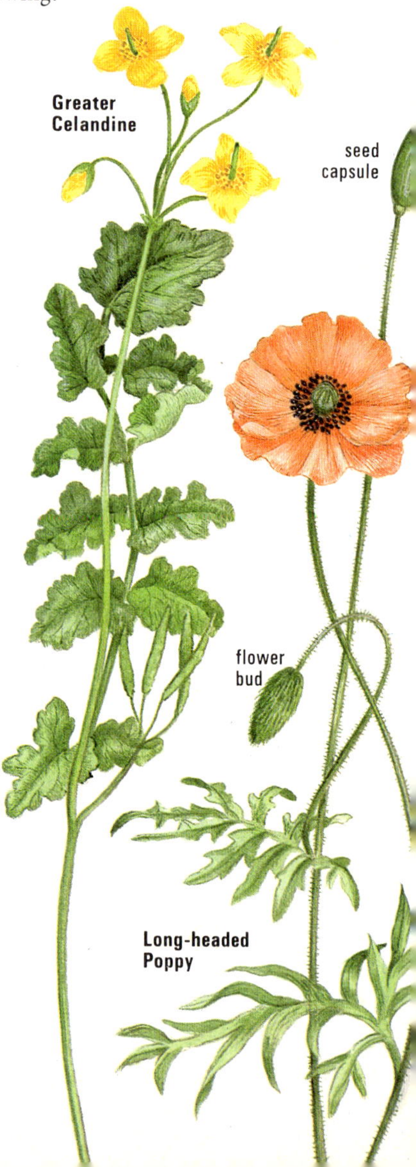

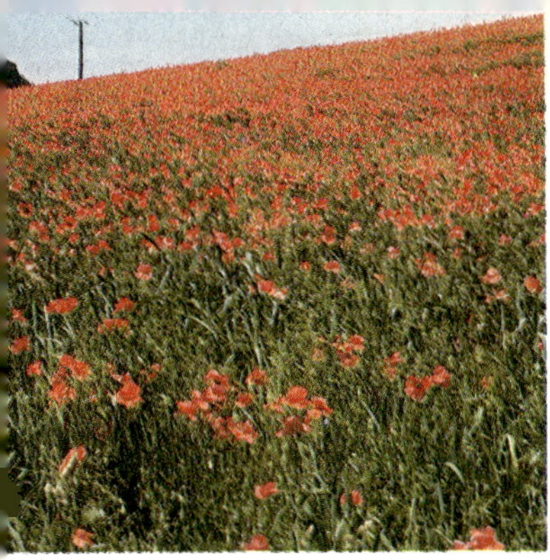

A sight that is becoming rarer: a cornfield reddened by Poppies.

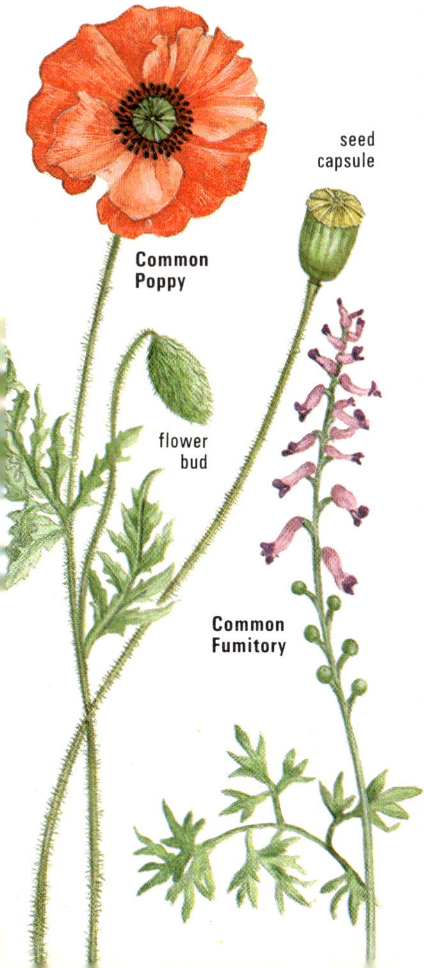

COMMON POPPY

Papaver rhoeas

The Common Poppy, with its large, scarlet flowers and covering of stiff hairs, grows 25-90 cm high. If cut, it exudes milky-white latex.

Flower: scarlet, often with dark blotch at petal-base; 7-10 cm across; petals thin; stamens many; stigma disc more or less flat with 8-12 radiating ridges.

Flower arrangement: on long stalks in the leaf axils.

Flowering time: June-August.

Leaf: stiffly hairy, 1- to 2-pinnate; segments coarsely toothed.

Fruit: capsule, rounded at base, top flat, length 1-2 cm, hairless, opening by pores under top.

Uses: Poppies were thought to cause headaches and thunderstorms, but were also used to treat headaches. Although slightly poisonous, the red Poppy does not contain the opium of the Opium Poppy (*P. somniferum*).

FUMITORY FAMILY
Fumariaceae

Fumitories are sprawling weeds of cultivated or disturbed ground. The leaves are finely cut, reminiscent of Maidenhair Fern. The small flowers are tubular and 2-lipped.

COMMON FUMITORY

Fumaria officinalis

Common Fumitory is a slender, glaucous, long-stemmed plant, climbing or almost erect. It is a weed of arable land and prefers light soils.

Flower: purplish pink, tips blackish red; tube-like corolla 7-9 mm long, spurred behind, 2-lipped; sepals 2, irregularly toothed.

Flower arrangement: raceme, usually of more than 20 flowers, longer than its stalk.

Flowering time: May-October.

Leaf: all arising from stem, finely divided into flat segments.

Fruit: more or less spherical, 2-3 mm.

CABBAGE FAMILY
Cruciferae

Members of the family characteristically have flowers with 4 petals resembling a cross, hence the Latin name. The flowers are very often yellow or white. Seed cases are arranged up the stem, which elongates as the seeds ripen, and are commonly long, narrow and upward-pointing, like candelabra. The many representatives of this family in North-West Europe include the relatives of such vegetables as cauliflower and turnip and many weeds of disturbed ground.

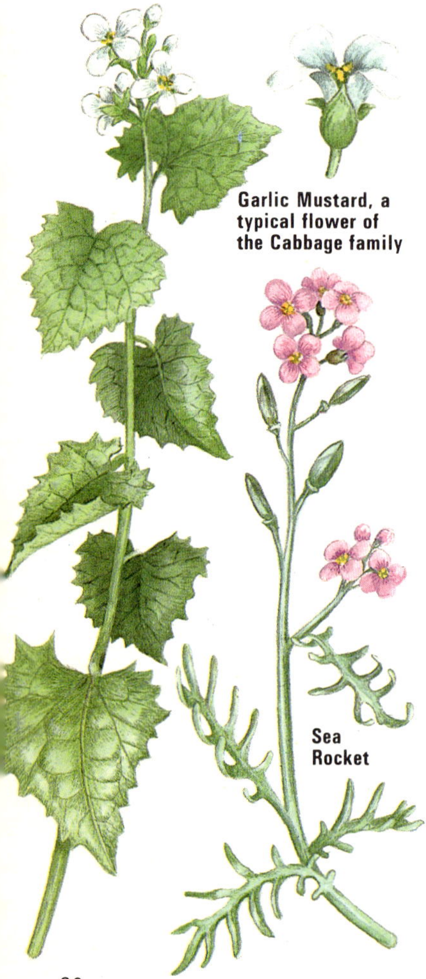

Garlic Mustard, a typical flower of the Cabbage family

Sea Rocket

GARLIC MUSTARD
Alliaria petiolata

A rather tall, upright plant, unbranched, up to 120 cm, Garlic Mustard smells faintly of garlic when crushed. The plant can be seen along hedgerows, walls and wood margins.

Flower: white, 6 mm across.

Flower arrangement: compact raceme.

Flowering time: April-June.

Leaf: pale, rather bright green, heart-shaped, toothed; basal leaves long-stalked, shape reminiscent of nettle leaf.

Fruit: long, very narrow capsule, 2-7 cm long, opening by 2 valves from below.

Uses: a sauce was formerly made from the leaves to accompany salted fish. An old name for the plant is Sauce Alone.

SEA ROCKET
Cakile maritima

This is a good-looking seaside plant of sand and shingle. The plant is succulent, pale bluish-green and 15-45 cm high. The fruits are dispersed by sea water.

Flower: pale lilac, occasionally purple or white, 1-2 cm across; petals narrowed at base; sepals 4, erect not spreading; stamens 6.

Flower arrangement: many flowers, closely spaced at end of branches.

Flowering time: June-August.

Leaf: deeply pinnately lobed or not; lower leaves 3-6 cm with short stalk; upper leaves stalkless.

Fruit: 1-2·5 cm, bulbous, narrowed at tip.

SHEPHERD'S PURSE

Capsella bursa-pastoris

Hardly a walk can be taken, whether in town or country, without seeing Shepherd's Purse, a plant 3-40 cm high, of wayside, cultivated land and waste places. It is distributed throughout the world, having followed man as a weed of agriculture.

Flower: white, about 2·5 mm across.

Flower arrangement: flowers crowded at the top of a raceme, becoming less dense in fruit.

Flowering time: all the year.

Leaf: basal leaves in rosette, deeply lobed or not; base of upper leaves clasping stem.

Fruit: heart-shaped, 6-9 mm across, the 2 valves breaking apart to disperse pale brown seeds – the 'money' in the 'purse'.

CUCKOO FLOWER

Cardamine pratensis

A very pretty plant of damp places and stream sides, the Cuckoo Flower grows 30-55 cm high, usually unbranched. The clustered flowers are pale lilac and open in the spring. Seeds are catapulted up to 2 m.

Flower: lilac, rarely white, 12-18 mm across; petals may be slightly notched.

Flower arrangement: clusters of 7-20 flowers.

Flowering time: April-June.

Leaf: pinnate, up to 7 oval or circular leaflets usually with widely spaced teeth; end leaflet enlarged; basal leaves in rosette.

Fruit: 2·5-4 cm, thin, on long stalks pointing upward, opening from below by 2 valves.

Uses: the plant may be eaten in the same way as Water-cress.

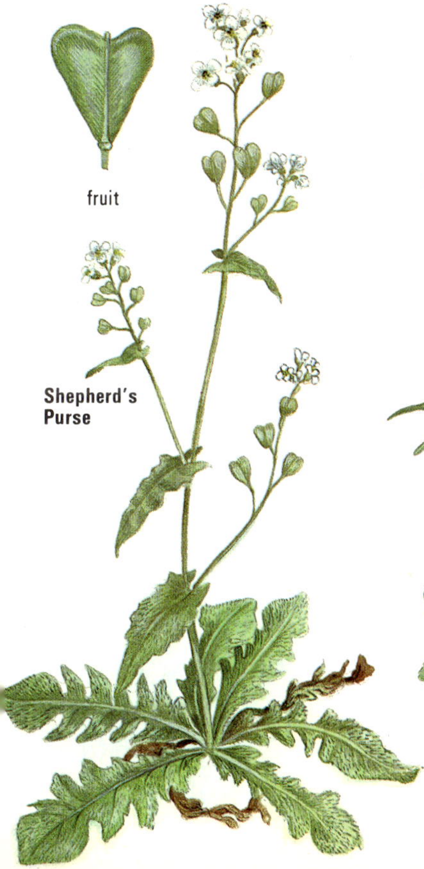

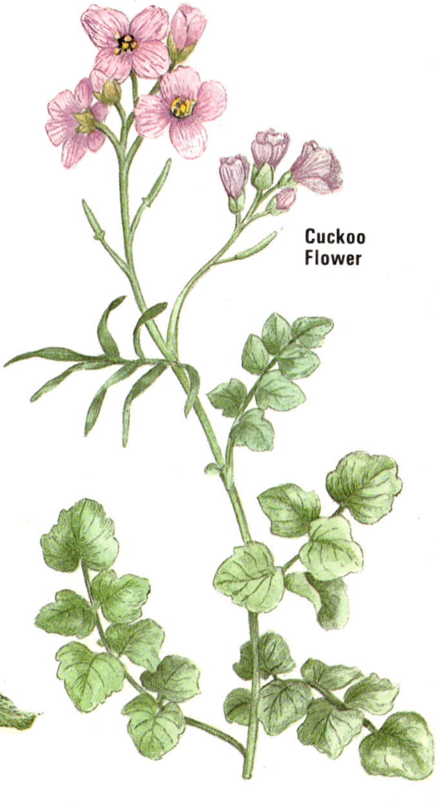

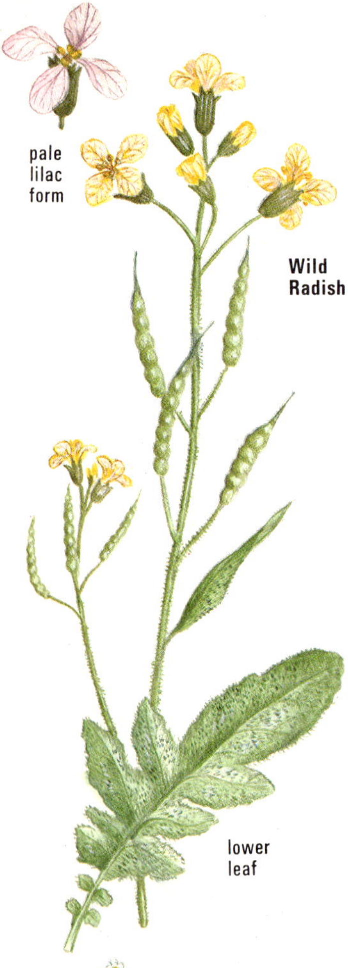

WILD RADISH

Raphanus raphanistrum

This arable weed is bristly, erect, branched and grows 15-150 cm high. The cultivated Radish (*R. sativus*) has the well-known edible swollen root and occasionally escapes from gardens.

Flower: yellow, lilac or white with dark veins, 2·5-4 cm across; petals narrowed at base, twice as long as sepals; stamens 6.

Flower arrangement: raceme.

Flowering time: May-September.

Leaf: lower leaves deeply lobed; end lobe rounded, enlarged; upper leaves lobed or toothed.

Fruit: long, narrow, abruptly narrowed into long spike at tip; contracted between each of the 4-7 seeds, breaking readily into 1-seeded units.

WATER-CRESS

Rorippa nasturtium-aquaticum

Water-cress grows in masses in wet places where there is fresh, moving water. It is 10-60 cm high, hairless, creeping, often rooting and ascending at the tip.

Flower: white, 4-6 mm across, petals about twice as long as sepals.

Flower arrangement: clustered at the top of a raceme.

Flowering time: May-October.

Leaf: pinnate, lower leaves with 1-3 circular or broadly ovate leaflets; upper leaf with 5-9.

Fruit: 13-18 mm, curving slightly upward.

Uses: commercial cultivation as a salad crop started at the beginning of the 19th century.

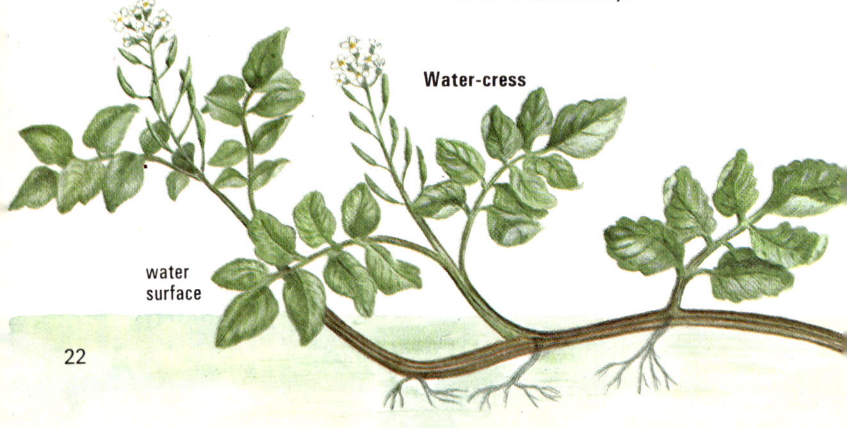

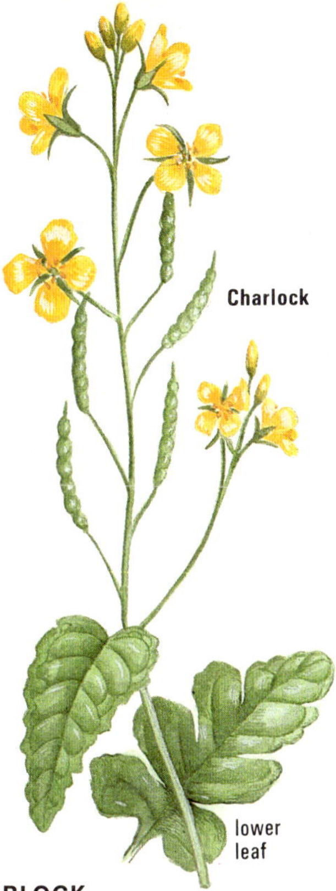

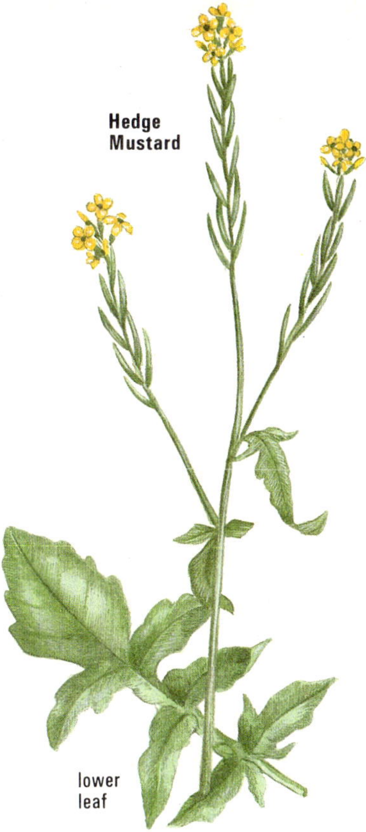

CHARLOCK

Sinapis arvensis

Charlock grows up to 80 cm and often has stiff hairs on the base of the stem. It is a serious weed of arable land.

Flower: bright yellow, 1·5-2 cm; petals narrowed at base; sepals 4; stamens 6.

Flower arrangement: dense raceme.

Flowering time: May-July.

Leaf: up to 20 cm, alternate, roughly hairy; lower leaf stalked, deeply lobed; end lobe large, coarsely toothed; upper leaves stalkless, without lobes.

Fruit: 2·5-4·5 cm long, narrow, abruptly narrowed at tip, indented between seeds, smooth or stiffly hairy, containing dark reddish-brown seeds.

HEDGE MUSTARD

Sisymbrium officinale

Hedge Mustard, familiar if not pleasing to the eye, grows in waste places in town and country to a height of 90 cm. The plant is stiffly erect and branched above, like candelabra.

Flower: pale yellow, small.

Flower arrangement: in small clusters on ends of branches.

Flowering time: June-July.

Leaf: lower leaves in a rosette, deeply lobed; end lobe larger than rest.

Fruit: very thin, cylindrical, 10-20 mm, straight, pressed to the stem, which elongates in fruit.

VIOLET FAMILY
Violaceae

The flowers are of 5 unequal petals, the lowest spurred. The sepals have small flaps or appendages. After producing normal flowers in spring, Violets often produce flowers which do not open and are self-fertilizing. Many tropical members of this family are shrubs.

SWEET VIOLET
Viola odorata

Although cultivated in gardens and often escaping, the scented Sweet Violet is also a native of Europe. It grows in hedgebanks, scrub and woods, and is 5-15 cm high, with a rosette of leaves and creeping, rooting runners.
Flower: deep violet or white with lilac spur, about 1·5 cm, scented; petals 5, unequal, lower petal forming spur behind; spur longer than sepal appendages; sepals rounded at tip.
Flower arrangement: solitary, on long stalks.
Flowering time: February-April.
Leaf: heart-shaped, rounded or pointed at tip, blunt-toothed, sparsely hairy, long-stalked.
Fruit: capsule, spherical, downy.
Uses: a flower prized for its sweet scent, it may also be candied for cake decoration.

COMMON DOG-VIOLET
Viola riviniana

This Violet can be very variable in size. It lacks creeping stems and grows in woods, on hedgebanks or in grassland.
Flower: usually blue-violet though varying; spur paler; lower petal with many long, dark veins; unscented, 1-2·5 cm; spur 2-5 mm, stout, often curved up, notched at tip; sepals with appendages about 2-3 mm.
Flower arrangement: solitary, on axillary branches.
Flowering time: April-June.
Leaf: in loose rosette; stalked, heart-shaped, blunt-toothed, up to 8 cm; stipules toothed.
Fruit: capsules opening by 3 valves; explosive.

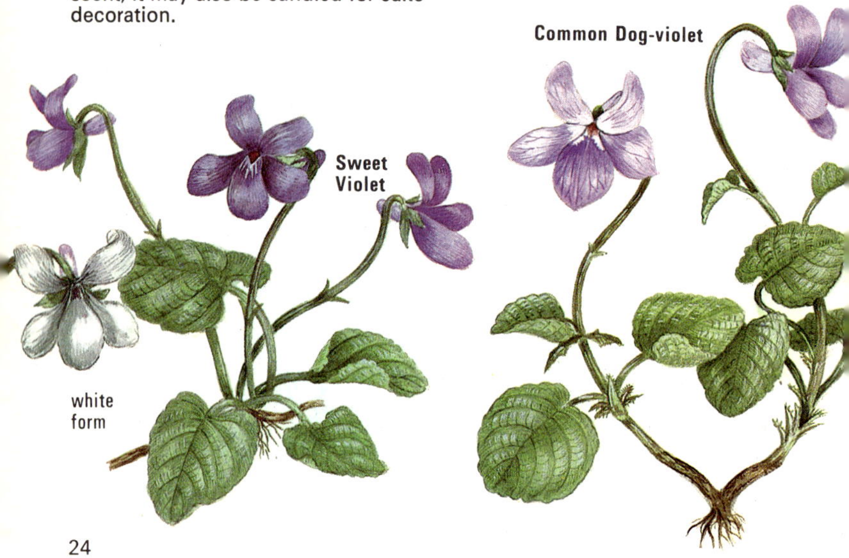

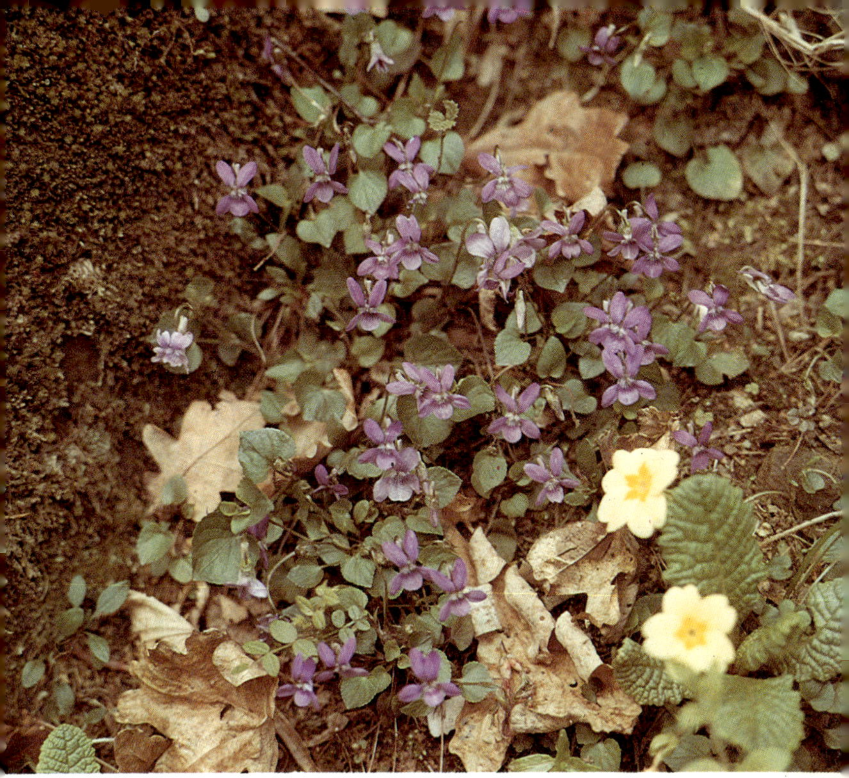

Violets can often be seen on damp, shady banks and under hedgerows.

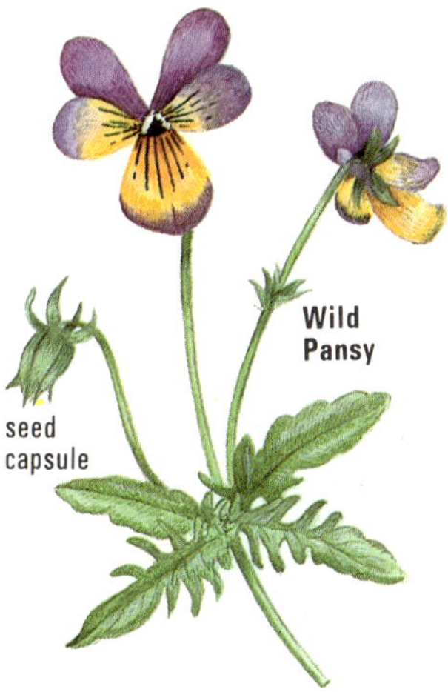

WILD PANSY

Viola tricolor

The Violet from which the older garden Pansies were bred is found on cultivated and waste ground and short grassland. It is 15-45 cm high and usually branched. A low-growing form (3-15 cm) occurs on dunes and grassland near the sea.

Flower: blue-violet or yellow, or both colours combined; scentless, 1-3 cm vertically; petals 5, unequal, usually longer than sepals, lower petal forming spur behind; sepals pointed, rather shorter than spur with appendage immediately below each sepal.

Flower arrangement: solitary, several arising from each stem.

Flowering time: April-September.

Leaf: alternate; lower leaf ovate or heart-shaped, blunt-toothed; upper leaf narrower; stipules leaf-like deeply lobed.

Fruit: 3-valved capsule.

MILKWORT FAMILY
Polygalaceae

This world-wide family includes shrubs and small trees but all the North European members are small plants growing in short grassland. The 3 true petals of the flowers are enclosed within the 5 petal-like sepals.

COMMON MILKWORT
Polygala vulgaris
This is a rather low, much branched plant, 10-30 cm high, to be found in short grassland, heaths and dunes. The tiny flowers are almost enclosed by 2 enlarged, coloured sepals.
Flower: blue, pink or white, 6-8 mm; sepals 5, the two inner enlarged, coloured, petal-like.
Flower arrangement: many-flowered raceme.
Flowering time: May-September.
Leaf: alternate, narrow, entire, more or less pointed; lower leaves 5-10 mm, upper leaves longer.
Fruit: flat, heart-shaped capsule, about 5 mm.
Uses: herbalists formerly prescribed this little plant for nursing mothers, to increase the flow of milk.

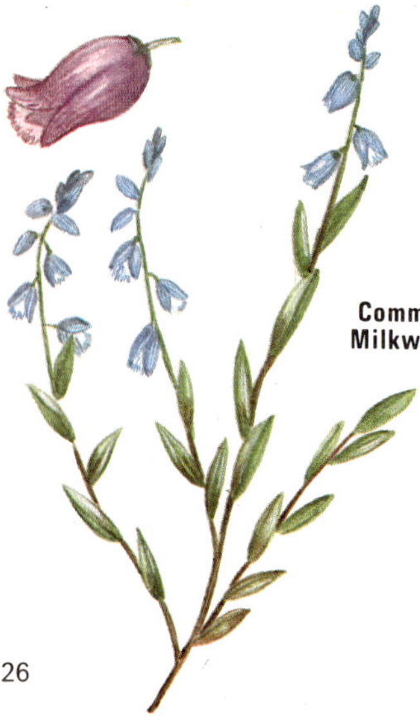

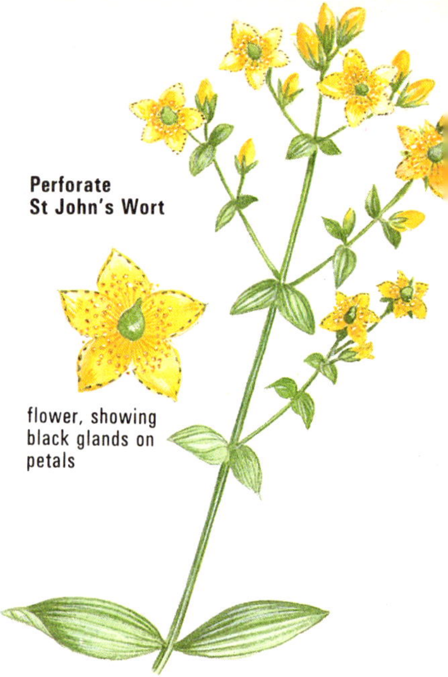

ST JOHN'S WORT FAMILY
Guttiferae

A family mainly of temperate regions. Glands, appearing as black or translucent dots on the plants, are characteristic of this family. There are 5 petals, and the many stamens are joined at their bases into bundles.

PERFORATE ST JOHN'S WORT
Hypericum perforatum
There are tiny translucent dots (seen if the plant is held to the light) and black dots to look for on this plant. Running down the stem are 2 raised lines. The plant is hairless, erect and 10-100 cm high, growing in grassland and scrub.
Flower: yellow, about 2 cm across; petals 5, tiny black dots around margins; sepals 5, pointed, with or without black dots; stamens many.
Flower arrangement: branched cyme.
Flowering time: June-September.
Leaf: alternate, with many trans-

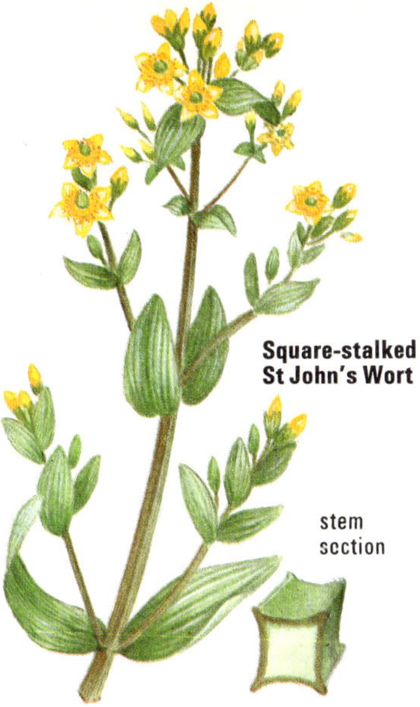

lucent dots; 1-3 cm, elliptic to linear, shortly or not stalked.
Fruit: capsule, seeds pitted.
Uses: once an important protective and healing plant, it was smoked over fires lit on 23rd June, St John's Eve, thus strengthening its powers. The ceremony included leaping over the flames, and may date from pre-Christian times.

SQUARE-STALKED ST JOHN'S WORT

Hypericum tetrapterum
The square cross-section of the stem, flanged at each angle, is the main feature of this St John's Wort. The plant is hairless, 10-100 cm high and grows in damp places. It is absent from Norway and the greater part of Sweden.
Flower: pale yellow, 1 cm across; petals 5; sepals pointed, occasionally with 1-2 black dots; stamens many.
Flower arrangement: many-flowered, branched cymes.
Flowering time: June-September.
Leaf: opposite, ovate, stalkless, weakly clasping stem at base, with some small, translucent and black dots.
Fruit: capsule, seeds pitted.

STITCHWORT FAMILY
Caryophyllaceae

This large family includes Carnations, Pinks and many other garden plants, as well as widespread weeds such as the Chickweeds. The flowers have 4 or 5 petals, which are notched, except in the case of Sandworts and Spurreys.

PROCUMBENT PEARLWORT

Sagina procumbens
As a result of its moss-like size and creeping habit, this common plant is easily overlooked. The stems spread out from a central rosette of needle-like leaves. It is found in lawns, grass verges and paths.
Flower: white, minute; petals 4 or 5; sepals much larger than petals.
Flower arrangement: solitary on long stalks.
Flowering time: May-September.
Leaf: 5-12 mm, needle-like, in tufts along stem.
Fruit: capsule.

Procumbent Pearlwort

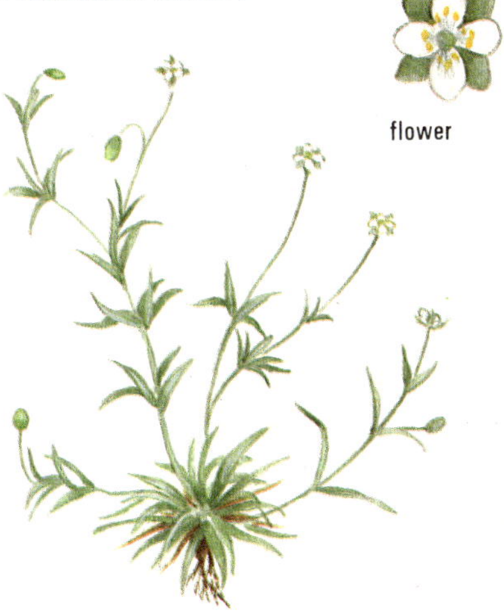

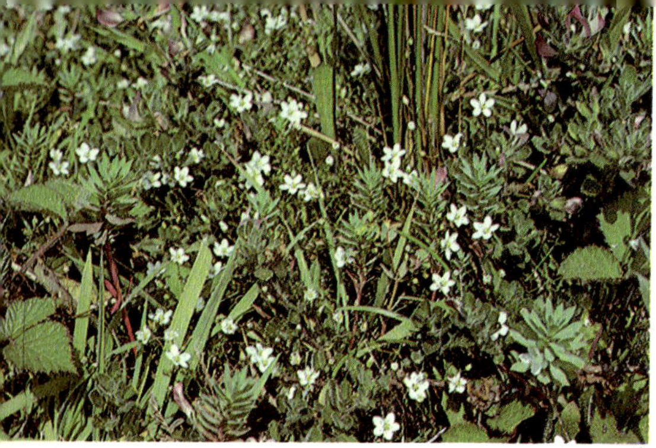

The conspicuous white flowers of a member of the Stitchwort family.

flower

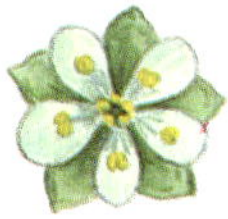

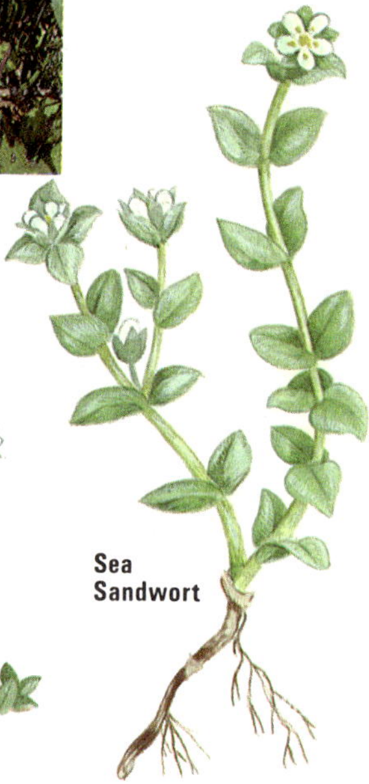

Sea Sandwort

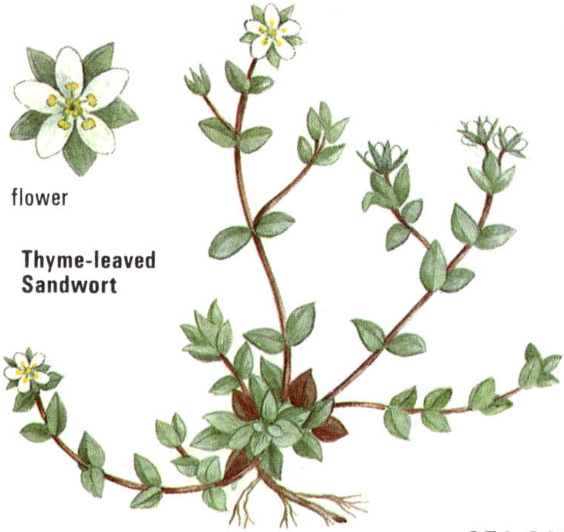

flower

Thyme-leaved Sandwort

THYME-LEAVED SANDWORT

Arenaria serpyllifolia

The lower parts of this small plant are often more densely branched than the upper. It is 3-30 cm high, with scattered hairs, and is slightly rough to the touch. Its habitat is arable and bare ground and walls. It seems to be ignored by rabbits and is common around their burrows.

Flower: white, 5-8 mm; petals 5, shorter than sepals; sepals hairy; anthers yellow.

Flower arrangement: cyme.

Flowering time: June-August.

Leaf: opposite, ovate; lower leaves shortly stalked, upper stalkless.

Fruit: capsule, flask-shaped; seeds tiny, black.

SEA SANDWORT

Honkenya peploides

The Sea Sandwort is a small, fleshy plant, 5-25 cm high, partly creeping on sand and shingle by the sea. It can withstand brief immersion in salt water.

Flower: greenish white, 6-10 mm; petals 5, rounded, as long as or shorter than the sepals.

Flower arrangement: solitary, in leaf axils and forks of branches.

Flowering time: May-August.

Leaf: opposite, ovate, fleshy, stalkless.

Fruit: capsule, spherical, opening by 3 teeth; seeds large, pear-shaped, reddish-brown.

Uses: in Yorkshire the whole plant was used as a pickle.

CORN SPURREY

Spergula arvensis

Corn Spurrey is a pale green plant, 5-70 cm high, slightly to very sticky, with weak, branched stems and whorls of leaves. It is a weed of cultivated land, preferring sandy soils.

Flower: white, 4-7 mm across; petals 5, rounded, slightly longer than sepals.

Flower arrangement: forked or umbel-like panicle, the stalks turning down in fruit.

Flowering time: June-August.

Leaf: 1-3 cm long, needle-shaped, in whorls, slightly fleshy, channelled beneath, sticky.

Fruit: capsule, 5 mm, opening by 5 teeth; seeds blackish, warty.

Uses: various forms of this weed are grown in Germany and the Netherlands as a nutritious fodder crop for sheep and cows. When cultivated it may grow 90 cm high.

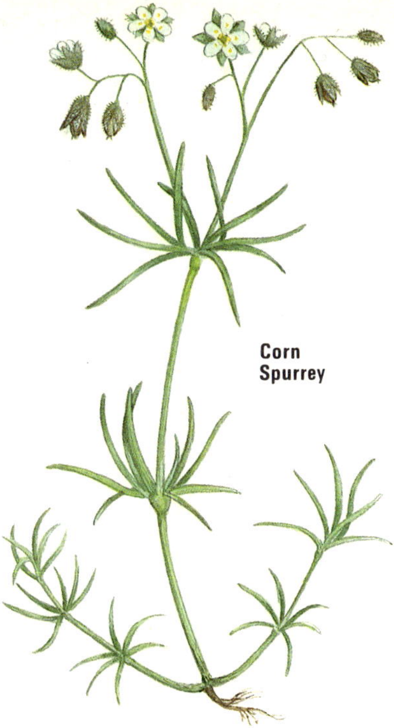

Corn Spurrey

SAND SPURREY

Spergularia rubra

Sand Spurrey, with its tiny, pink flowers, is a straggling plant, 5-25 cm high, found on sandy soils in open ground. The upper parts of the plant have slightly sticky hairs.

Flower: pink, paler at base of petals, 3-5 mm, petals 5; sepals longer than petals.

Flower arrangement: few-flowered cyme.

Flowering time: May-September.

Leaf: in clusters along stem, very narrow, tapering to stiff, sharp point, not fleshy; stipules silvery, conspicuous.

Fruit: capsule, 4-5 mm, opening by 3 teeth; seeds tiny, dark brown.

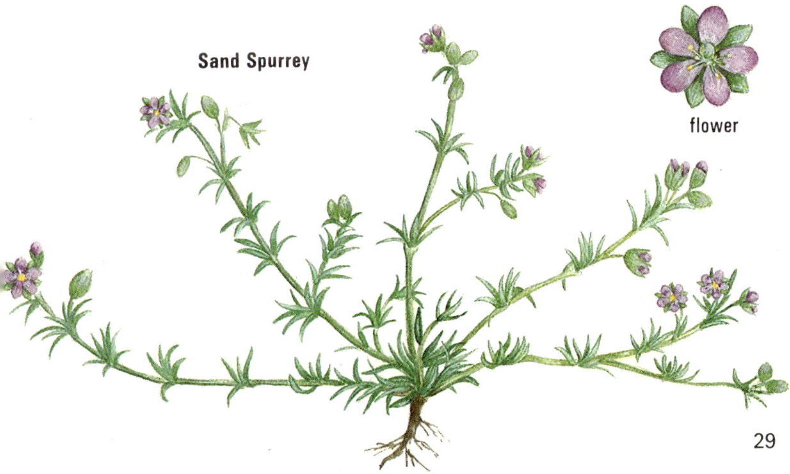

flower

Sand Spurrey

WHITE CAMPION

Silene alba

The White Campion is a branched, softly hairy weed of cultivated land and grows to 80 cm. As with the Red Campion, the flowers are unisexual. They open in the evening when they are slightly scented to attract moths as pollinators.

Flower: white, 2·5-3 cm across; petals 5, deeply cleft, narrowed at base; calyx-tube hairy, sticky.

Flower arrangement: cyme.

Flowering time: May-September.

Leaf: opposite, ovate, stalked; stem leaves stalkless.

Fruit: capsule 1-1·5 cm, ovoid, opening by 10 teeth.

RED CAMPION

Silene dioica

The Red Campion grows in woods and hedgerows. The whole plant is softly hairy and grows up to 80 cm high. There are separate male and female flowers. Red Campion interbreeds readily with White Campion, the offspring having pale pink flowers.

Flower: bright rose, 18-25 mm across; petals 5, deeply cleft, narrowed at base; calyx-tube hairy, slightly sticky.

Flower arrangement: cyme.

Flowering time: May-June.

Leaf: opposite, broadly ovate; the basal leaf blade continuous as thin border down each side of stalk; upper leaves stalkless.

Fruit: capsule 1-1·5 cm, spherical or ovoid, opening by 10 teeth which curve back.

Uses: Campions were associated with snakes, the pounded seed being used to treat snake bite.

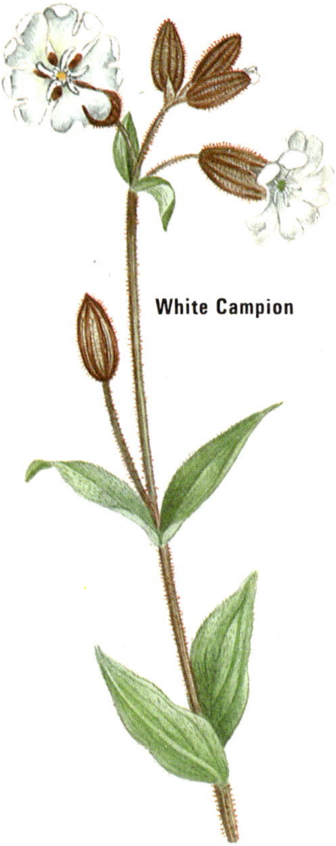

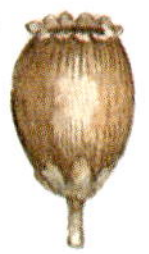

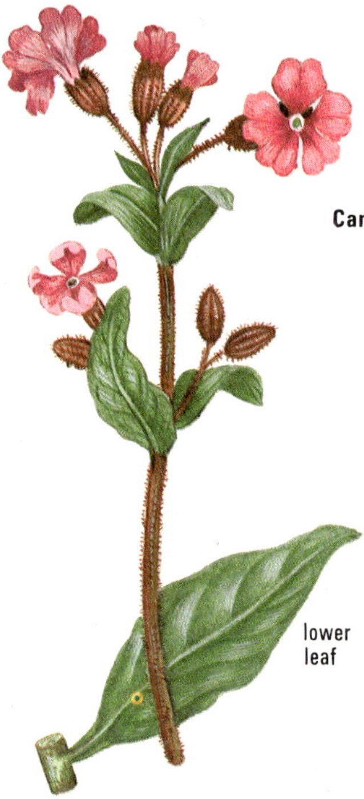

BLADDER CAMPION

Silene vulgaris

This erect, often grey-green, branching plant is usually without hairs and grows up to 90 cm high. The 'bladder' is the inflated calyx-tube. It is found in grassland and arable land, and along roadsides.

Flower: white, about 1·5 cm across; petals 5, deeply cleft, narrowed at base; calyx-tube inflated, net-veined; bracts papery.

Flower arrangement: loose cyme.

Flowering time: June-August.

Leaf: often greyish-green, opposite, ovate; lower leaves short-stalked, upper stalkless.

Fruit: capsule, with 6 erect teeth, enclosed by persistent calyx.

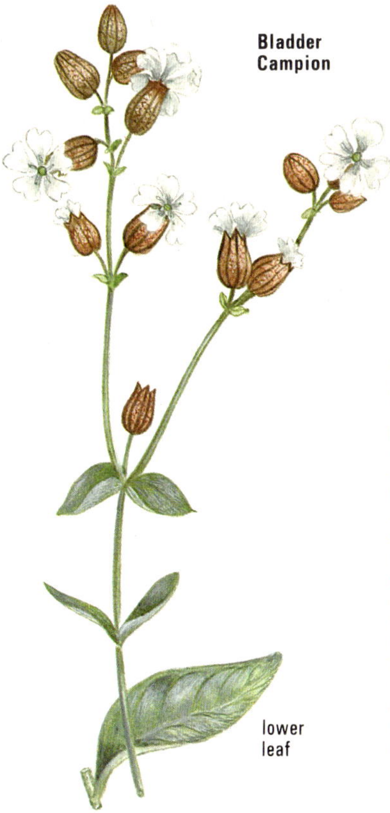

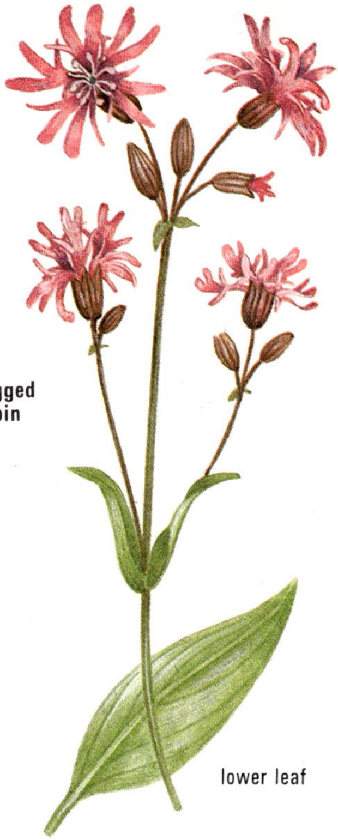

RAGGED ROBIN

Lychnis flos-cuculi

The rose-red, finely dissected flower petals of the Ragged Robin are striking. The stem and leaves are slightly rough to the touch. The height of the branched stem is 20-90 cm. The plant is a lover of damp places.

Flower: rose-red, 3-4 cm across; petals deeply cut into thin segments; calyx-tube 5-toothed; stamens 10.

Flower arrangement: cyme.

Flowering time: May-June.

Leaf: opposite; basal leaves ovate, stalked, slightly rough to touch; upper leaves stalkless.

Fruit: capsule 6-10 mm, opening by 5 teeth.

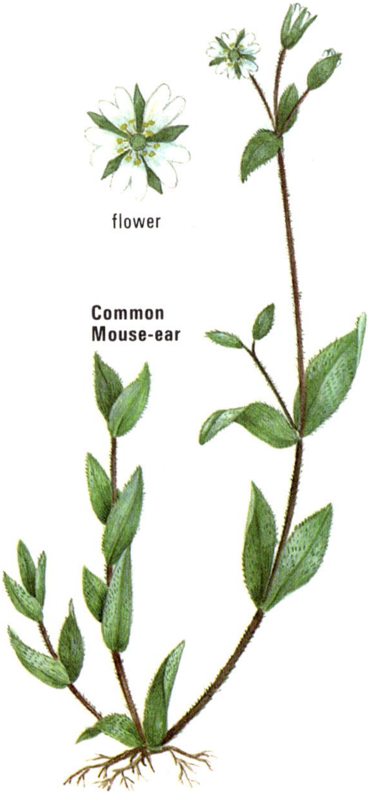

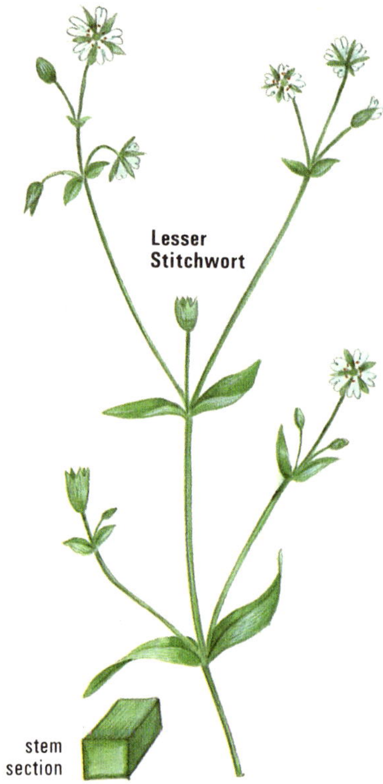

COMMON MOUSE-EAR

Cerastium holosteoides

The flowering stems of this very common little plant, up to 45 cm high, are longer than the non-flowering stems. It is found almost everywhere, growing in loose, straggling tufts. The leaves and stem are hairy.

Flower: white; petals 5, deeply notched, equalling sepals; sepals with narrow, papery margins and showing between petals of open flower; stamens 10 or 5.

Flower arrangement: loose clusters.

Flowering time: April-September.

Leaf: 10-25 × 3-15 mm, stalkless, tip pointed or rounded.

Fruit: capsule, curved; seeds warty.

LESSER STITCHWORT

Stellaria graminea

Lesser Stitchwort is 20-90 cm high, and the 4-angled stem is smooth to the touch. The leaves are a bright green and the flowers smaller than those of Greater Stitchwort. It grows in woods and grassland and on heaths.

Flower: white, 5-12 mm, long-stalked; petals 5, notched to more than half their length (looking like 10 petals); sepals with narrow, papery margins; stamens 10.

Flower arrangement: loose clusters.

Flowering time: May-August.

Leaf: bright green, opposite, 1·5-4 cm long, lanceolate, tapering to sharp point, stalkless.

Fruit: capsule, ovoid; seeds reddish-brown.

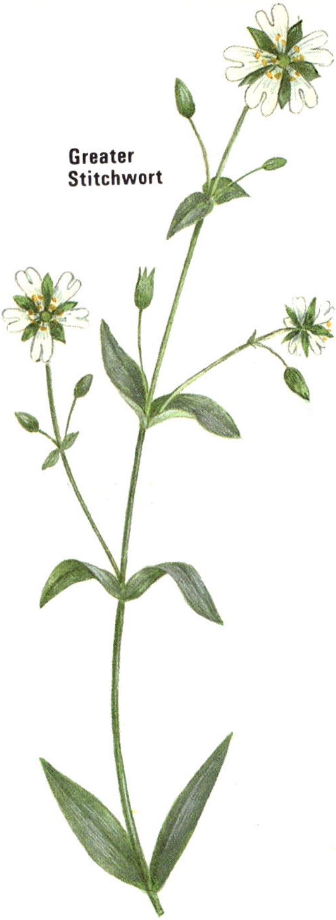

Greater Stitchwort

GREATER STITCHWORT

Stellaria holostea

The slender, flowering stems are 15-60 cm high and 4-angled, the angles being slightly rough to the touch. The plant is slightly greyish-green and grows in hedgerows and woods.

Flower: white, 2-3 cm, long-stalked; petals 5, notched to about half their length; sepals with narrow, papery margins; stamens 10.

Flower arrangement: loose clusters.

Flowering time: April-June.

Leaf: rather greyish-green, opposite, 4-8 cm long, lanceolate, tapering to sharp point, stalkless.

Fruit: capsule, spherical; seeds reddish-brown, warty.

Uses: seed of Stitchwort was powdered, added to wine and used against pains or 'stitches' in the side.

COMMON CHICKWEED

Stellaria media

The straggling, branching stems of this world-wide weed are 5-40 cm long. The tiny flowers are inconspicuous and there is a single line of hairs running down the stem.

Flower: white, 8-10 mm; petals very deeply cleft; sepals same length as petals with narrow, papery margins, showing between petals of open flower.

Flower arrangement: loose clusters.

Flowering time: all year.

Leaf: opposite, ovate; lower leaves stalked, upper stalkless.

Fruit: capsule, stalk curved down.

Uses: young plants can be eaten in salads and sandwiches. Small birds love the seed.

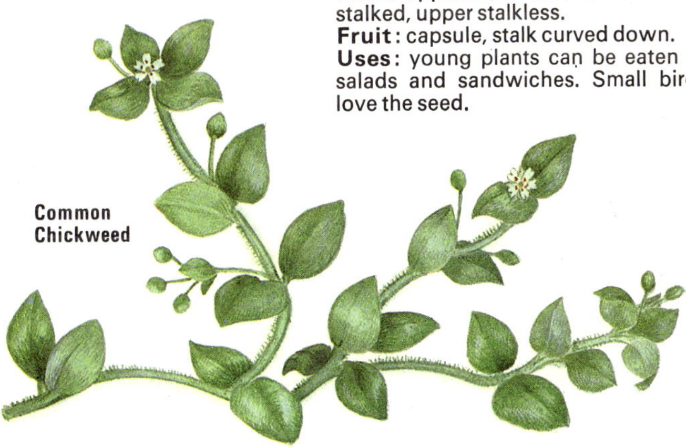

Common Chickweed

PURSLANE FAMILY
Portulacaceae

Plants belonging to this family are hairless and more or less fleshy. The pairs of opposite leaves are without teeth and may be joined into a cup shape surrounding the stem. There are 5 flower petals and only 2 sepals. Many of the species are natives of North America.

BLINKS
Montia fontana

A small and straggling plant, Blinks grows up to 50 cm high in fresh water. When growing on mud, the plant is more compact and tufted. The often reddish stem and green to yellow-green leaves are hairless and slightly fleshy. The plant is absent from most of N. France.

Flower: white, very inconspicuous, about 2 mm across, long-stalked; petals 5; sepals 2; stamens 3.
Flower arrangement: cyme.
Flowering time: May-October.
Leaf: 3-20 mm long, opposite, oval, entire, base tapering into stem.
Fruit: capsule, 1·5-2 mm, spherical; seeds usually 3.

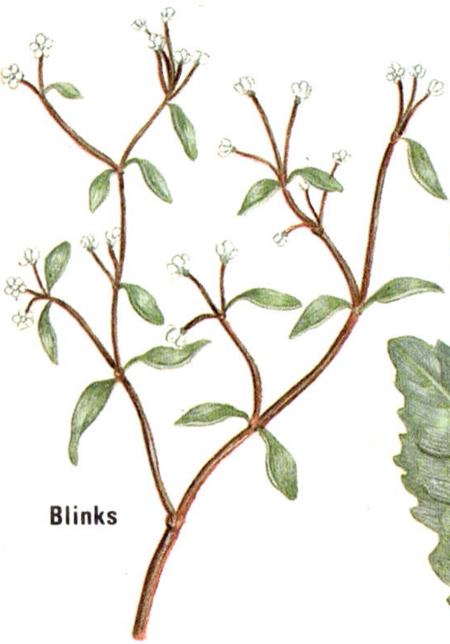

GOOSEFOOT FAMILY
Chenopodiaceae

Economic crop plants in this family include beetroot and spinach. Flowers are inconspicuous and clustered into small spikes, and are wind-pollinated. The pale mealiness on the leaves is composed of minute, bladder-like hairs. Many of the species grow in dry, salty conditions, either in coastal areas or inland.

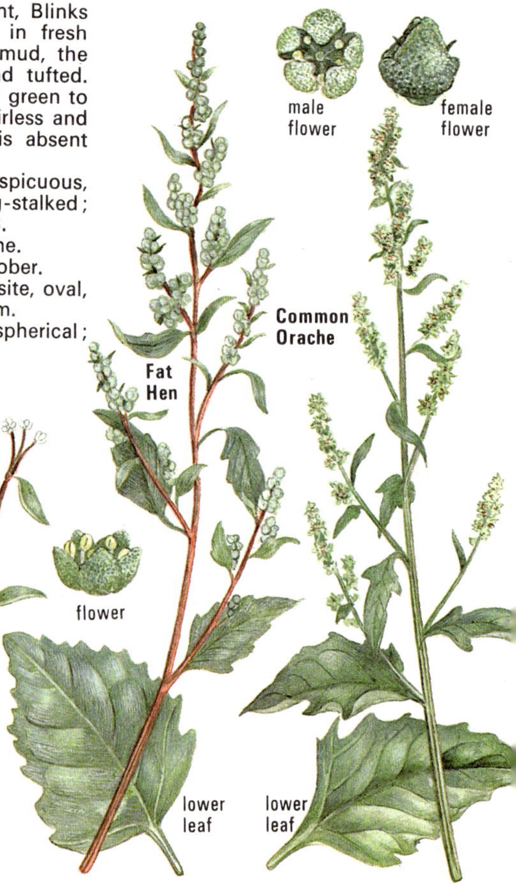

FAT HEN
Chenopodium album
Growing 10-150 cm high, Fat Hen often has a red tinge to the grooved stem. The plant is deep green with a mealy covering and grows on cultivated and waste land. It is very variable and there are several other similar species.
Flower: green, inconspicuous, bisexual.
Flower arrangement: spikes, arising from leaf-axils.
Flowering time: July-October.
Leaf: alternate, mealy, diamond-shaped to narrowly ovate, stalked, toothed, sometimes nearly 3-lobed or entire.
Fruit: black.

COMMON ORACHE
Atriplex patula
The plant is branched, up to 150 cm high and slightly mealy. The stems are ridged and striped white and green or red and green. This is a weed of waste places and cultivated ground. Although similar to Fat Hen, Common Orache can be distinguished by its separate male and female flowers.
Flower: green, inconspicuous, unisexual, males with 5 green 'petals' and 5 stamens, females with 2 stigmas and enclosed by 2 diamond-shaped bracts.
Flower arrangement: spikes arising from leaf-axils.
Flowering time: July-September.
Leaf: alternate, diamond-shaped, base tapering into leaf-stalk, toothed or entire; upper leaves narrow, entire, stalkless.
Fruit: black, enclosed by 2 bracts.

MALLOW FAMILY
Malvaceae

Mallows, Cotton and Hollyhock are all members of this family. The 5 flower petals are twisted in bud, and the many stamens are bunched centrally on a single stalk. Seen through a hand lens, the hairs on most of the species are branched in a star shape.

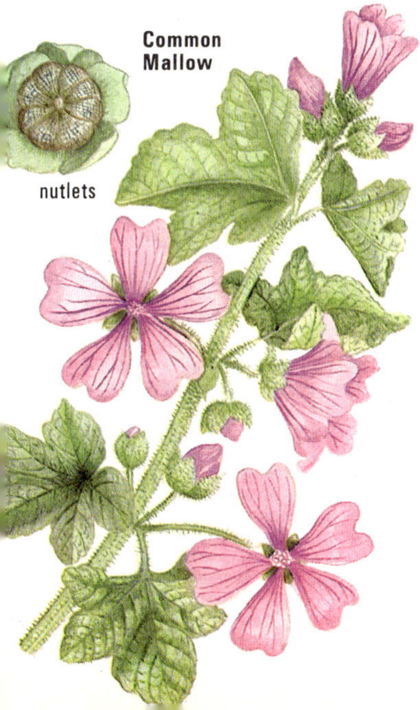

COMMON MALLOW
Malva sylvestris
This plant is erect or straggling, up to 150 cm high, and the stem is woody at the base. The habit, hairiness and leaf shape are all variable. The plant favours dry, open places on waste and cultivated land.
Flower: rose-purple, dark-striped, 2·5-4 cm across; petals 5, thin, narrowed at base, notched, 3 or 4 times as long as sepals; 5 sepals joined at base, with 3 smaller beneath; stamens many, clustered on a single stalk.
Flower arrangement: several stalked flowers arising from each leaf-axil.
Flowering time: June-September.
Leaf: palmately lobed, blunt-toothed, often folded along main veins; basal leaves long-stalked.
Fruit: nutlets, arranged in circle, covered by network of ridges, sharp-angled.

FLAX FAMILY
Linaceae

Members of this small family are often slender and hairless. Flax is the most important member, from which comes linseed oil and a fibre used for good-quality paper.

PURGING FLAX
Linum catharticum

Slender, hairless and not usually more than 15 cm high, the Purging Flax is found in grass or on rocks, especially on limey or sandy soils.
Flower: white, yellow at petal-base, 4-6 mm across, nodding in bud, on thin stalks; petals 5, round-tipped; sepals 5, pointed at tip, with a few glandular hairs on margin; stamens 5.
Flower arrangement: loose cymes.
Flowering time: June-September.
Leaf: opposite, oval, stalkless, single-veined; the pairs widely spaced, pointing up.
Fruit: capsule, spherical.
Uses: as the common name suggests, this particular Flax was commonly used as a purge.

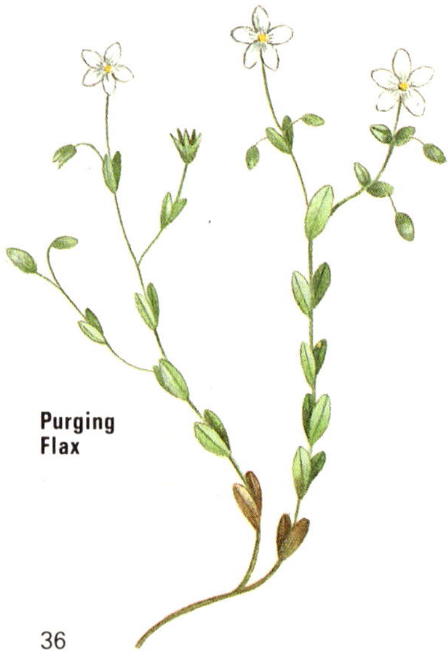

Purging Flax

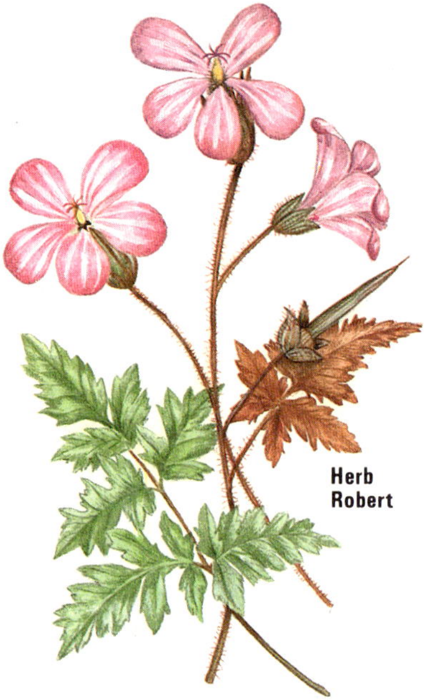

Herb Robert

GERANIUM FAMILY
Geraniaceae

Many species in the Geranium family have long, soft hairs, and the flowers are usually brightly coloured, with 5 petals. The seeds of the characteristic fruit are arranged around the base of the stiff, persistent style.

HERB ROBERT
Geranium robertianum

The stem and leaves of Herb Robert are hairy and often turn bright red. The plant grows 10-50 cm high, is branched and erect or straggling. If bruised, it smells unpleasant. It is most often found in hedgerows but also grows among rocks, on walls and in woodland.
Flower: bright pink-mauve, 2 cm across, long-stalked; petals 5, narrowed at base; sepals erect, with bristle-like tips; stamens 10, anthers orange or purple.
Flower arrangement: in pairs.
Flowering time: May-September.

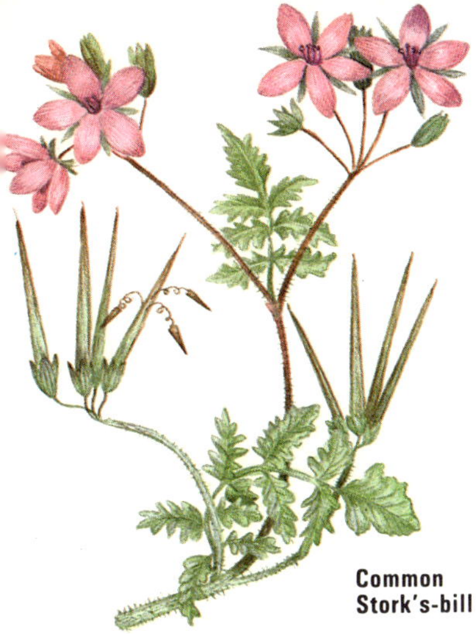

Common Stork's-bill

Leaf: in 3 main segments, each deeply and repeatedly dissected; long-stalked.
Fruit: arranged around base of stiff, persistent style to which fruits are attached by thin strands.

COMMON STORK'S-BILL
Erodium cicutarium
This plant looks rather similar to Herb Robert but differs in the clustered flowers, the pinnate leaf-segments and the spiralling strands attached to the fruits. The stem and leaves are slightly to very hairy. The plant grows up to 60 cm high in dry, open places, particularly near the sea.
Flower: bright rose-purple; petals 5, 12-14 mm across, upper 2 sometimes with black spot at base, especially on plants growing inland; sepals spreading, not erect, with bristle-like tips.
Flower arrangement: 3-12 flowers in umbel-like cluster.
Flowering time: June-September.
Leaf: doubly pinnate.
Fruit: arranged around base of stiff, persistent style to which fruits attached by thin, spiralling strands.

WOOD-SORREL FAMILY
Oxalidaceae

The flowers in this family have 5 petals and 10 stamens. The family is mainly distributed in the tropics. Some *Oxalis* species are grown as ornamentals in gardens, and a few have edible tubers. The leaflets of the Clover-like leaves often fold down at night or in cold weather.

WOOD SORREL
Oxalis acetosella
A small plant of woodland and shaded hedgebanks, Wood-sorrel has leaves composed of 3 leaflets, like Clover leaves but a paler, more delicate green. In cold weather and at night the leaves fold down. The stem creeps, bearing the long-stalked leaves and flowers in small clusters. Although Wood-sorrel contains oxalic acid, livestock rarely eat sufficient quantities for it to prove fatal.
Flower: white, lilac-veined, bell-shaped, nodding; petals 5, 8-15 mm long; sepals 5.
Flower arrangement: solitary.
Flowering time: April-May.
Leaf: in 3 rounded, notched leaflets, pale yellow-green.
Fruit: capsule, rounded, 5-angled, 3-4 mm long; seeds light brown.

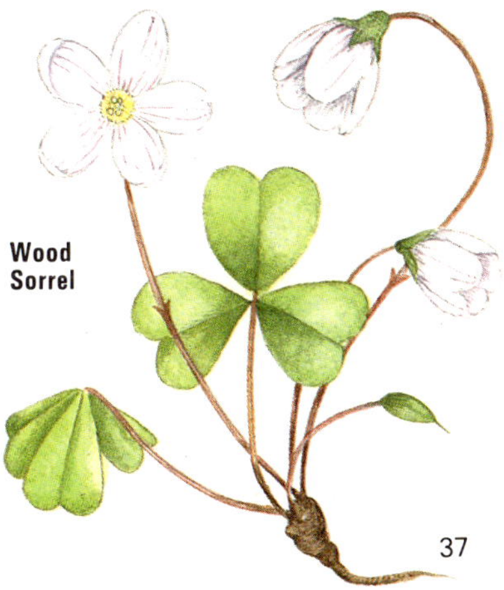

Wood Sorrel

BALSAM FAMILY
Balsaminaceae

The Balsams are hairless plants with juicy, easily broken, translucent stems often with stalked, sticky glands. The flowers are irregular in shape, with 5 petals forming a broad lip, a hood and a curved spur behind. Typically the flower dangles from the flower stalk. The fruits explode on being touched. The house plants known as Busy Lizzies (*Impatiens* species) are in this family.

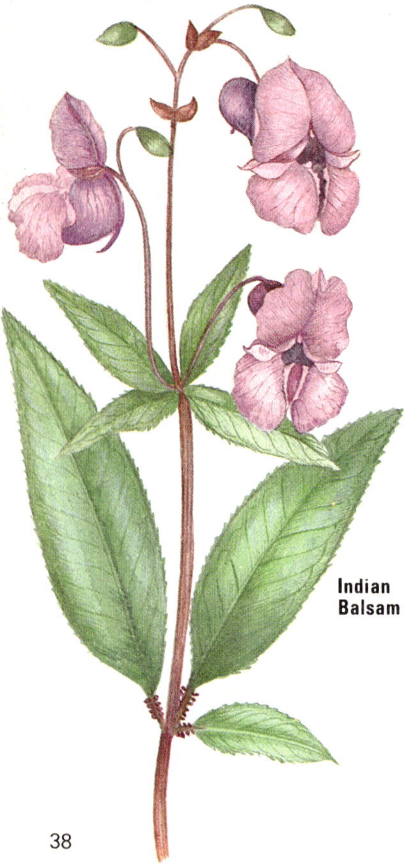

Indian Balsam

INDIAN BALSAM
Impatiens glandulifera

Introduced as a garden plant from the Himalayas in 1839, and naturalized along waterways and in waste places, this tall, stout-stemmed species grows 100-200 cm high. It is hairless and the stems reddish. There is no mistaking the rather Orchid-like, mauve, dangling flowers.

Flower: purplish pink, 2·5-4 cm, petals 5, forming a broad, lower lip and hood; sepals 3, lower forming a mauve, spurred bag.

Flower arrangement: long-stalked racemes arising from leaf-axils.

Flowering time: July-October.

Leaf: opposite or in threes, 5-18 cm long, elliptic, toothed; reddish glands along basal margins.

Fruit: capsule, club-shaped, opening by 5 valves which spring into coils, shooting out seeds.

PEA FAMILY
Leguminosae

The flowers in this very large family are easily recognizable, being composed of an upright 'standard' petal, 2 side 'wing' petals and a pair of fused, boat-shaped petals under the standard, as in the Sweet Pea. The 5 sepals are fused into a calyx tube, and stamens and style are usually enclosed by the petals. The flowers are loosely clustered or in small, dense heads. Leaves are usually alternate and pinnate, sometimes with a tendril, or with 3 leaflets. The fruit is typically a pod and many important food crops such as soybeans and peas belong to this family. Clover and Lucerne are very widely grown as fodder and green manure. The roots form nodules which contain nitrogen-fixing bacteria and act as a natural fertilizer.

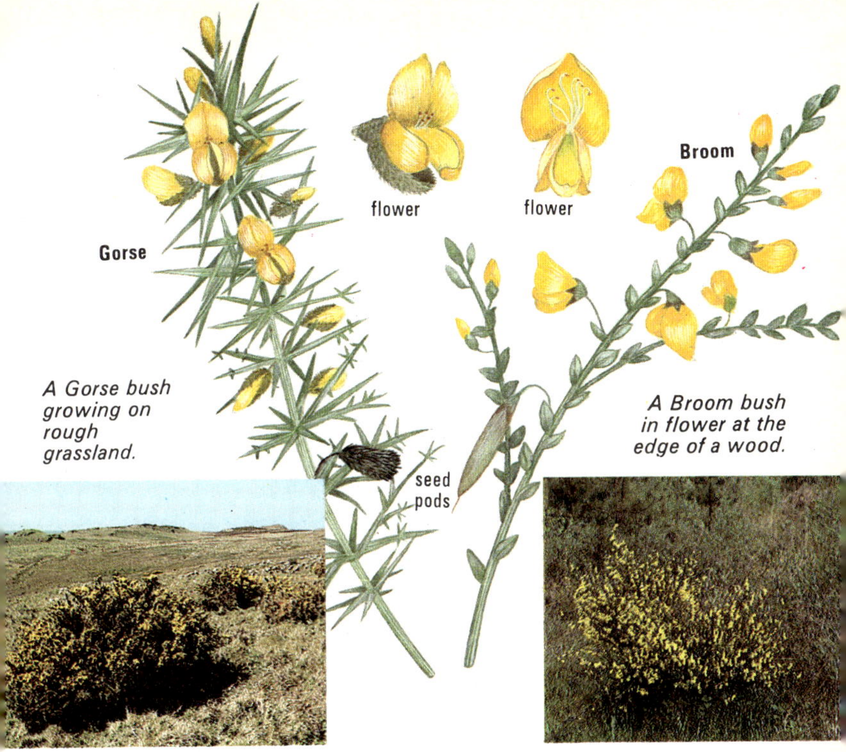

A Gorse bush growing on rough grassland.

A Broom bush in flower at the edge of a wood.

GORSE

Ulex europaeus

Gorse is a spiny shrub which can cover large areas of heath and rough grassland. Its golden, scented flowers are favoured by bees. On being touched, the flowers explode pollen onto the visiting insect.

Flower: golden yellow, about 1·5 cm, on short, velvety stalks; calyx yellowish, 2-lipped, hairy.

Flower arrangement: in leaf-axils toward ends of shoots.

Flowering time: mainly in spring or late winter.

Leaf: a stiff, branched spine, 1·5-2·5 cm long, deeply grooved, slightly grey-green.

Fruit: pod, black, 11-20 mm long, hairy, barely longer than the calyx, bursting open when ripe to expel seeds.

Uses: an old use for Gorse was as a fuel and, after crushing, as fodder.

BROOM

Sarothamnus scoparius

A shrub similar to Gorse but without spines, the Broom grows up to a height of 2 m. The twigs are 5-ridged and hairless. The flowers respond to the landing of visiting insects by expelling pollen onto their undersides. The shrub is found on heaths, mountains and dunes, and in woods.

Flower: golden-yellow, about 2 cm, on stalks up to 1 cm; style forming loop; calyx 2-lipped, hairless.

Flower arrangement: solitary or in pairs in leaf-axils.

Flowering time: May-June.

Leaf: composed of 3 elliptic leaflets, short-stalked or stalkless, slightly hairy.

Fruit: pod, black, 2·5-4 cm long; hairs on margins only.

Uses: the shoots are still used to stimulate urine production, and the long, supple branches were made into brooms for sweeping.

COMMON REST-HARROW

Ononis repens

A shrubby, hairy plant of 40-70 cm, this species is prostrate, often with upturned tips bearing the pink flowers. The stems are hairy all round and the roots are long and very tough. The plant grows in rough grassland and dunes.

Flowers: pink, 1·5-2 cm long, on shortly hairy stalks; wing petals as long as keel; calyx tube with 5 long teeth, densely hairy.

Flower arrangement: in the leaf-axils.

Flowering time: June-September.

Leaf: 1-3 leaflets, oval, finely toothed, hairy, short-stalked; stipules 3-5 mm, finely toothed, clasping stem at base.

Fruit: pod, hidden by calyx.

COMMON BIRD'S-FOOT TREFOIL

Lotus corniculatus

This plant is usually almost hairless and grows in grassland. Plants growing on the coast may have small, fleshy leaves. The stems, 5-35 cm long, are prostrate, turning up at the tips.

Flowers: yellow, often tinged or streaked with red, 1-1·5 cm long; petals 2 or 3 times as long as calyx-tube.

Flower arrangement: 2-7 flowers in outward-facing ring on erect stalk up to 8 cm.

Flowering time: June-September.

Leaf: of 5 elliptic or almost circular leaflets, each 3-10 mm long, rounded at tip or with a short point; short leaf-stalk often between lower and upper leaflets.

Fruit: pod, 1·5-3 cm long, cylindrical, straight; seeds many.

BLACK MEDICK

Medicago lupulina

The leaves of Black Medick are Clover-like and the flowers yellow. The plant is sprawling, 5-50 cm high and downy, growing in open places such as roadsides, cultivated fields and at the coast.

Flower: bright yellow, 2-3 mm.

Flower arrangement: grouped into small, round heads 3-8 mm across, on stalks longer than the leaf-stalks.

Flowering time: April-August.

Leaf: of 3 leaflets, each narrowed towards base, finely toothed, often shallowly notched at tip in which is a minute bristle; stipules finely toothed.

Fruit: tightly curved disc, about 2 mm across, containing 1 seed, covered by network of ridges.

Uses: this Medick is sometimes grown for fodder.

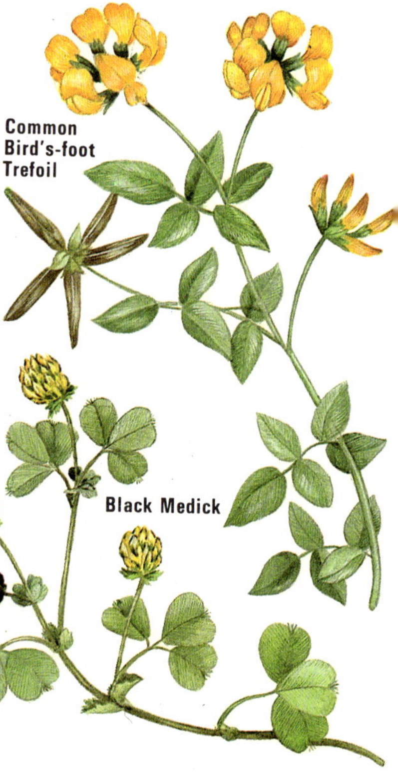

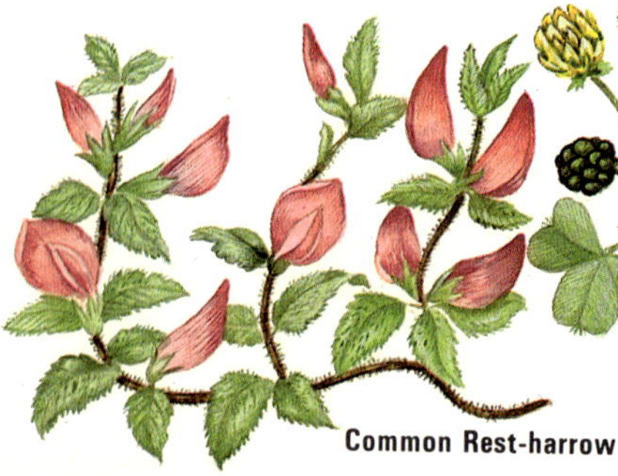

RED CLOVER

Trifolium pratense

Red Clover grows erectly 5-100 cm high in grassland, and is more or less hairy.

Flower: pink-purple; individual flowers 15-18 mm long.

Flower arrangement: in compact, rounded or ovoid heads of 2-4 cm.

Flowering time: May-September.

Leaf: of 3 elliptic leaflets, each 1-3 cm long, often with pale crescent, usually rounded at tips; leaf-stalk up to 20 cm; pair of short-stalked leaves immediately below flower head; stipules conspicuous, joined up the leaf-stalk, with 2 free points, each ending in bristle.

Fruit: pod, about 2 mm.

Uses: a variety with hollow stems is widely grown for fodder.

WHITE CLOVER

Trifolium repens

A very familiar little plant of grassland, including lawns and verges. The stems of White Clover creep along the ground rooting at intervals. The plant is hairless and may grow as long as 50 cm.

Flower: white or pink-tinged, scented, individual flowers 8-13 mm, turning down and becoming brown from base of head upwards; calyx-tube white, green-veined with narrow, pointed teeth.

Flower arrangement: round head on long, grooved stalk.

Flowering time: June-September.

Leaf: of 3 rounded leaflets, minutely toothed, each 1-3 cm long, each often with pale crescent; stipules joined, sheathing stem, with 2 free points.

Fruit: pod, hidden by dead flower.

Uses: bees use the nectar to produce clover honey, and several varieties are grown for fodder.

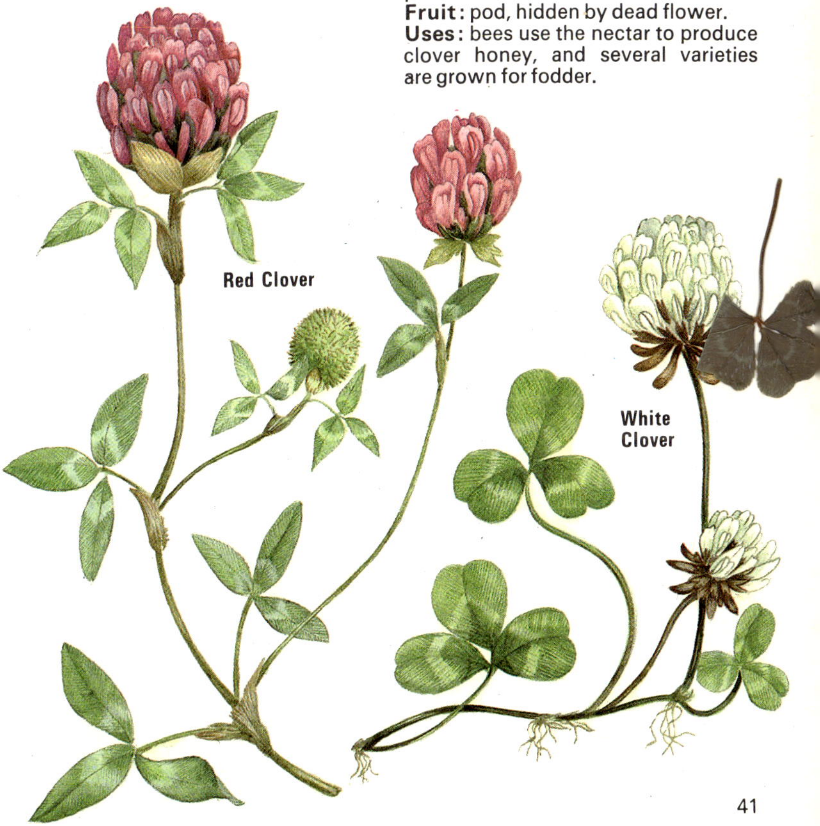

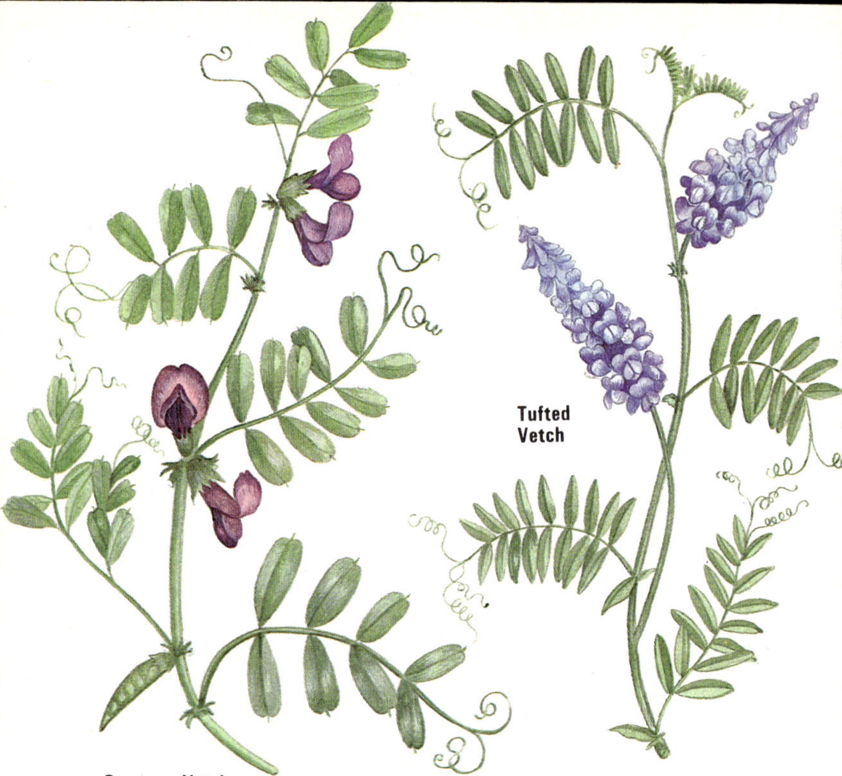

COMMON VETCH

Vicia sativa

The Common Vetch is a slightly hairy plant, scrambling or climbing in hedges or grassy places. It can grow up to 120 cm.

Flower: purplish red, 1-3 cm long; calyx teeth about equal.

Flower arrangement: solitary or in pairs, on very short stalks or stalkless.

Flowering time: May-September.

Leaf: pinnate, with 3-8 pairs of narrow leaflets, each 1-2 cm long, often wider at tip than base, with minute bristle, notched or pointed; tendrils branched or not; stipules toothed or not, often with dark spot.

Fruit: pod, 2·5-8 cm long, yellow-brown to black, hairless or slightly hairy; seeds 4-12.

Uses: a form of this Vetch is often grown as a fodder crop.

TUFTED VETCH

Vicia cracca

Tufted Vetch is a weak-stemmed plant which gains support by clambering over other vegetation. It is 60-200 cm long, slightly hairy and grows in hedges and bushy places. The long, crowded racemes of flowers are characteristic of this species.

Flower: blue-purple, 8-12 mm long, each drooping on short stalk; style equally hairy all round; upper teeth of calyx-tube minute; lower teeth about as long as calyx-tube.

Flower arrangement: dense raceme of 10-40 flowers on stalk 2-10 cm long.

Flowering time: June-August.

Leaf: pinnate, with 6-15 pairs of narrow leaflets, each 1-2·5 cm long, pointed or with minute bristle; leaf ends in branched tendril; stipules untoothed.

Fruit: pod, brown, hairless, 1-2·5 cm long; seeds 2-6.

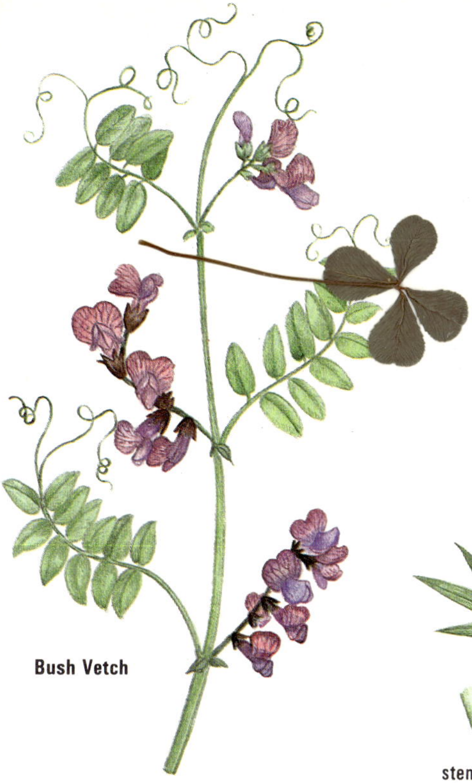

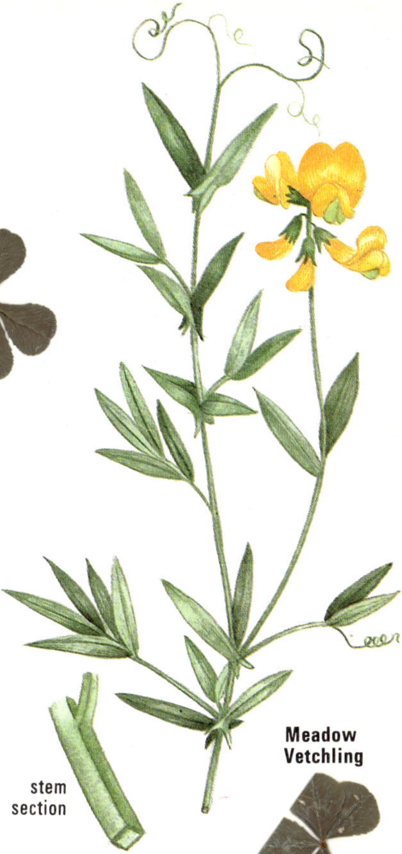

BUSH VETCH

Vicia sepium

Climbing or scrambling in grassy or bushy places, the Bush Vetch grows 30-100 cm long. The leaves and stem have short hairs or are almost hairless.

Flower: pale purple, 1-1·5 cm; lower calyx teeth much shorter t han calyx-tube, and tips curving toward each other.

Flower arrangement: raceme of 2-6 flowers, very shortly stalked.

Flowering time: May-August.

Leaf: pinnate, with 3-9 pairs of leaflets, each 1-3 cm long, variably shaped; tips rounded or pointed, with or without minute bristle at centre of slight notch at leaflet-tip; tendrils branched; stipules sometimes toothed, with black spot.

Fruit: pod, 2-3·5 cm long, black, hairless; seeds 3-10.

MEADOW VETCHLING

Lathyrus pratensis

This Vetchling, with or without short hairs, scrambles over vegetation in grassy or bushy places. It is 30-120 cm in length and has a sharply angled stem.

Flower: yellow, 10-18 mm long; teeth of calyx-tube narrowly triangular.

Flower arrangement: raceme of 5-12 flowers on long stalk.

Flowering time: May-August.

Leaf: 1-2 pairs of narrow, pointed leaflets, 1-3 cm long; tendril branched or not; stipules leaf-like, 1-2·5 cm, arrow-shaped.

Fruit: pod, 2-4 cm long, black; seeds 5-12.

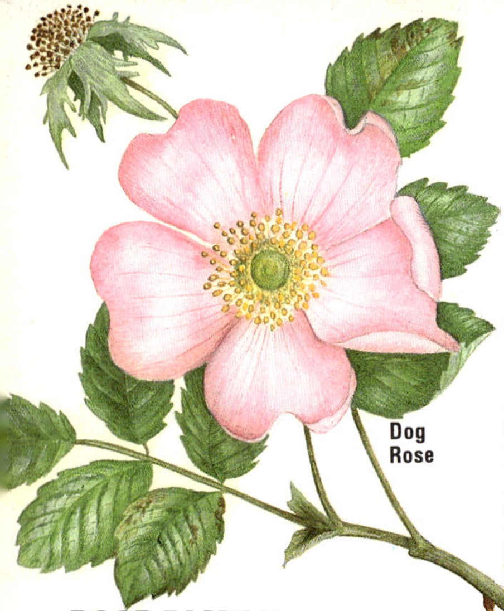

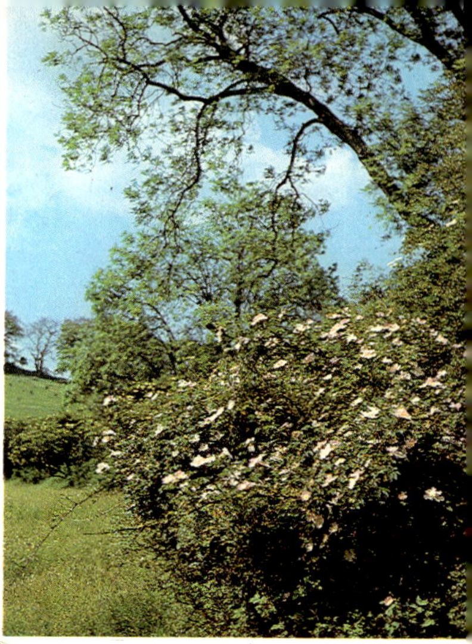

A Dog Rose adds colour to a hedgerow on chalk downland.

ROSE FAMILY
Rosaceae

This ancient family is among the more primitive of the flowering plant families. The flowers are often conspicuously coloured, but very rarely blue. The regular, unspecialized flowers attract a wide range of insects. There are 5 petals and many stamens. The fruits are varied and include achenes, follicles and the commercially very important tree fruits – apples, pears and plums. The popular modern roses of gardens are complicated hybrids, far from their wild ancestors.

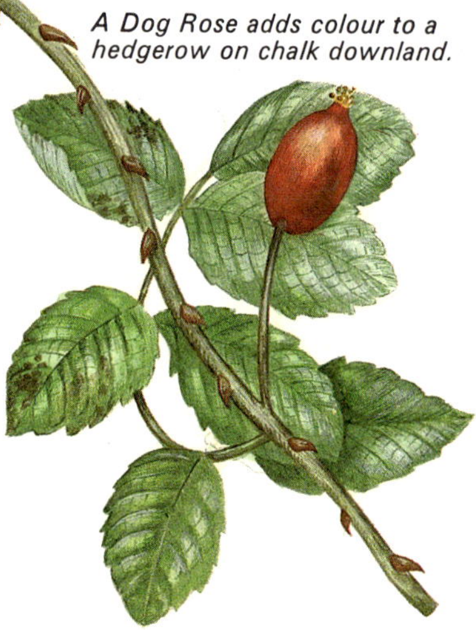

DOG ROSE
Rosa canina

The Dog Roses are extremely variable shrubs, 1-3 m high, with stems that arch and scramble in hedgerow and scrub. The prickles are hooked.
Flower: pink or white, 4-5 cm across; petals 5, notched; sepals 5, lobed, falling before fruit ripens; stamens many; stigmas in a head.
Flower arrangement: cluster of 1-4 flowers, stalks hairless.
Flowering time: June-July.
Leaf: pinnate, with 2-3 pairs of elliptic, toothed, usually hairless leaflets; stipules joined to leaf-stalk.
Fruit: rose hip, scarlet, about 1·5-2 cm long, spherical or ovoid.
Uses: jelly and syrup may be made from the fruit, which is rich in vitamin C. More than 500 tons of hips were collected in Britain in 1943 as part of the war effort, to provide children with rose-hip syrup.

BRAMBLE

Rubus fruticosus

The stems of these woody shrubs often arch over, rooting at the tip and bearing hooked prickles, some of which may be straight. The Brambles are extremely variable. About 2,000 micro-species may be recognized in the *Rubus fruticosus* group. This huge number is thought to have arisen by a combination of hybridization and self-fertilization.

Flower: pink or white, 2-3 cm across; petals 5; stamens many.

Flower arrangement: solitary or clustered.

Flowering time: May-September.

Leaf: of 3-5 toothed leaflets.

Fruit: the 'blackberry'.

Uses: blackberries have been eaten and enjoyed for thousands of years. Healing powers were associated with the leaves and stems, mainly for relieving burns and swellings.

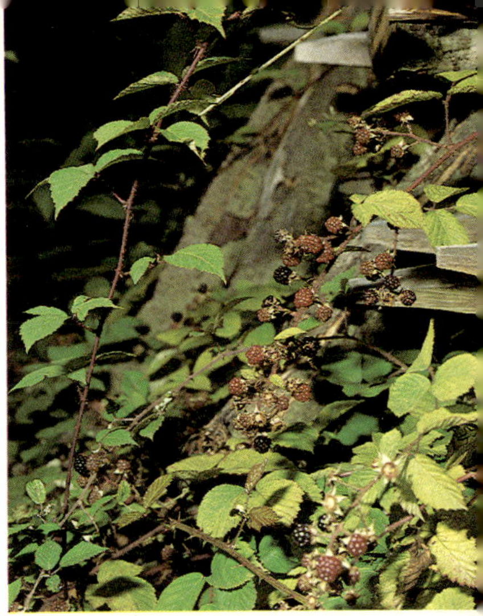

The spines of the Bramble help it to scramble up into the sunlight.

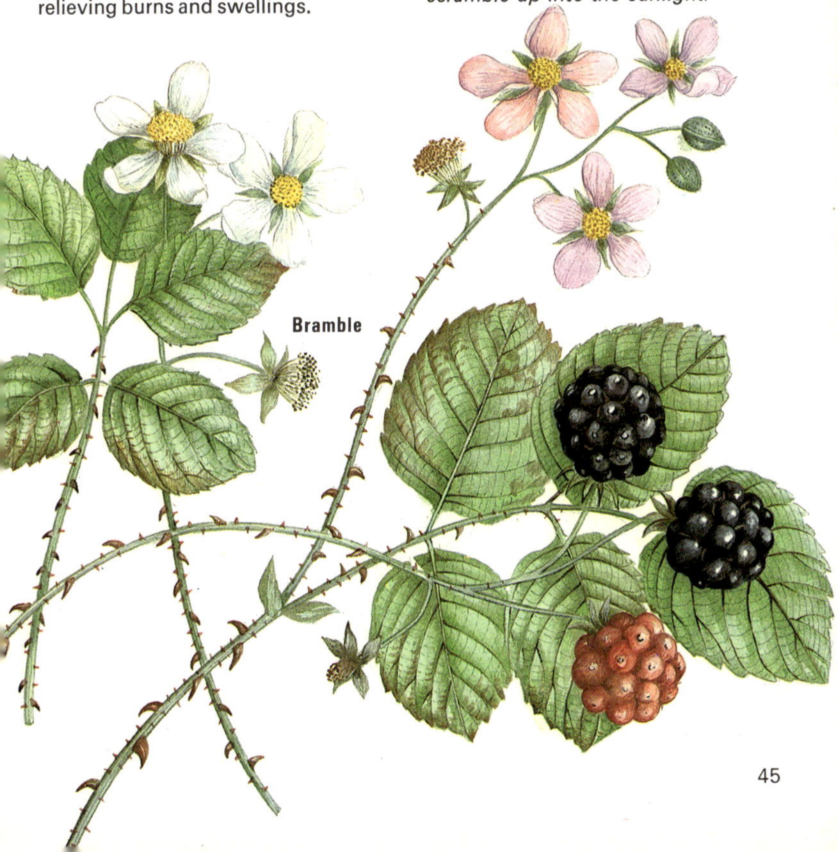

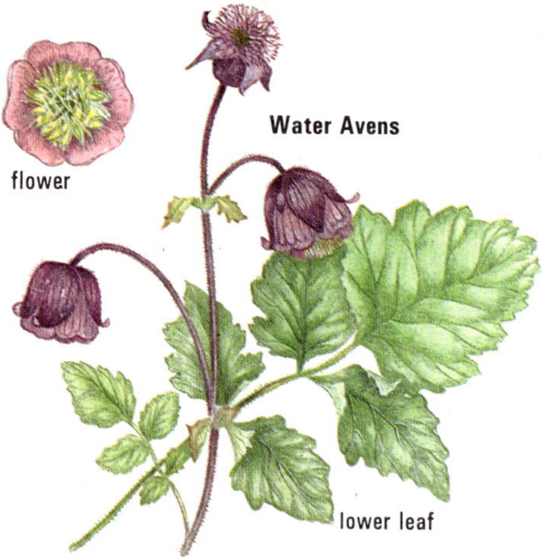

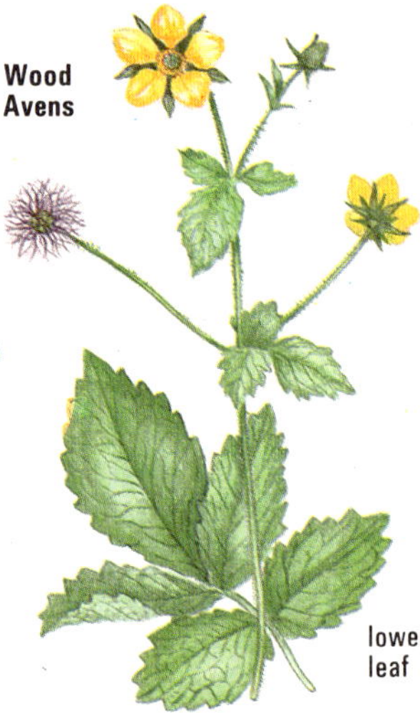

WATER AVENS

Geum rivale

A plant of shady, wet places and cleared woodland, the Water Avens is 20-60 cm high and shortly hairy. The flowers may easily be overlooked due to their nodding habit.

Flower: orange-pink, nodding; petals 5, 1-1·5 cm long, shallowly notched, abruptly narrowed at base; sepals purple, 5 as long as petals alternating with 5 shorter; stamens many; styles many, in central tuft.

Flower arrangement: few-flowered cyme.

Flowering time: May-September.

Leaf: pinnate, with 3-6 pairs of toothed leaflets; end leaflets enlarged, more or less rounded; leaf-stalk long; upper leaves smaller with fewer leaflets.

Fruit: head of achenes; styles persistent, becoming hooked; dispersed by clinging to fur of passing animals.

WOOD AVENS or HERB BENNETT

Geum urbanum

Growing erect in shady places, the Wood Avens is 20-60 cm tall and shortly hairy. Where Wood Avens and Water Avens grow together, hybrids between the two often occur.

Flower: yellow, 10-18 mm across; petals 5, oval; sepals 10, 5 as long as petals, alternating with 5 shorter; stamens many; styles many, in central tuft.

Flower arrangement: long-stalked, few-flowered cyme.

Flowering time: June-August.

Leaf: basal leaves pinnate, stalked, with 2-3 pairs of toothed leaflets, 5-10 mm long; end leaflet enlarged; stipules leaf-like.

Fruit: head of hooked achenes, dispersed by catching on clothing of passers-by and fur of animals.

Uses: the roots are said to smell and taste of cloves and were used to flavour ale.

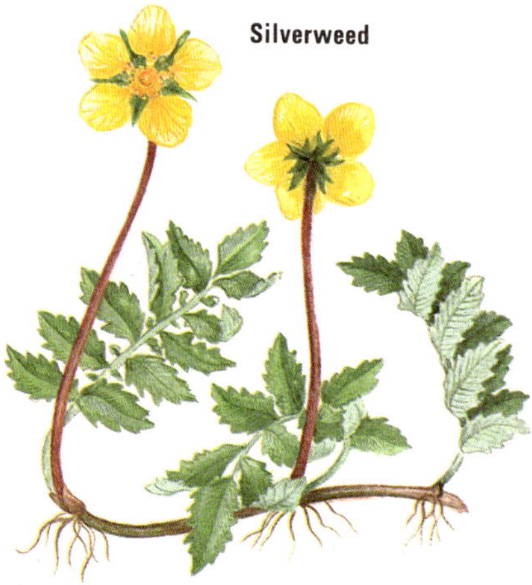

SILVERWEED

Potentilla anserina

The name describes the silvery, silky hairs with which this plant is covered. The leaves form a rosette from which creep rooting runners up to 80 cm long. The plant grows in damp roadside places and meadows.

Flower: yellow, 1·5-2·0 cm across; petals 5, rounded; sepals 10, in 2 layers, outer layer toothed and half as long as petals; stamens many.

Flower arrangement: solitary, on long stalk.

Flowering time: June-August.

Leaf: pinnate, 5-25 cm, with 7-12 pairs of deeply toothed leaflets, alternating with much smaller leaflets; dense, silver, silky hairs beneath or silky both sides.

Fruit: achenes hairless, in a head.

Uses: the fleshy roots were eaten in the poorer parts of Britain as a vegetable or made into meal for bread and porridge.

TORMENTIL

Potentilla erecta

Erect or creeping but not rooting, Tormentil is 10-30 cm high. It grows in grassland and may be found on mountains to a height of about 1,000 m.

Flower: yellow, 7-11 mm across; petals 4, shallowly notched, longer than sepals; sepals 8; stamens many.

Flower arrangement: on long slender stalks in loose cymes.

Flowering time: June-September.

Leaf: of 3 toothed segments; stalked basal leaves in rosette, often withering before flowering; stem leaves stalkless with large, toothed, leaf-like stipules (leaf appearing 5-segmented).

Fruit: achenes, hairless, in a head.

WILD STRAWBERRY

Fragaria vesca

This plant grows 5-30 cm high, with long runners which root and form new plants. It grows in woods and on hedgebanks. The Alpine Strawberry is a form of the Wild Strawberry.

Flower: white, 12-18 mm across; petals 5, rounded, not notched, edges touching or overlapping; sepals 10, in 2 layers; stamens many.

Flower arrangement: long-stalked cyme; stalk hairs lie flat.

Flowering time: April-July.

Leaf: divided into 3 toothed segments, each 1-6 cm long, ovate, bright green, paler with silky hairs beneath; leaf-stalks long, hairy.

Fruit: strawberry.

Uses: although the fruits are smaller than the cultivated strawberry, their flavour makes them very good to eat.

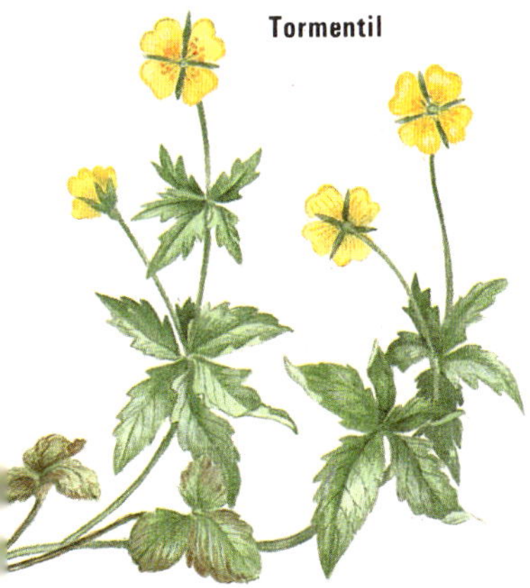

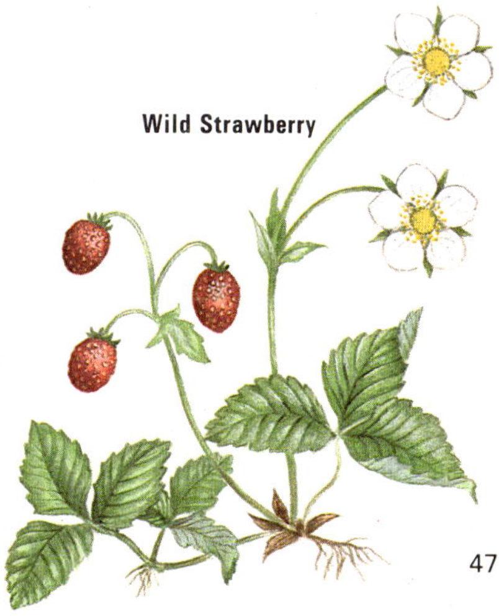

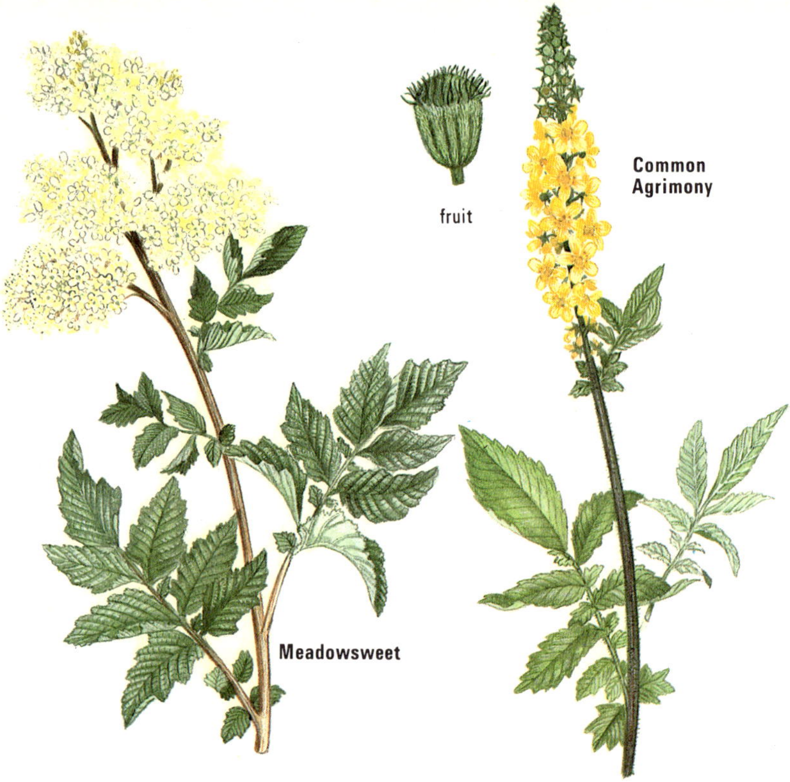

MEADOWSWEET

Filipendula ulmaria

This is a rather tall, erect plant, 60-200 cm high, of wet places, including damp meadows. The small, cream-coloured flowers with long stamens are in frothy, irregular masses. The stems are often reddish.

Flower: cream, scented, 4-10 mm across; stamens many, twice length of petals.

Flower arrangement: in loose, irregular masses.

Flowering time: June-September.

Leaf: pinnate, with 2-5 pairs of large, ovate, toothed leaflets with small leaflets between; usually white, downy beneath.

Fruit: carpels becoming twisted together to form achene about 2 mm.

Uses: Meadowsweet was formerly used against malaria when forms of that disease were common in undrained lowland areas.

COMMON AGRIMONY

Agrimonia eupatoria

This is an erect plant, 30-60 cm high, with a slender spike of yellow flowers above and densely leafy below. The reddish stems have long hairs, and the plant favours dry roadsides and field edges.

Flower: yellow, 5-8 mm across; petals 5; sepals 5, hairy; ring of hooked bristles immediately below; stamens many.

Flower arrangement: slender spike.

Flowering time: June-August.

Leaf: pinnate, with 3-6 pairs of toothed, elliptic leaflets, 2-6 cm long; hairy, greyish beneath, not glandular; smaller leaflets between; stipules leaf-like.

Fruit: grooved; top covered with hooked bristles which point forward; dispersed by catching onto clothing, or fur of passing animals.

STONECROP FAMILY
Crassulaceae

Members of this family are adapted to dry habitats such as walls and stony places, and have fleshy, hairless stems and leaves. The leaves are often closely spaced, and regeneration from fallen buds or leaves is common. The small flowers are of 5 pointed petals and sepals, and the fruits are clusters of follicles containing tiny seeds.

ORPINE
Sedum telephium

Orpine is a fleshy, hairless, upright plant, 20-60 cm tall, with slightly grey-green leaves and a stem often tinged red. Although native in European woods and hedges, it may also be found as a garden escape.
Flower: red-purple, star-shaped, 9-12 mm across; petals 5, pointed; sepals 5; stamens 10.
Flower arrangement: in dense clusters at the top of the stems.
Flowering time: July-September.
Leaf: fleshy, oval, alternate, up to 8 cm long, stalkless or shortly stalked, irregularly toothed.
Fruit: group of follicles.

BITING STONECROP
Sedum acre

Growing in mats on dry, stony or sandy ground or on walls, the Biting Stonecrop gets its name from the burning taste of its small, fleshy leaves.
Flower: bright yellow, star-shaped, about 12 mm across; petals 5, pointed; sepals 5; stamens 10.
Flower arrangement: at the ends of the branches.
Flowering time: June-July.
Leaf: very fleshy, hairless, rounded, 3-6 mm long, overlapping on non-flowering shoots.
Fruit: group of spreading follicles.

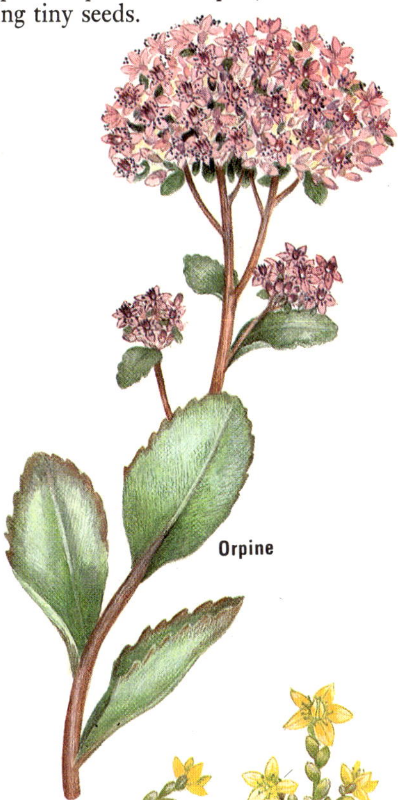

Orpine

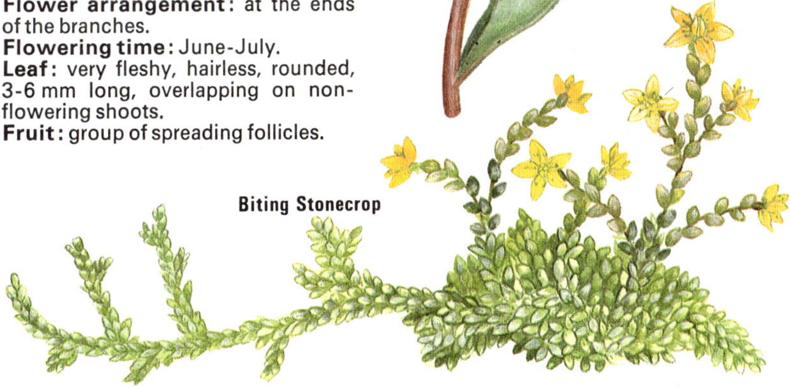

Biting Stonecrop

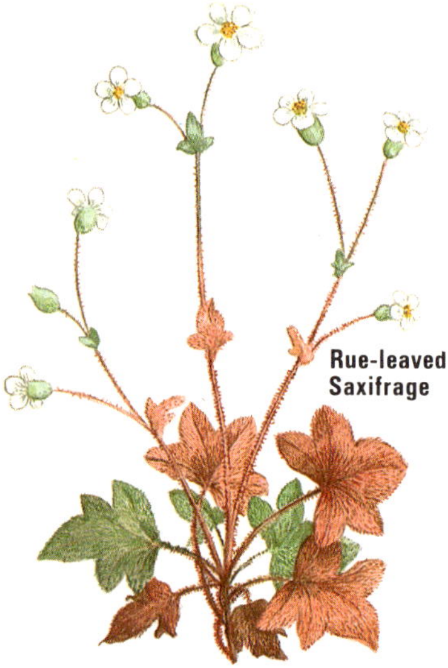

SAXIFRAGE FAMILY Saxifragaceae

Many species of Saxifrage are short, mountain plants and several are commonly grown in gardens. The flowers have 5 petals and sepals and 10 stamens. The alternate leaves often form rosettes.

RUE-LEAVED SAXIFRAGE

Saxifraga tridactylites

This is a slender, often red-tinged plant of 3-8 cm, though sometimes taller, often branched and covered in sticky hairs. In sunshine the ring-shaped nectaries at the flower centres exude glistening nectar. Although this Saxifrage inhabits mainly dry walls in lowland areas, many others are mountain-dwellers.

Flower: white, 4-6 mm across; petals 5, rounded; sepals 5, joined at base, erect; stamens 10; nectary yellow, ring-shaped.

Flower arrangement: loose cyme.

Flowering time: April-June.

Leaf: 3-5-lobed; basal leaves not forming rosette, often withered at flowering time.

Fruit: 2-lobed capsule; seeds brown.

GRASS-OF-PARNASSUS FAMILY Parnassiaceae

There is only one European species in this family. The plant name was first used by a Flemish botanist in the 16th century, who identified it as the Grass-of-Parnassus of Dioscorides, the founder of medicine according to ancient Greek mythology.

GRASS-OF-PARNASSUS

Parnassia palustris

The habitat of this very pretty, slightly grey-green plant is wet moorland and bogs. The plant is hairless, growing in a loose tuft and 5-40 cm high, the white, veined flowers smelling faintly of honey.

Flower: white, 1·5-3 cm across; petals 5, clearly veined, oval; sepals 5; fertile stamens 5; infertile stamens fan-shaped, lying against petals.

Flower arrangement: solitary.

Flowering time: July-October.

Leaf: all basal, heart-shaped, stalked, except for single, stalkless leaf about a third of the way up flower stem.

Fruit: capsule, opening by 4 valves.

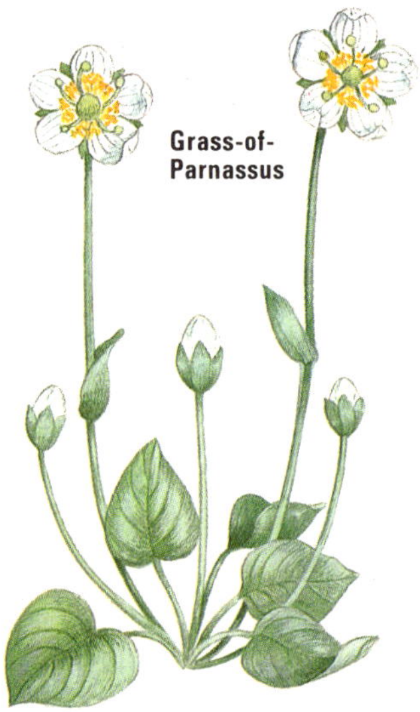

SUNDEW FAMILY
Droseraceae

As well as the Sundews, this family of insectivorous plants includes the Venus' Fly Trap. Sundews have long, sticky glands on the leaves, which trap insects and digest them with secreted enzymes. This may be a response to a lack of nitrogen in the boggy, waterlogged conditions in which these plants grow.

ROUND-LEAVED SUNDEW
Drosera rotundifolia

Stalked, sticky red glands on the leaves of this little plant often lend a red tinge to the ground of bogs and wet moors where it grows. Insects stick to the glands which slowly bend toward the leaf centre, further enmeshing the insect. Eventually the prey is digested and the glands return to their former positions.

Flower: white, 5 mm across; petals 5 or 6.
Flower arrangement: spike, slender, on long stalk.
Flowering time: June-August.
Leaf: circular, long-stalked, in a rosette, upper surface covered in sticky, red, stalked glands.
Fruit: capsule.

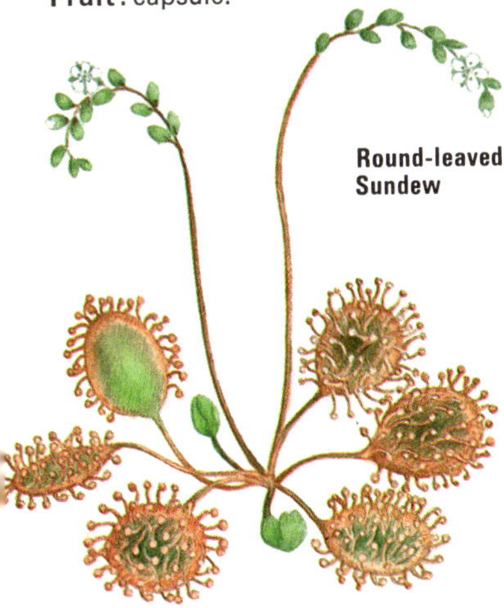

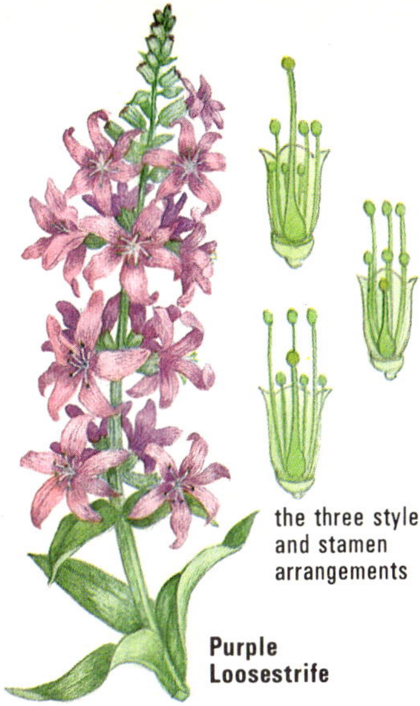

LOOSESTRIFE FAMILY
Lythraceae

This is a small family of plants which favour damp places. The flowers have 4-6 petals which are crumpled in bud. Some species in this family produce dyes, one of the best known being henna.

PURPLE LOOSESTRIFE
Lythrum salicaria

This is an erect plant, 50-150 cm tall with a 4-angled stem and varying from almost hairless to densely hairy. It is found in damp places such as river banks. The flowers are insect-pollinated and are of 3 kinds, differing in the relative lengths of their styles and stamens. Each plant bears only one kind of flower.

Flower: red-purple, 1-1·5 cm across; petals 6, flimsy; calyx tubular, ribbed, with 12 teeth; stamens 12.
Flower arrangement: in whorls on a tall spike.
Flowering time: June-August.
Leaf: opposite or in threes; narrow, pointed, without teeth, 4-7 cm long, stalkless.
Fruit: capsule, ovoid, enclosed by calyx.

WILLOWHERB FAMILY
Onagraceae

This family is widespread throughout the world and includes some shrubs and water plants as well as such garden ornamentals as the Evening-primroses (*Oenothera* species). The flowers have 4 petals, which may be formed into a tube as in Fuchsias. There are commonly 8 stamens and the stigma is 4-lobed or undivided. Many are pollinated by moths. The fruit is usually a capsule.

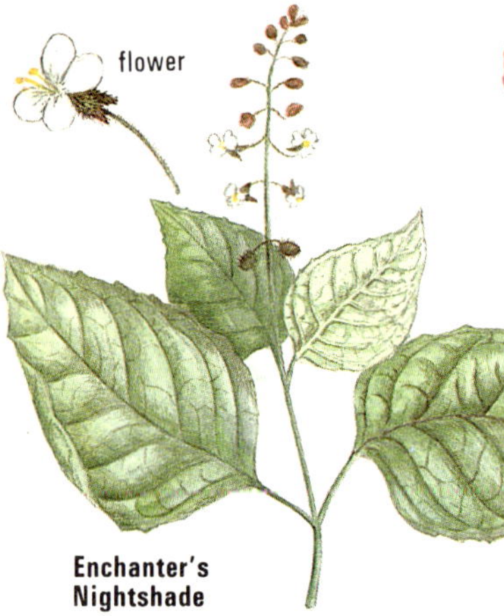

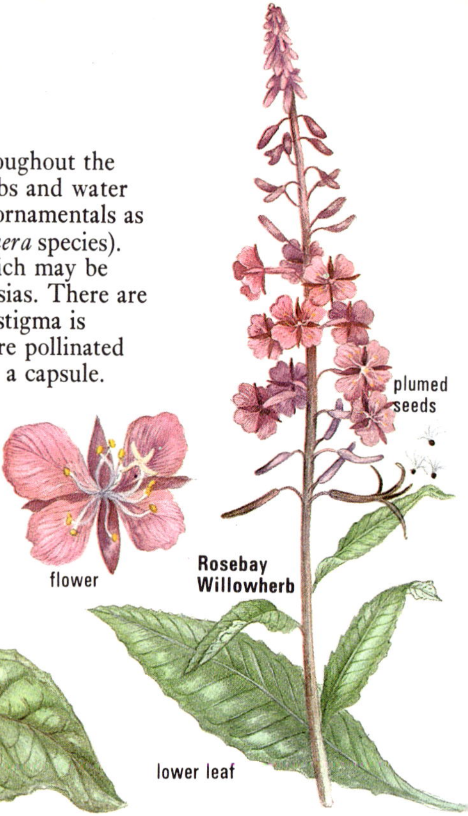

ENCHANTER'S NIGHTSHADE
Circaea lutetiana

Standing 15-70 cm high, this shade-loving plant of woods and gardens often grows in patches. The stem and leaves have scattered glandular hairs.
Flower: white or pink-tinged, 4-8 mm; petals 2, deeply notched, appearing as 4; sepals 2, glandular, hairy; stamens 2.
Flower arrangement: raceme.
Flowering time: June-August.
Leaf: opposite, ovate, sparsely toothed, 4-10 cm long, stalked, dull above, shiny beneath.
Fruit: rounded, covered with hooked bristles, 2-4 mm; stalks turning down; dispersed by clinging to fur of small animals, especially cats.

ROSEBAY WILLOWHERB
Epilobium angustifolium

The tall, almost hairless plants are up to 120 cm high. In Britain a century ago this species was confined to certain localities but has since spread widely. It has a preference for burnt ground, and covered bombed sites in World War II.
Flower: rosy-purple, 2-3 cm across; petals 4, upper 2 slightly larger; sepals 4, narrow, purple; stamens 8; stigma 4-lobed.
Flower arrangement: raceme, long, many-flowered.
Flowering time: July-September.
Leaf: narrow, pointed, alternate, 5-20 cm long, entire or with small, widely spaced teeth.
Fruit: capsule, long (2·5-8 cm), narrow, opening by 4 long slits, downy; seeds with plume of hairs.

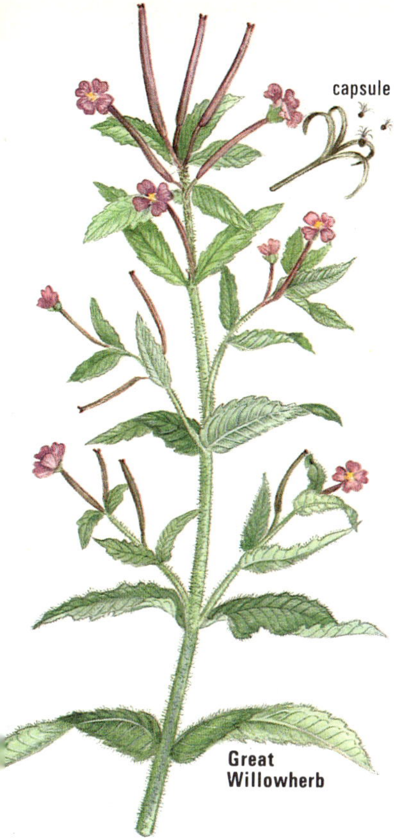

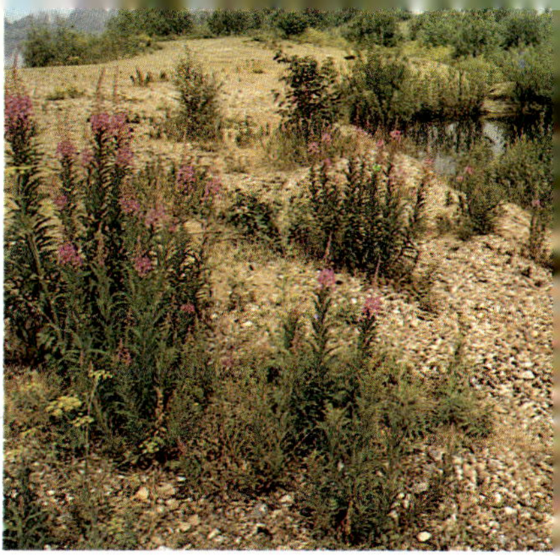

Rosebay Willowherb colonizing a gravel pit.

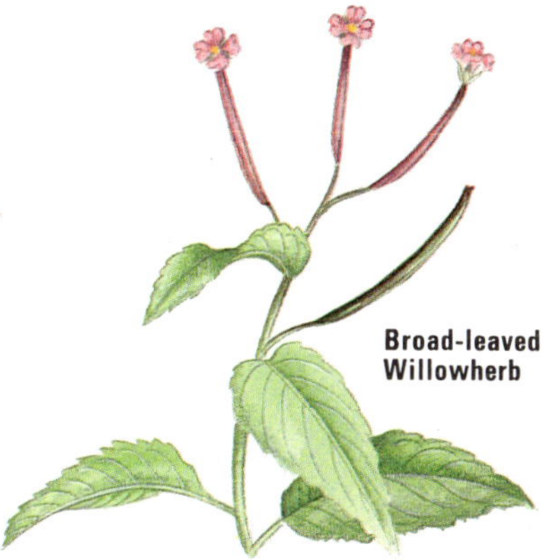

GREAT WILLOWHERB

Epilobium hirsutum

This Willowherb is tall, up to 150 cm, erect and densely covered in soft hairs. It often forms stands in moist places such as marshes and stream-sides. It is absent from N.W. Scotland and most of Sweden and Norway.

Flower: deep purplish pink, 1·5-2·5 cm across; petals 4, notched; sepals 4, erect, pointed; stamens 8; stigma cream-coloured, 4-lobed; buds erect.

Flower arrangement: raceme, flower stalks arising from leaf-axils.

Flowering time: July-August.

Leaf: rather narrow, opposite, pointed, teeth curved forward; stalk-less, leaf base weakly clasping stem.

Fruit: capsule, long (5-8 cm), narrow, opening by 4 long slits, downy; seeds with plume of hairs.

BROAD-LEAVED WILLOWHERB

Epilobium montanum

This is a small, sparsely hairy plant. The stems are erect, 20-60 cm high and reddish. It is found in gardens as a weed, and in woods, hedges and stony places.

Flower: pale mauve, 6-9 mm across; petals 4, notched; sepals 4, erect, pointed; stamens 8; stigma 4-lobed; buds nodding.

Flower arrangement: raceme, flower stalks arising from leaf-axils.

Flowering time: June-August.

Leaf: ovate, opposite, toothed, shortly stalked.

Fruit: capsule, long (4-8 cm), narrow, opening by 4 longitudinal slits, downy; seeds with plume of hairs.

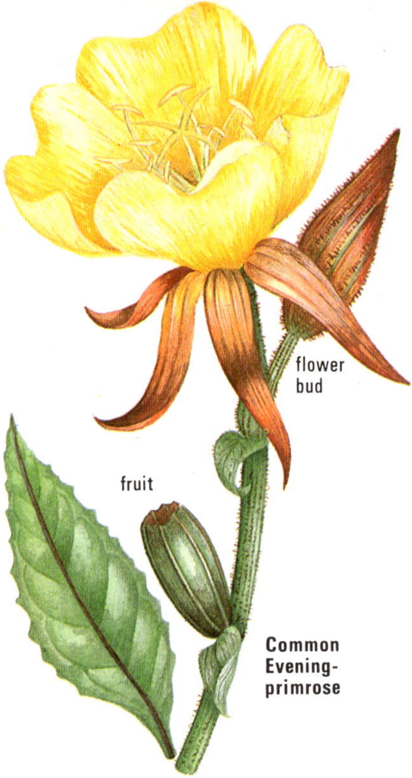

MARE'S TAIL FAMILY
Hippuridaceae

There is only one species, *Hippuris vulgaris*, in this family.

MARE'S TAIL
Hippuris vulgaris
Growing 25-75 cm high in still or slow-moving fresh water, the unbranched shoots of Mare's Tail bear many whorls of narrow leaves. The leaves are flattened, not tubular as in the superficially similar Horsetails, which are relatives of the ferns.
Flower: inconspicuous, without petals, greenish, wind-pollinated.
Flower arrangement: in the leaf-axils of aerial shoots.
Flowering time: June-July.
Leaf: very narrow, 1-7·5 cm long, in whorls, stalkless; submerged leaves very thin, pale, limp.
Fruit: nut, green, 2-3 mm.

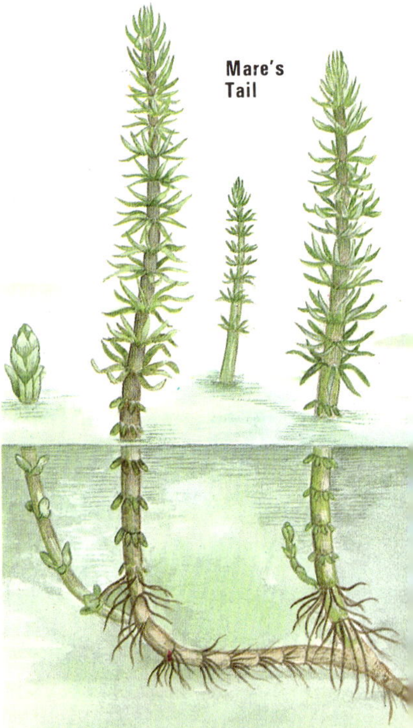

COMMON EVENING-PRIMROSE
Oenothera biennis
This species grows 50-150 cm high. The stems are stout and often shortly hairy. The flowers open at dusk and exude scent to attract pollinating moths. Evening-primroses were originally introduced from N. America. This one occurs on dunes and in dry, waste places.
Flower: yellow, 5-6 cm across; petals 4, broadly heart-shaped; sepals 4, narrow, tapered to point, bent sharply down; stamens 8; stigma deeply 4-lobed.
Flower arrangement: raceme, flower stalks arising from leaf-axils.
Flowering time: June-September.
Leaf: elliptic, alternate, sparsely toothed, stalkless or shortly stalked, main vein becoming reddish.
Fruit: capsule, 3-3·5 cm long, opening by 4 valves; seeds angled.

STARWORT FAMILY
Callitrichaceae

The Starwort family consists of one genus of 17 species. They are small, slender water plants. Some species grow and are pollinated underwater, some grow in or beside water and others only on wet mud. The flowers are minute and unisexual.

WATER-STARWORT
Callitriche stagnalis

These small, hairless water plants may be found creeping and rooting on wet mud, or floating or submerged in ponds, streams or lakes. The stems grow 1-25 cm long on land and to 100 cm in water. The species in this aggregate group are extremely variable and difficult to separate. Leaf shape depends on whether the plants are submerged or not and on water depth and movement.
Flower: inconspicuous, green, without petals, unisexual.
Flower arrangement: in leaf-axils.
Flowering time: April-October.
Leaf: oval or strap-shaped, opposite, often forming rosettes at tips of emerging shoots.
Fruit: 4-lobed.

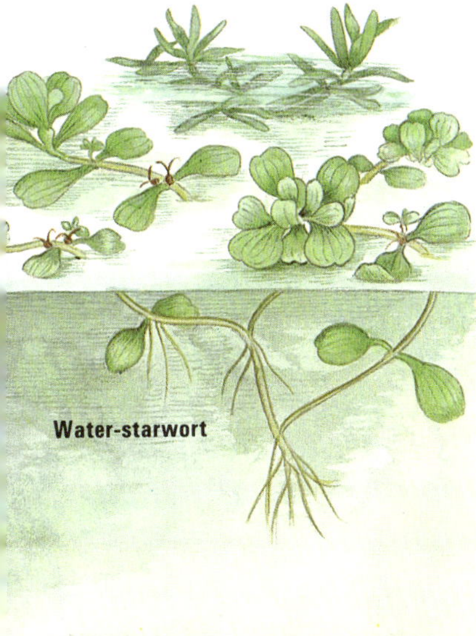

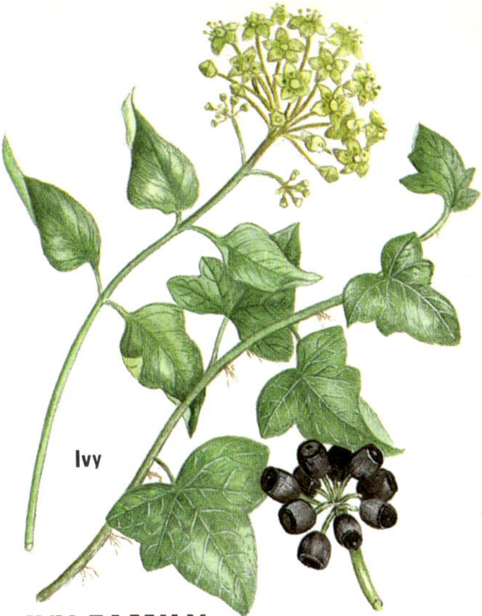

IVY FAMILY
Araliaceae

This is a family of mainly tropical herbs, shrubs and trees. The small flowers are green or white, and the fruits are berry-like. Climbing species often have modified, clinging aerial roots.

IVY
Hedera helix

The familiar, evergreen Ivy climbs to 30 m on trees, cliffs and buildings. Short, thick roots up one side of the stem help it to cling to a support. It may also be found carpeting the ground in woods.
Flower: yellow-green; petals 5, 3-4 mm long, pointed; calyx with 5 tiny teeth; stamens 5; style surrounded by nectar-secreting disc.
Flower arrangement: in rounded, umbel-like clusters on unshaded, high parts of plant.
Flowering time: September-November.
Leaf: glossy, stalked, of 2 kinds: those on non-flowering branches 3-5-lobed, those on the flowering not lobed, ovate or more or less diamond-shaped.
Fruit: black, berry-like, 8-10 mm.

CARROT FAMILY
Umbelliferae

Among the most easily recognizable features of this large family is the arrangement of tiny flowers in umbels. These are flat-topped clusters of flowers, with the bases of the stalks (*rays*) all joining at one point. Many species have compound umbels. These are umbels formed, in turn, of smaller umbels. Bracts may be present at the base of a compound (*primary*) umbel and smaller bracts (*bracteoles*) at the bases of the individual (*secondary*) umbels. The fruits and bracts are important for identification. There are many herbs and spices in the family, including parsley, fennel and dill, as well as many poisonous plants.

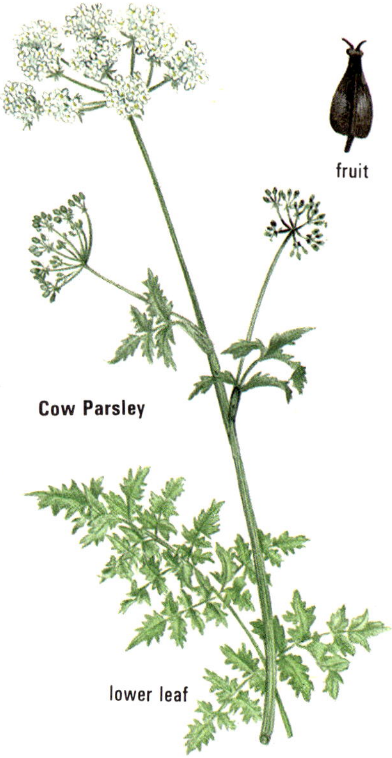

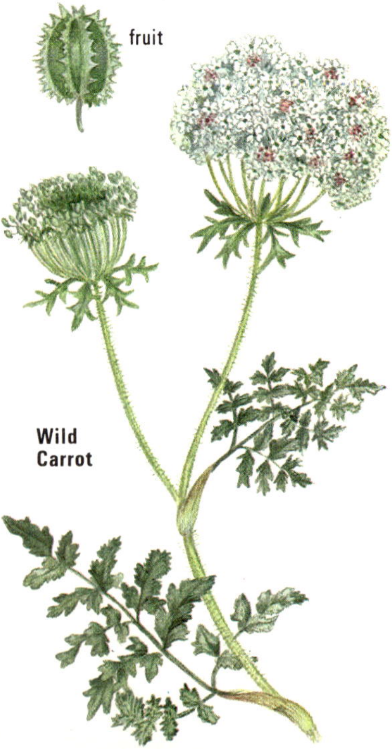

WILD CARROT
Daucus carota

The Wild Carrot usually has stiffly hairy stems, ridged, not hollow and 30-100 cm high. It grows in grassy places, and at the coast. The middle flower of each umbel is often red. The widely cultivated carrot with a swollen edible tap root is a form of the Wild Carrot.

Flower: white, middle flower of umbel often red; petals 5, tips incurved; petals of outer flowers enlarged.

Flower arrangement: compound umbel, 3-7 cm across; rays many; bracts conspicuous, each of 3 or more long points; bracteoles similar.

Flowering time: June-August.

Leaf: finely dissected, often fleshy if growing by the sea.

Fruit: ovoid; ridges spiny; 2-4 mm; umbel becoming hollow in fruit.

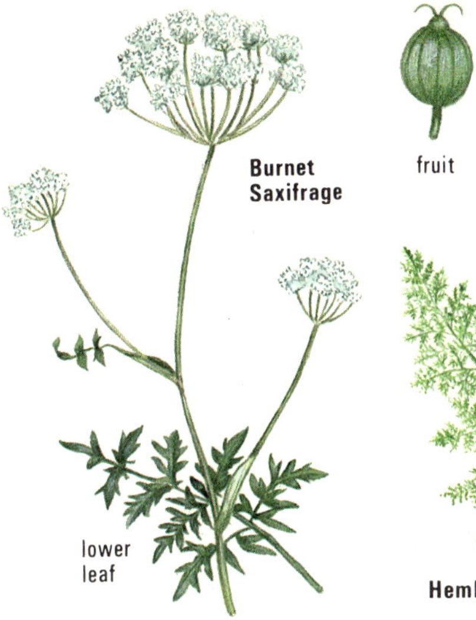

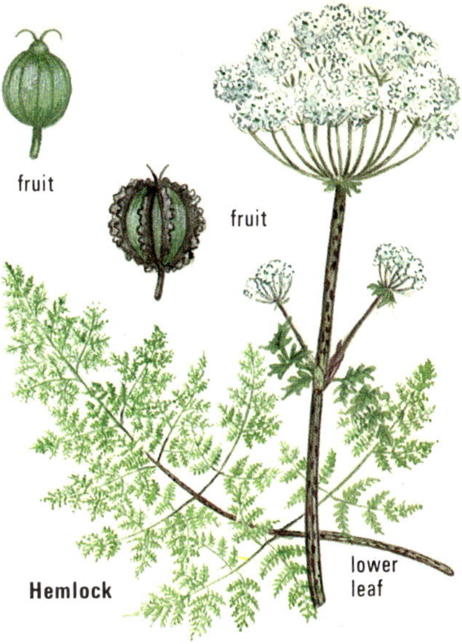

COW PARSLEY

Anthriscus sylvestris

One of the commonest white-flowered umbels, Cow Parsley is also among the earliest to flower. A tall, slightly downy plant, it grows up to 150 cm high in hedges and wood borders. The stems are hollow, grooved and may be tinged red.
Flower: white, 3-4 mm across; petals 5, tip often slightly notched and curved inward.
Flower arrangement: in compound umbels, 2-6 cm across; no bracts; bracteoles 5 or 6.
Flowering time: April-June.
Leaf: 2- or 3-pinnate, up to 30 cm long, shortly hairy beneath, leaf-stalk sheathing stem at base.
Fruit: of 2 oblong, joined carpels, black, smooth, 5-10 mm, each bearing short, persistent style.

BURNET SAXIFRAGE

Pimpinella saxifraga

This species has a downy and tough but slender stem, weakly ridged. It grows 30-100 cm high in dry grassland, very often on chalk or limestone. The seed of a Mediterranean species of Pimpinella is the aniseed of seed cake and sweets.
Flower: white, 2 mm across; petals 5, tips incurved.
Flower arrangement: compound umbel, 2-5 cm across, flat-topped; rays 10-20; no bracts or bracteoles.
Flowering time: July-August.
Leaf: pinnate; leaflets ovate, coarsely toothed, stalkless; upper leaves doubly pinnate, leaflets narrow.
Fruit: ovoid, 2-3 mm.

HEMLOCK

Conium maculatum

Hemlock is extremely poisonous in all parts. It can be recognized by the smooth, purple-spotted stem and a 'mousy' smell if the plant is crushed. The hairless plant grows up to 2·5 m in damp habitats, near water and on waste land.
Flower: white, 2 mm across; petals 5, tips shortly incurved.
Flower arrangement: compound umbel, 2-5 cm across; rays 10-20; bracts 5-6; bracteoles on outer sides of secondary umbels.
Flowering time: June-July.
Leaf: finely dissected, up to 30 cm.
Fruit: spherical, 2·5-3·5 mm, ridges bumpy.
Uses: traditionally this was the drug used to poison Socrates. Medicinal use of Hemlock was revived in the late 18th century but discontinued due to the uncertain effects.

WILD ANGELICA

Angelica sylvestris

Often stout and up to 200 cm or more high, this Umbellifer is almost hairless. It favours damp, shady places. The hollow, grooved stem is often purple with a whitish cast or bloom.

Flower: white or pink, 2 mm across; petals 5, incurved.

Flower arrangement: compound umbel, rounded, 3-15 cm across; rays many, slightly hairy; few or no bracts; bracteoles few, bristle-like.

Flowering time: July-September.

Leaf: doubly or trebly pinnate; leaflets 2-8 cm, ovate, toothed, leaf-stalks deeply grooved on upper side, widely sheathing stem at base.

Fruit: ovoid, 4-5 mm, flattened, winged; persistent styles curved.

GROUND ELDER

Aegopodium podagraria

The leaves of Ground Elder have broad, undissected leaflets, unlike the finely dissected leaves of many other Umbellifers. The plant is hairless, with hollow, grooved stems, and grows in shady places and gardens, where it can be a stubborn weed.

Flower: white, sometimes pink, 1 mm across; petals 5, tips incurved.

Flower arrangement: in compound umbels, 2-6 cm across; rays 15-20; few or no bracts or bracteoles.

Flowering time: May-July.

Leaf: of 3 leaflets, each 4-8 cm, ovate, toothed, on long, 3-angled leaf-stalk sheathing stem at base.

Fruit: ovoid, 4 mm, ridged; persistent styles curved down.

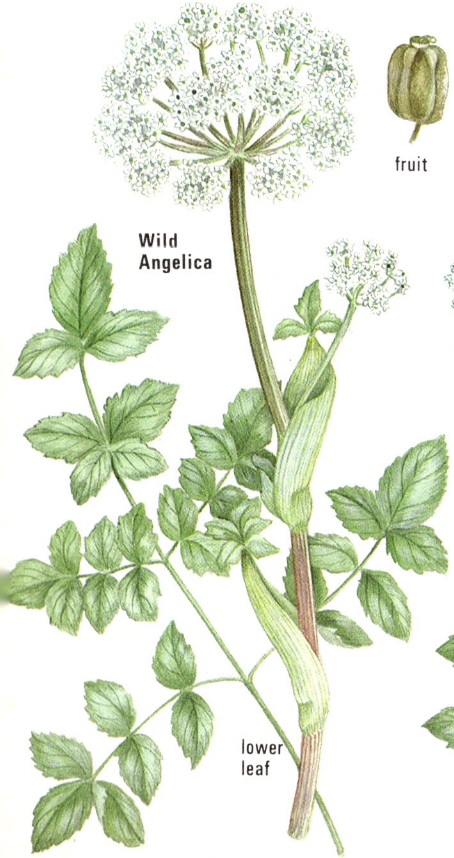

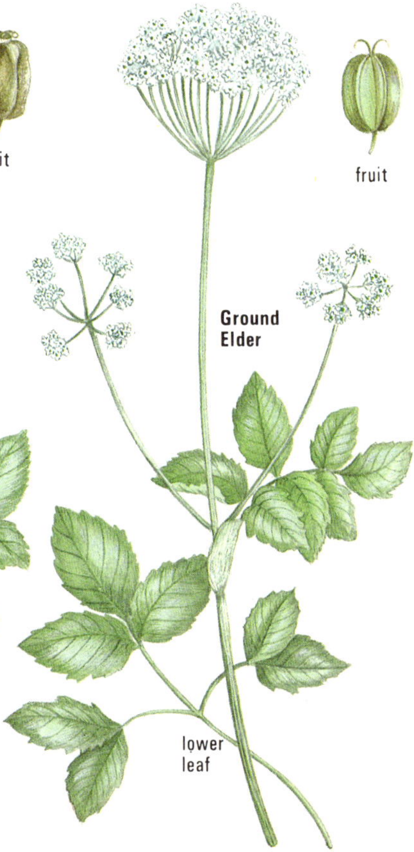

HOGWEED

Heracleum sphondylium

The stout stem of Hogweed is grooved, hollow and stiffly hairy, the hairs bent sharply down. The plant is found in grassland, hedges and woods, growing 50-200 cm high. The Giant Hogweed (*H. mantegazzianum*) is up to 3·5 m and has a red-blotched stem.

Flower: white or pink, 5-10 mm across; petals 5, incurved, enlarged in outer flowers.

Flower arrangement: compound umbel, 5-15 cm across; rays 7-20, few or no bracts; bracteoles bristle-like.

Flowering time: June-September.

Leaf: pinnate, 15-60 cm; leaflets broad, toothed and lobed, stiffly hairy; bases of stalks widely sheathing stem.

Fruit: ovoid, flattened, whitish, 7-8 mm; persistent styles short, curved.

Uses: the leaves are fed to pigs.

LESSER WATER-PARSNIP

Berula erecta

These hairless plants, 30-100 cm high, grow in shallow fresh water, often forming sprawling masses. The stems are hollow and ridged. Fool's Water-cress (*Apium nodiflorum*) is similar to this species. They cannot easily be told apart unless flowers or fruit are present.

Flower: white, 2 mm across; petals 5, tips incurved.

Flower arrangement: compound umbel, 3-6 cm across, on long stalk; rays 10-20; bracts and bracteoles many, often with a few teeth.

Flowering time: July-September.

Leaf: pinnate, up to 30 cm long; 7-14 pairs ovate, toothed leaflets; dull, blue-green.

Fruit: 2-lobed, 1·5-2 mm, a little wider than high; persistent styles curved.

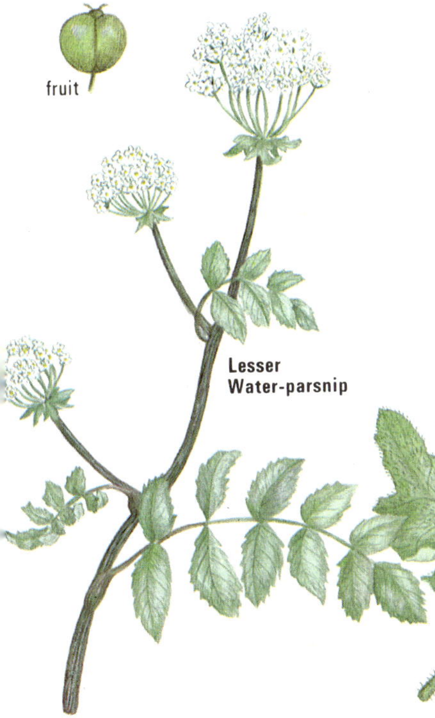

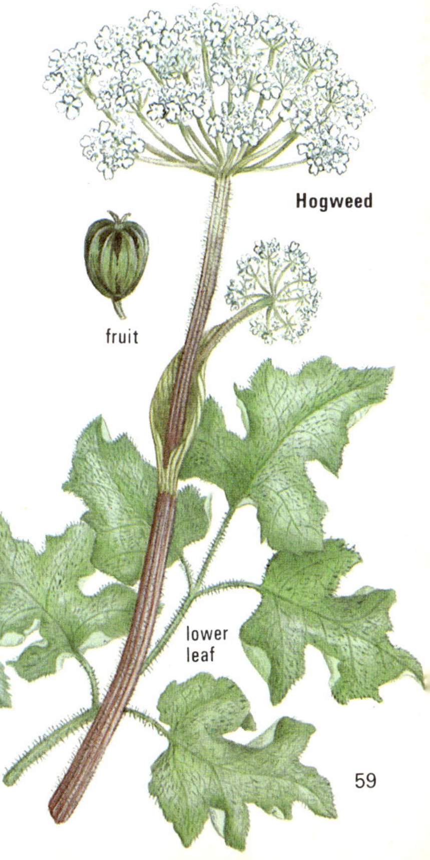

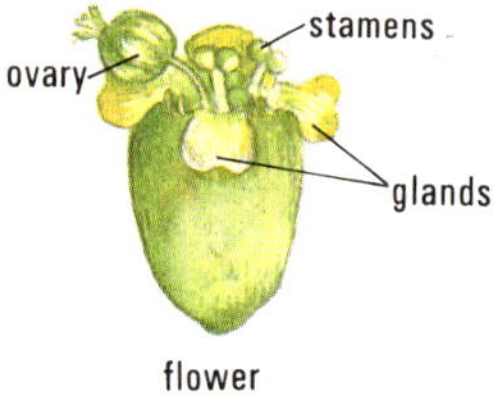

SPURGE FAMILY
Euphorbiaceae

This large, mainly tropical family includes species which produce rubber and castor oil. The Spurges have very distinctive flowers without petals, consisting of a little cup in which are several stamens and a single style and ovary. Glands around the rim attract insects. Poisonous, sometimes milky sap is characteristic of the family.

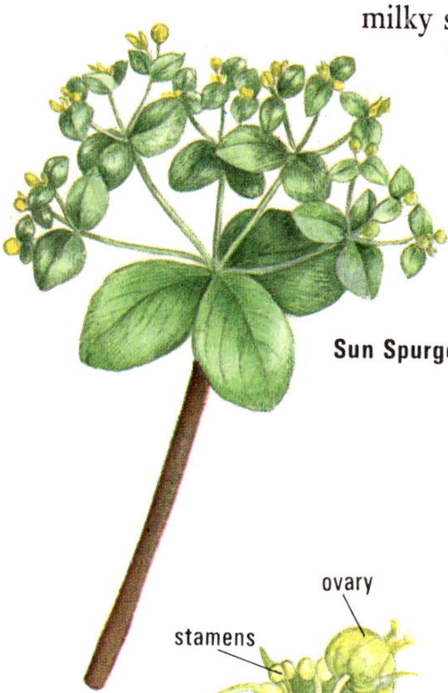

Sun Spurge

SUN SPURGE
Euphorbia helioscopia

The whole plant is hairless, 10-50 cm high and erect. The characteristic yellowish bracts of the flowers lend a yellow-green look to the plant. The stem is often red and if broken exudes white latex containing irritant poison. Disturbed ground is the habitat of this Spurge.

Flower: minute; glands on rim green; kidney-shaped, surrounded by yellowish, leaf-like bracts.
Flower arrangement: in umbel-like, 5-stalked clusters.
Flowering time: May-October.
Leaf: rounded, lower leaf often tapering at base; minutely toothed, alternate.
Fruit: capsule, smooth, 3-5 mm, stalked, nodding over rim of flower; seeds brown, wrinkled.

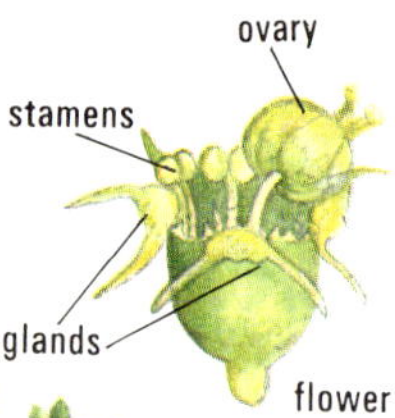

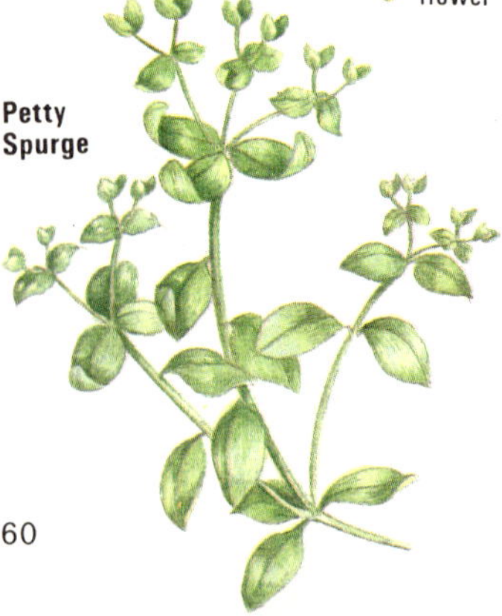

Petty Spurge

PETTY SPURGE
Euphorbia peplus

Growing 10-30 cm high in cultivated ground, the Petty Spurge is hairless and light green. The minute flowers are surrounded by leaf-like bracts. If broken the plant oozes white latex, which can irritate the skin.

Flower: minute; glands on rim crescent-shaped with long, pointed tips, surrounded by opposite, leaf-like bracts.
Flower arrangement: flower stalks repeatedly dividing in two.
Flowering time: April-November.
Leaf: oval, not toothed, alternate.
Fruit: capsule, ridged, 2 mm, stalked, nodding over rim of flower; seeds pale grey, pitted.

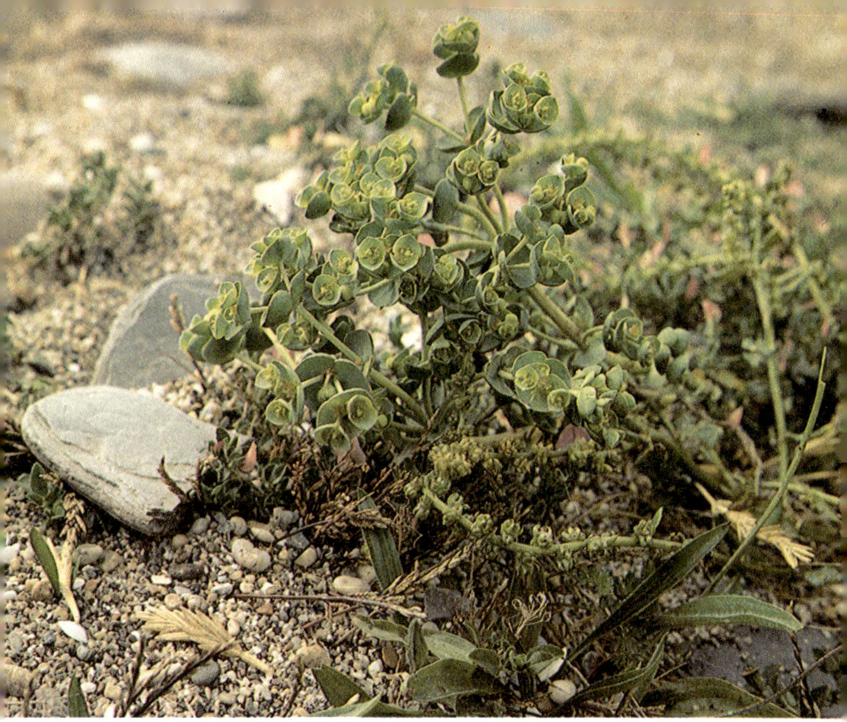

Sea Spurge (Euphorbia paralias) *sharing a stony beach with other seaside plants.*

DOG'S MERCURY

Mercurialis perennis

Poisonous to humans and livestock, Dog's Mercury is erect, up to 40 cm, unbranched and shortly hairy. The plant smells unpleasant if crushed, and grows in woods and shady places. The spikes of inconspicuous flowers open in spring, each plant bearing either all-male or all-female flowers. The very similar species, Annual Mercury (*M. annua*), differs by being hairless and summer-flowering.

Flower: inconspicuous, green; male and female on separate plants.

Flower arrangement: males in slender spikes, females in small, stalked clusters.

Flowering time: February-April.

Leaf: elliptic, blunt-toothed, opposite, 2-8 cm long, shortly stalked.

Fruit: spherical, hairy, 6-8 mm.

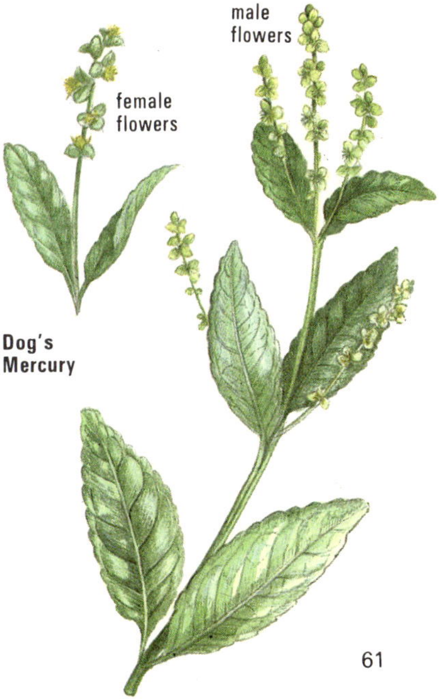

DOCK FAMILY
Polygonaceae

Most members of this large family are from northern temperate areas. Useful species include Rhubarb and Buckwheat. The leaves have a characteristic papery sheath called an *ochrea* encircling the stem at the leaf-base. The small flowers have no true petals and are white, green or pink. The fruit, enclosed by the persistent flower, is important in identification.

AMPHIBIOUS BISTORT
Polygonum amphibium

The stems and leaves of this water plant float on the surface of still or slow-moving water. The stems grow 30-75 cm long and root along their length. A slightly differing form, with short, stiff hairs on the leaves and ochreae, grows at the water's-edge and in damp grassland.

Flower: pink; petal-like lobes 5; stamens 5, red.

Flower arrangement: dense, short spike, 2-4 cm long, stalked.

Flowering time: July-September.

Leaf: long—ovate, hairless, shiny stalked, alternate; ochreae hairless (leaves and ochreae hairy in land form).

Fruit: nut, shiny, brown.

REDSHANK
Polygonum persicaria

The stem, often reddish, is more or less erect, branched and 25-80 cm high. There are dense spikes of tiny pink flowers, and the leaves often bear a dark blotch. The whole plant is almost hairless and grows on waste and cultivated ground.

Flower: pink; petal-like lobes 5.

Flower arrangement: compact spike, up to 3·5 cm long.

Flowering time: June-October.

Leaf: narrow, tapering to point, often dark-blotched, alternate, margin fringed with hairs; ochreae brownish, fringed with hairs.

Fruit: nut, black, shiny.

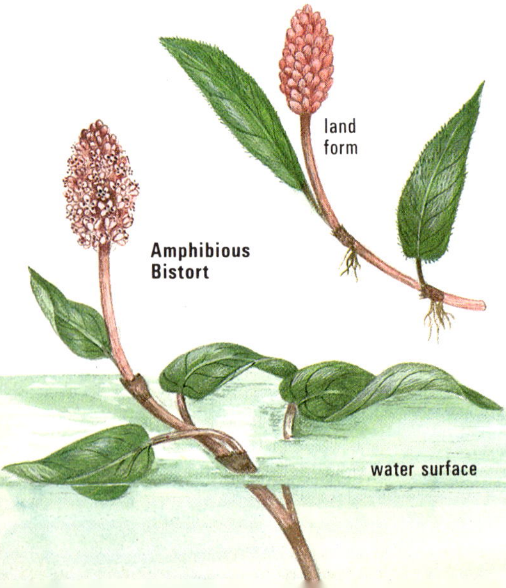

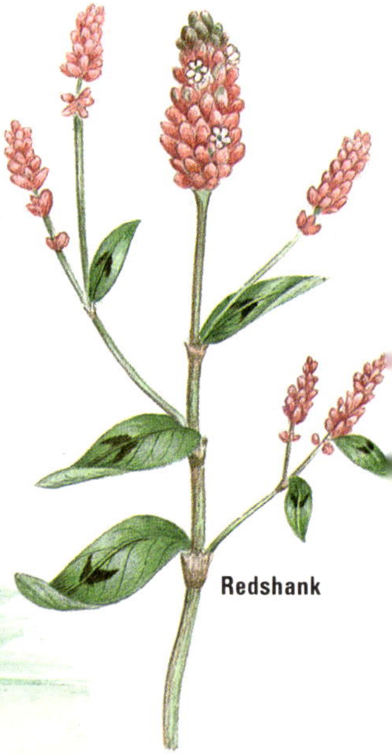

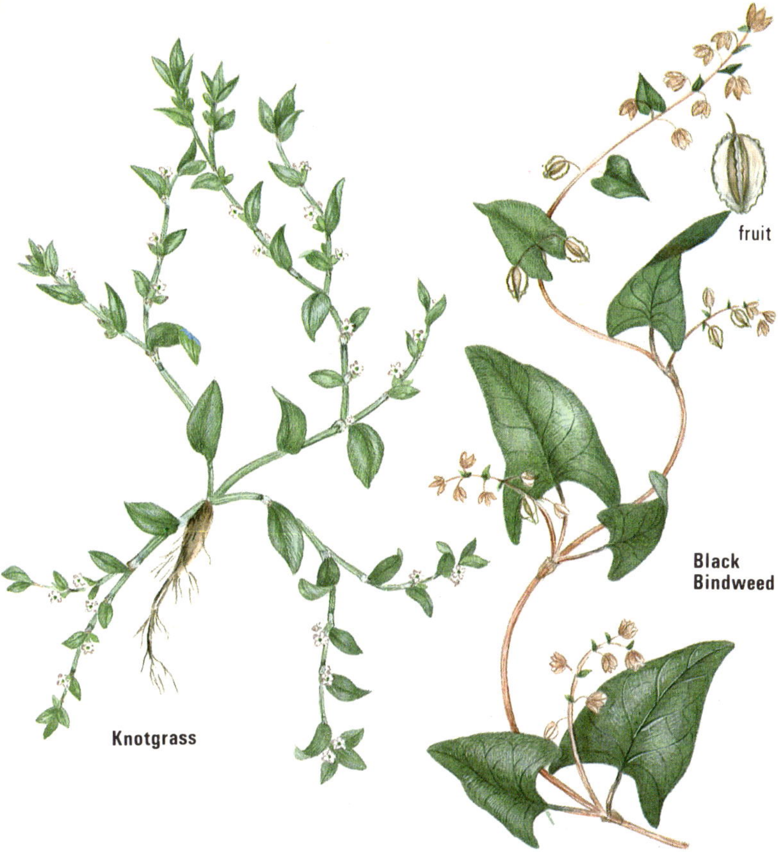

KNOTGRASS

Polygonum aviculare

Knotgrass is a ragged-looking species, erect (up to 2 m high) or straggling in mats on trampled ground and at the coast. The plant is hairless and branched, and the ochreae are ragged and silvery.

Flower: pink or white; petal-like lobes 5.

Flower arrangement: 1-6 flowers in the leaf-axils.

Flowering time: July-October.

Leaf: elliptic to very narrow, tips more or less pointed, almost stalkless; leaves on main stem larger than branch leaves; ochreae silvery, torn.

Fruit: nut, 3-angled, hidden by dead flower.

BLACK BINDWEED

Polygonum convolvulus

The grooved stem of the climbing Black Bindweed twines clockwise around its support to a height of 30-120 cm. It grows on waste or cultivated land.

Flower: greenish white; petal-like lobes 5, 3 outer with ridge; each flower stalk 1-2 mm, jointed above middle.

Flower arrangement: loose spike or raceme in the leaf-axils.

Flowering time: July-October.

Leaf: spear-shaped, stalked, powdery white beneath, usually alternate; ochrea rim at an angle.

Fruit: nut, dull, black, enclosed by persistent flower.

COMMON SORREL

Rumex acetosa

Growing up to 100 cm but usually much smaller, this almost hairless plant grows in grassland, to which the flowers and fruits can give a reddish tinge.

Flower: green and red, tiny; male and female flowers on separate plants; wind-pollinated.

Flower arrangement: in whorls on branched raceme.

Flowering time: May-July.

Leaf: spear-shaped, basal lobes pointing down, acid-tasting, up to 10 cm long; upper leaves almost stalkless; ochreae fringed.

Fruit: 3-4 mm, with 3 papery wings, tinged red, enclosing 3-angled nut.

Uses: a sharp-tasting sauce, to be eaten with fish or pork, can be made from the leaves simmered in butter with salt and black pepper.

BROAD-LEAVED DOCK

Rumex obtusifolia

This is a very common Dock, 50-120 cm high, of waste places and cultivated land. There are several similar species of dock which can be distinguished by their fruits.

Flower: green, tiny, wind-pollinated.

Flower arrangement: in whorls, on branched raceme.

Flowering time: June-October.

Leaf: oblong, broad, tip pointed or rounded, lobed at base, alternate, up to 25 cm long, minutely blunt-toothed, often hairy on underside.

Fruit: 5-6 mm, with 3 green, deeply toothed wings alternating with 3 unequal red swellings enclosing 3-angled nut.

Uses: traditionally Dock leaves are rubbed on Nettle stings to reduce irritation.

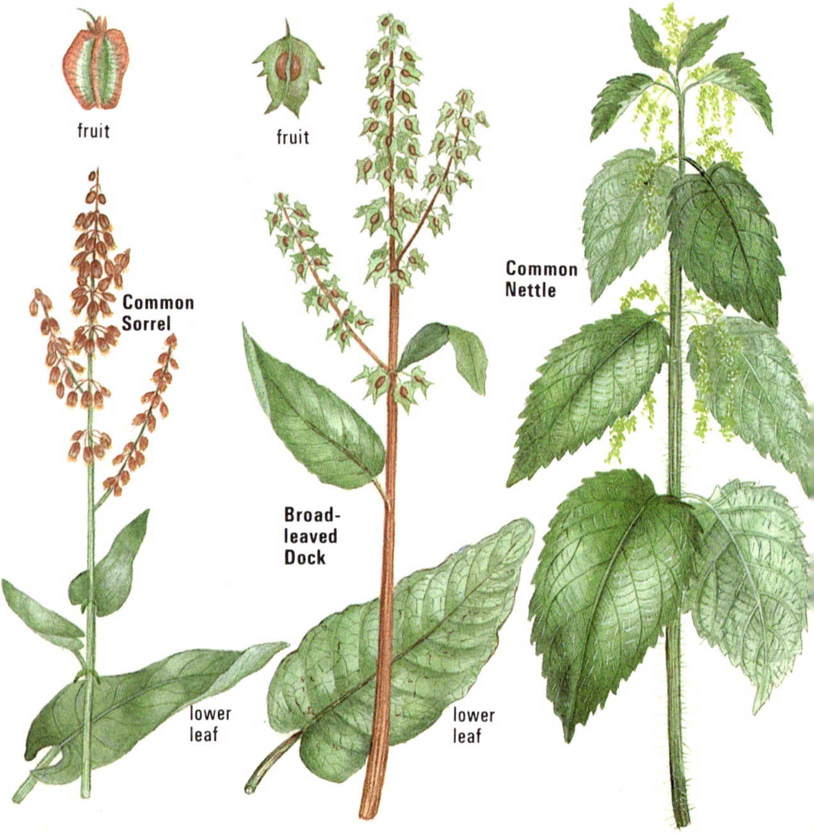

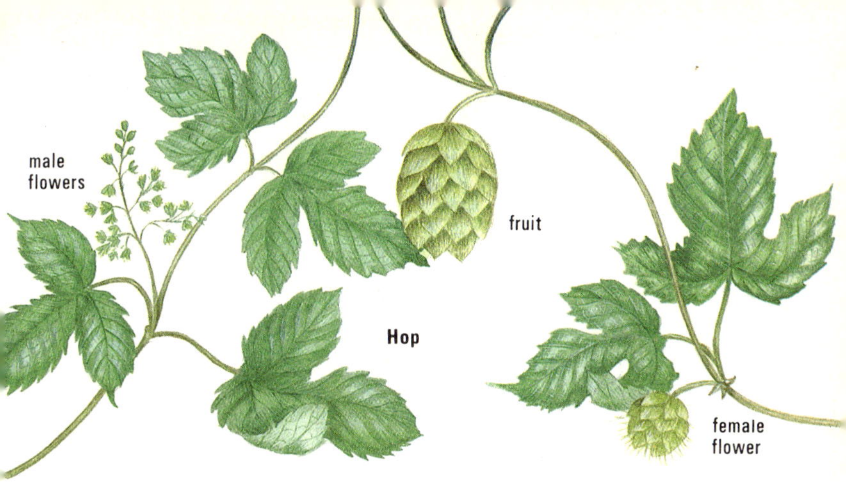

NETTLE FAMILY
Urticaceae

Stinging hairs crop up in many members of this family, including some Australian tree species. The flowers are inconspicuous and without petals. The stamens are flicked out as the flowers open, expelling pollen in puffs.

COMMON NETTLE
Urtica dioica

Notoriously covered in stiff, stinging hairs, the Common Nettle grows 30-150 cm high in waste places and woods. When touched, the hair-tip breaks off. The remaining hollow hair injects the skin with fluid containing an irritant poison. It is a major foodplant for the caterpillars of many butterflies.
Flower: green, tiny; male and female flowers on separate plants; wind-pollinated.
Flower arrangement: in loose hanging spikes in leaf-axils.
Flowering time: June-August.
Leaf: ovate, toothed, opposite, 4-8 cm long; lower leaves longer than their stalks.
Fruit: achene.
Uses: this unpromising plant has been made into nettle beer and in World War II the tough plant fibres were made into textiles.

HEMP FAMILY
Cannabiaceae

There are two main divisions in this family. One contains the Hops. The other contains species used for their plant fibre (hemp) and the drug cannabis. The flowers are either male or female, borne on separate plants.

HOP
Humulus lupulus

The Hop is found climbing with rough stems in hedges and, although native in N. Europe, is often an escape from cultivation. The 'cones' of pale bracts on the female plants are easy to recognize.
Flower: males and females on separate plants; females enclosed by yellow-green bracts; males tiny, green; petal-like lobes 5.
Flower arrangement: female bracts in hanging 'cone'; male flowers in branched clusters.
Flowering time: July-August.
Leaf: 3-5 lobed, coarsely toothed, roughly hairy, opposite, 10-15 cm, yellow glands dotting underside.
Fruit: enclosed by enlarged bracts dotted with yellow resin glands.
Uses: the female 'cones' are used to flavour beers. Cultivation of Hops began in Britain in about 1520, earlier in the rest of Europe.

HEATHER FAMILY
Ericaceae

As well as Heathers and Heaths, this family also contains the Rhododendrons. The members are small or large shrubs, mainly from temperate areas, with evergreen, often needle-like leaves. The flowers are normally bell-shaped. Most species prefer acid soils, and many have a fungus growing inside the roots.

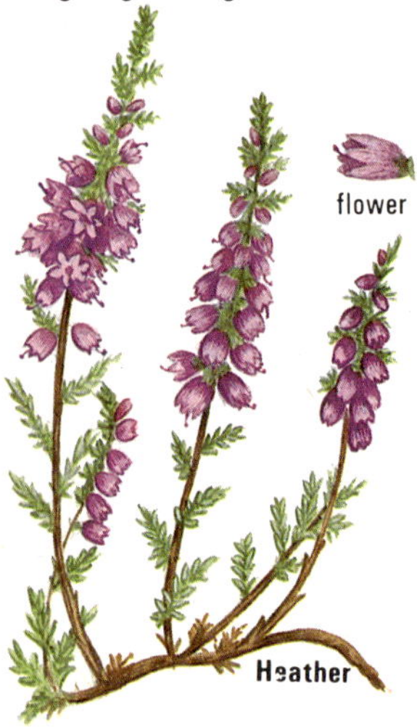

Lowland heaths and upland moors often support a thick, springy carpet of Heath and Heather.

HEATHER
Calluna vulgaris

This low-growing, wiry shrub grows 15-80 cm high, preferring acid soil and carpeting large tracts of heath, moor and open woods. Heather differs from the similar species of Heath in that the flower petals are not joined into a bell and the leaves are opposite, not whorled.

Flower: mauve, scented; petals 4, hidden by 4 petal-like sepals, about 4 mm long.

Flower arrangement: spikes, 3-15 cm.

Flowering time: July-September.

Leaf: needle-like, opposite, pressed to stem, 1-3·5 mm long, overlapping on short, side shoots.

Fruit: capsule.

Uses: hives of bees are kept on Heather moors in late summer, the resulting honey being particularly good. Heather also feeds sheep and shelters red grouse.

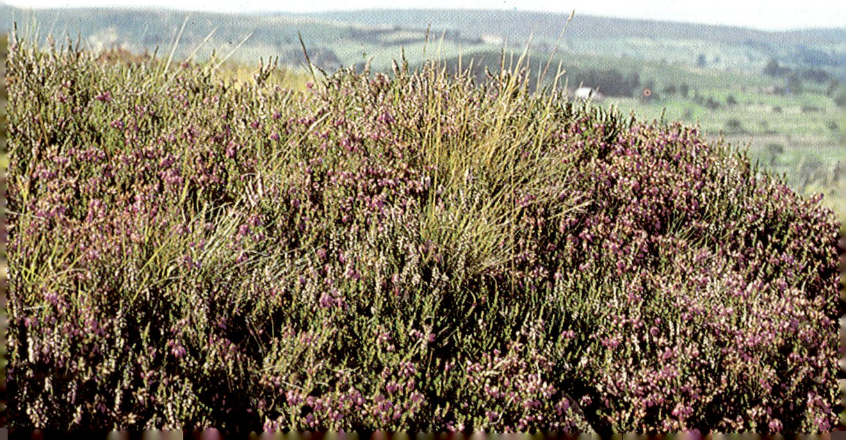

THRIFT FAMILY
Plumbaginaceae

Many members of this family, such as the Thrifts and Sea Lavenders, grow on the coast. The remainder are alpine and arctic species. The flowers have 5 petals and papery bracts.

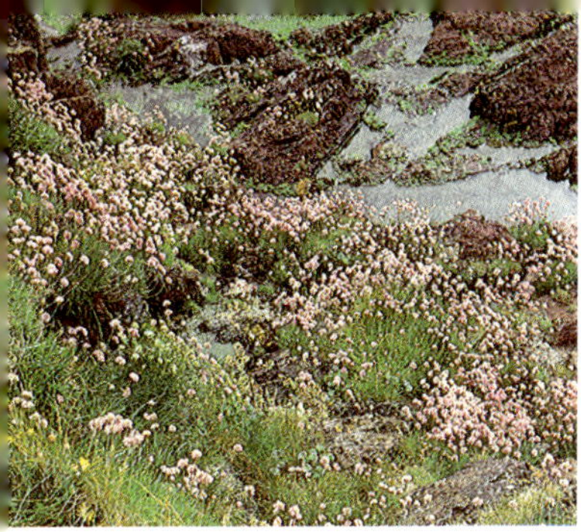

Flowering Thrift makes colourful cushions on rocky cliffs by the sea.

THRIFT
Armeria maritima

Thrift forms cushions of narrow leaves and pink flowers mainly in rocky places at the sea-side, in salt marshes, or inland on mountains and sandy places.
Flower: pale to deep pink; petals 5.
Flower arrangement: in dense, rounded head, 1·5-2·5 cm across; bracts below, greenish; flower stalk 5-30 cm high, surrounded by brown, papery sheath above.
Flowering time: April-October.
Leaf: grass-like, slightly fleshy, hairy or not, 2-15 cm long, up to about 4 mm wide.
Fruit: surrounded by papery calyx.

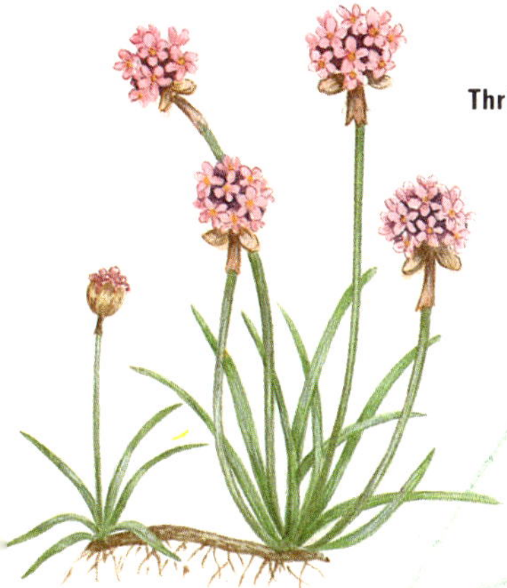

Thrift

BILBERRY
Vaccinium myrtillus

A low, hairless shrub 15-35 cm high, the Bilberry is known for its sweet, black berries. It grows in woods, and on moors and mountains to an altitude of over 1,200 m. The twigs are 3-angled and green.
Flower: pink, tinged green; petals joined into a globe shape, 4-6 mm.
Flower arrangement: solitary or paired.
Flowering time: April-June.
Leaf: ovate, tip pointed, minutely toothed, bright green, short-stalked, alternate, 1-3 cm long.
Fruit: berry, blue-black, edible.
Uses: the berries are worth the labour of gathering. If too bitter for eating raw then they make good tarts and jam.

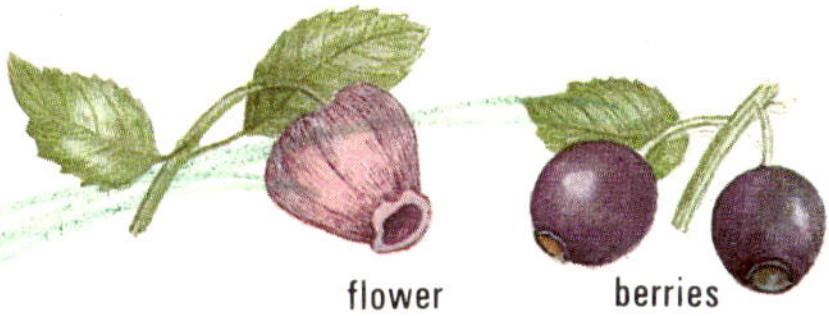

flower **berries**

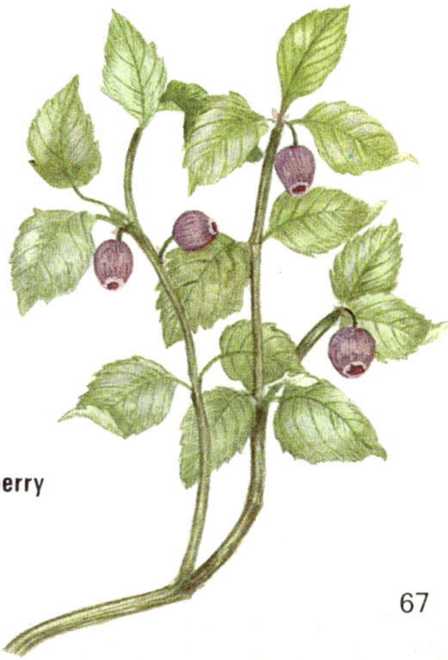

Bilberry

PRIMROSE FAMILY
Primulaceae

This is a large family, mainly from the northern hemisphere, in which are many garden ornamentals, such as the Primulas. Many species have flowers with either long styles (*pin-eye*), where the stigma shows in the throat of the flower, or short styles (*thrum-eye*), where the stigma does not show (see facing page).

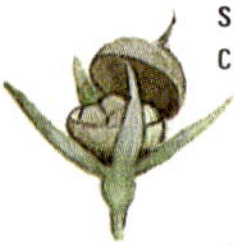
seed capsule

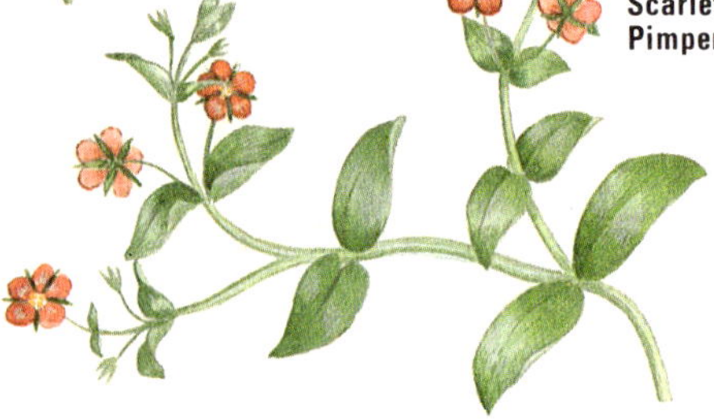
Scarlet Pimpernel

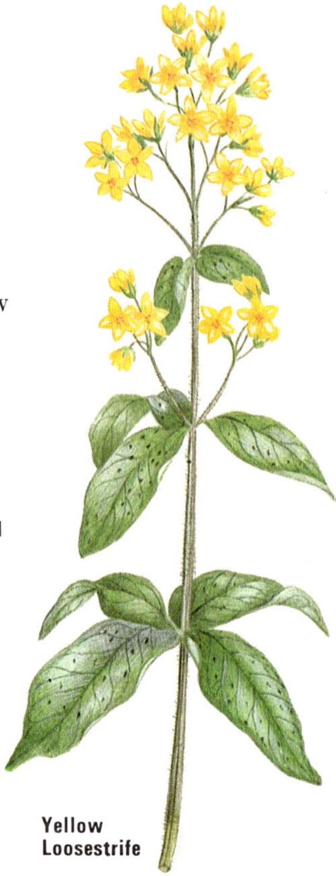
Yellow Loosestrife

SCARLET PIMPERNEL
Anagallis arvensis

One of the very few scarlet-flowered plants native to N. Europe, the Scarlet Pimpernel grows 6-30 cm on cultivated ground. The stems are square in section and prostrate.
Flower: scarlet or salmon pink, rarely blue, up to 14 mm across; petals 5, more or less rounded; sepals 5, sharply pointed.
Flower arrangement: on thin stalks, longer than leaves, arising from each leaf-axil.
Flowering time: June-August.
Leaf: ovate, pointed, opposite, stalkless, black glands beneath.
Fruit: capsule, spherical, with persistent style, splitting around middle.
Uses: the flowers can be used to tell the time and approaching weather. They open from about 8 am to 3 pm and close in the damp, cool air of impending rain.

YELLOW LOOSESTRIFE
Lysimachia vulgaris

The tall, erect, shortly hairy plants of Yellow Loosestrife grow 60-150 cm high. They are found along riversides and other damp places. This species is absent from N. Scotland, Sweden and much of Norway.
Flower: yellow, about 1·5 cm across; petals 5; sepals 5, orange-margined.
Flower arrangement: in loose, branched heads.
Flowering time: July-August.
Leaf: long, narrow, pointed, in pairs or whorls of 3 or 4; stalkless, dotted with black glands.
Fruit: capsule, spherical, opening by 5 valves.

PRIMROSE

Primula vulgaris

Less common in some areas than formerly, the well-loved Primrose has suffered much uprooting by 'gardeners'. The plants grow in grassy places, woods and hedges, flowering before the trees come into leaf and shade the ground.

Flower: pale yellow, deep yellow in throat, 2-3 cm across; petals joined at bases into tube with 5 spreading, notched lobes; calyx tubular, 5-toothed.

Flower arrangement: solitary on long, softly hairy stalks.

Flowering time: December-May.

Leaf: oblong, tip rounded, tapering gradually at base into stalk, wrinkled, shortly hairy beneath.

Fruit: capsule, ovoid, enclosed by calyx.

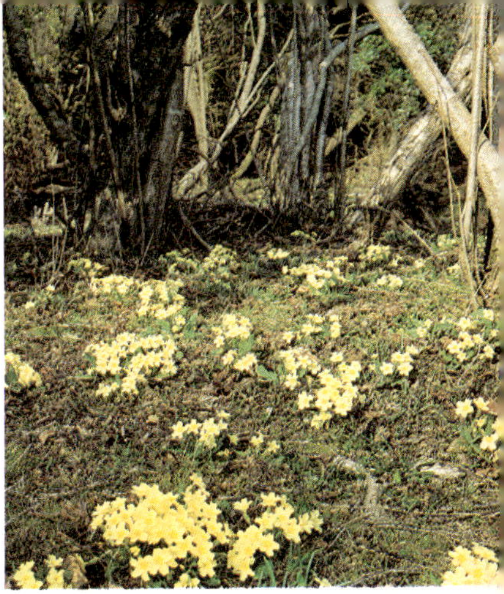

Clumps of Primroses in early spring sunshine at the margin of a wood.

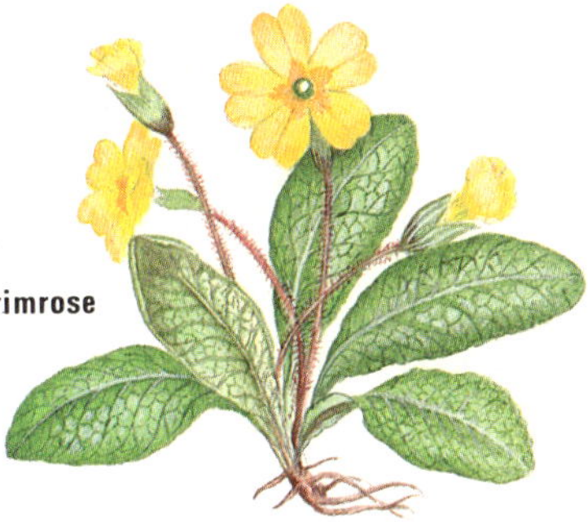

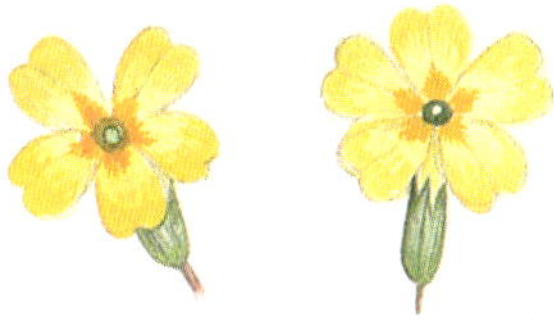

COWSLIP

Primula veris

Cowslip is only locally common and is decreasing owing to the ploughing of old pasture where it grows. The plants are 5-30 cm high.

Flower: pale or deep yellow, orange in throat, nodding; petals joined at bases into tube with 5 notched lobes; calyx tubular, pale green, 5-toothed.

Flower arrangement: 1-30 flowers in umbel-like cluster on shortly hairy stalk, 10-30 cm high.

Flowering time: April-May.

Leaf: oblong, rounded at tip, abruptly narrowed into stalk, wrinkled, shortly hairy all over.

Fruit: capsule, ovoid, hidden by calyx.

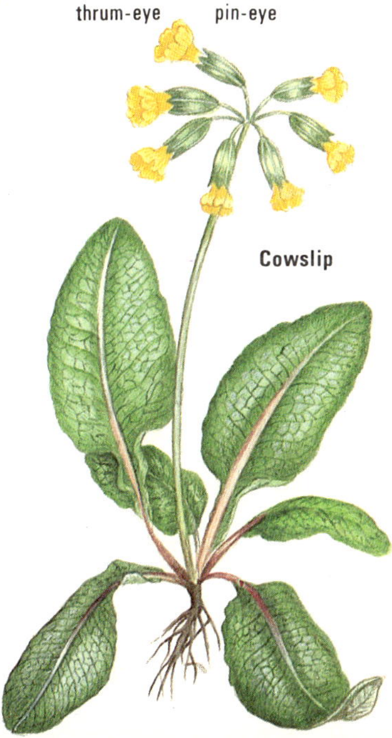

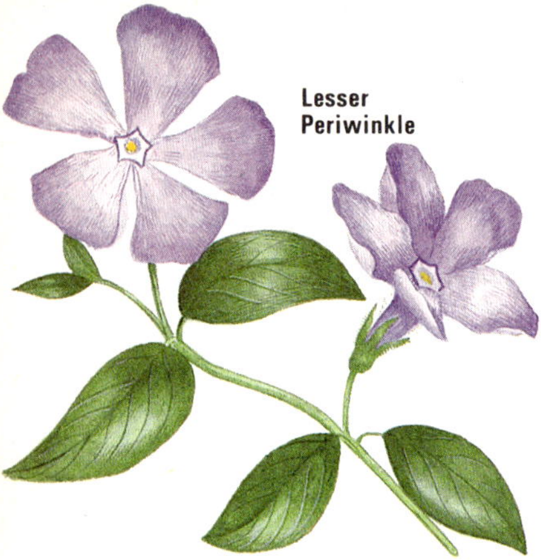

GENTIAN FAMILY
Gentianaceae

Many of the species in this family grow in arctic regions and on mountains. The flowers, of 5 joined petals, are often blue, bell-shaped and erect. The Gentian family is one in which a fungus commonly lives within the roots, benefitting both plant and fungus. The bitter roots have been much used medicinally and in the French aperitif, Suze.

PERIWINKLE FAMILY
Apocynaceae

Members of this large family are mainly tall rain-forest trees of the tropics, some of which have buttresses at the base of the trunk. The rest are shrubs and woody climbers, or herbs in northern Europe, with a milky, often poisonous latex, used in the tropics to tip arrows for hunting.

LESSER PERIWINKLE
Vinca minor

This species has long been grown in gardens. It has escaped and become naturalized in shady places and is truly native only in part of N. Europe. It is an evergreen plant with long, rooting stems of 30-60 cm covering the ground.
Flower: blue-purple or white, 2·5-3 cm across; petals 5, wide and blunt at tip, joined at base; calyx tube 5-toothed, hairless.
Flower arrangement: solitary, stalked, in leaf-axil.
Flowering time: March-May.
Leaf: elliptic, opposite, glossy, hairless, short-stalked.
Fruit: pair of follicles, rarely ripening in Britain, forked at tip.
Uses: Periwinkle wreaths were used in ancient ceremonies, especially at the funerals of children.

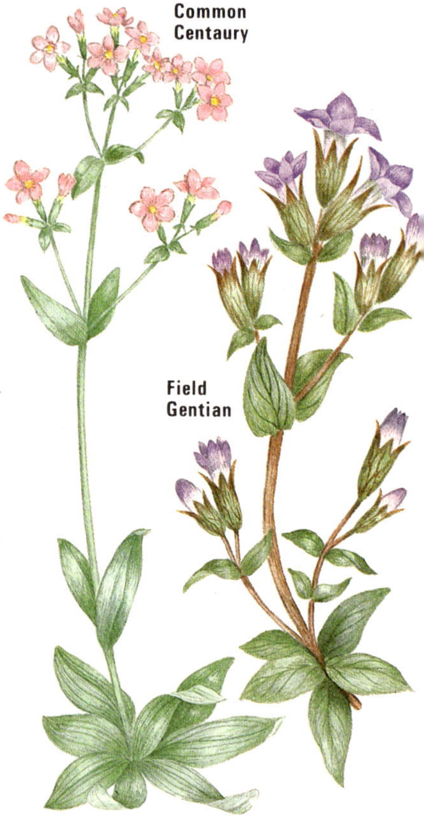

COMMON CENTAURY

Centaurium erythraea

Common Centaury varies between 2 and 50 cm high, with a branched stem bearing flat clusters of pink flowers. It is a hairless plant growing in dry grassland and dunes. It is absent from much of Scotland and Scandinavia.

Flower: rose-pink, 1-1·5 cm across; petals joined into tube below; lobes 5, spreading flat; calyx with 5 long, narrow teeth.

Flower arrangement: in more or less flat-topped clusters.

Flowering time: June-October.

Leaf: opposite, basal leaves in rosette; elliptic, tip rounded or pointed, stalkless.

Fruit: capsule.

Uses: Common Centaury has been called Gall of the Earth due to its bitterness. A tonic can be made from an infusion of dried plants.

FIELD GENTIAN

Gentianella campestris

Absent from much of southern Britain and the Low Countries, the Field Gentian inhabits grassland and dunes. The erect, sometimes branched stem is 10-30 cm high.

Flower: blue-purple; tube yellow-green, 1·5-2·5 cm long; petals joined into 4-lobed tube, fringed within; calyx of 4 unequal lobes, larger pair almost enclosing smaller.

Flower arrangement: clustered on stalks arising from leaf-axils.

Flowering time: July-October.

Leaf: ovate, opposite, stalkless, hairless.

Fruit: capsule, narrow.

Uses: this Gentian has been used in Sweden as a substitute for hops in beer-making.

BOGBEAN FAMILY
Menyanthaceae

This is a small family of water plants in which the 5 white, pink or yellow flower petals are often hairy.

BOGBEAN

Menyanthes trifoliata

The leaves and beautiful fringed, pink and white flowers of this hairless water plant are borne above the surface of shallow water, the stems creeping through the mud. It is found in marshes, lake-edges and upland pools.

Flower: pink, paler within, about 1·5 cm across; petals 5, covered in long, white hairs, joined at base; anthers reddish.

Flower arrangement: clustered, on long stalk.

Flowering time: May-July.

Leaf: of 3 rounded leaflets, 3·5-7 cm, alternate, on stalk with sheathing base.

Fruit: capsule, spherical, with persistent style.

Uses: the underground stem contains a bitter substance called menyanthin, which was used as a tonic and to bring down fever.

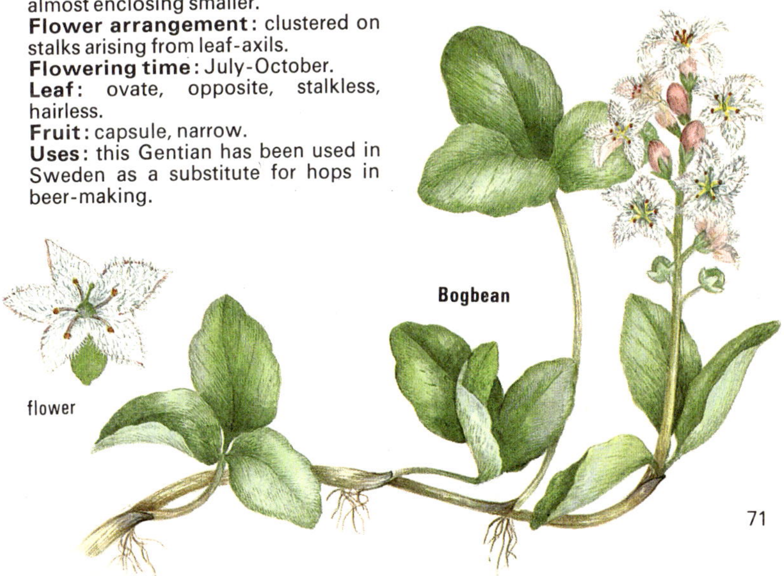

FORGET-ME-NOT FAMILY
Boraginaceae

Members of this family are almost always hairy, often stiffly so. The blue or mauve, sometimes white, flowers are very often pink in bud and arranged in one-sided racemes which uncoil as the flowers open.

FIELD FORGET-ME-NOT
Myosotis arvensis

The particular characteristics of this shortly hairy Forget-me-not are the concave petals and small flowers (5 mm or less). The plant grows 15-30 cm high in drier places than most other Forget-me-nots, such as roadsides and fields.

Flower: pale blue, yellow in throat, up to 5 mm across; petals joined into tube at base; lobes 5, concave; calyx 5-toothed with hooked hairs; buds pink.

Flower arrangement: cyme, uncoiling as flowers open, without bracts.

Flowering time: April-September.

Leaf: ovate to lanceolate, tips rounded or pointed; lower leaves shortly stalked, forming rosette; upper leaves stalkless.

Fruit: 4 nutlets, brown, shiny, enclosed by calyx.

WATER FORGET-ME-NOT
Myosotis scorpioides

Growing in damp or wet places, this Forget-me-not has a slightly ridged, hairy stem, 15-45 cm high, the base of which often creeps and roots. The important characteristics of this species are the flower size and the notched petal-lobes.

Flower: sky-blue, yellow in throat, 4-10 mm across; petals joined into tube at base; lobes 5, shallowly notched; calyx 5-toothed with straight hairs; buds pink.

Flower arrangement: cyme, uncoiling as flowers open, without bracts.

Flowering time: May-September.

Leaf: oblong, usually rounded at tip, stalkless, shortly hairy or almost hairless.

Fruit: 4 nutlets, black, shiny, enclosed by calyx.

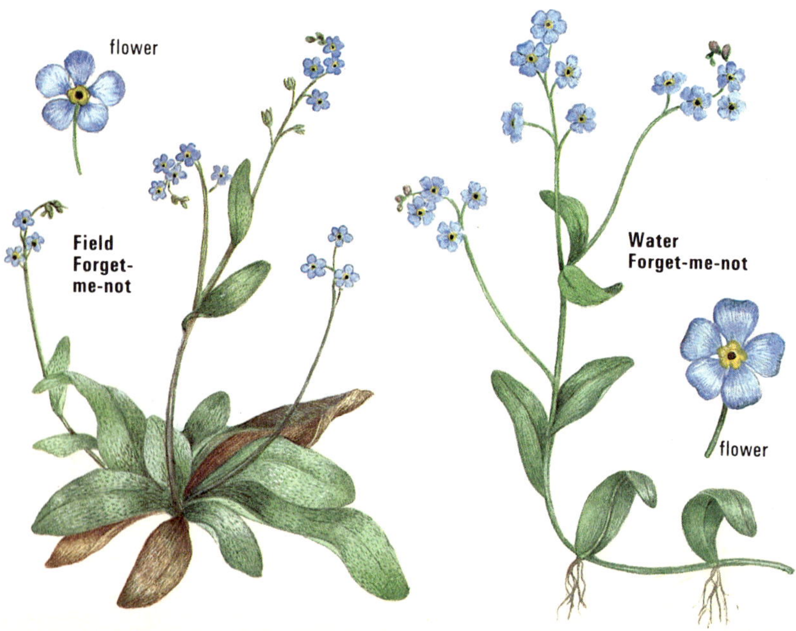

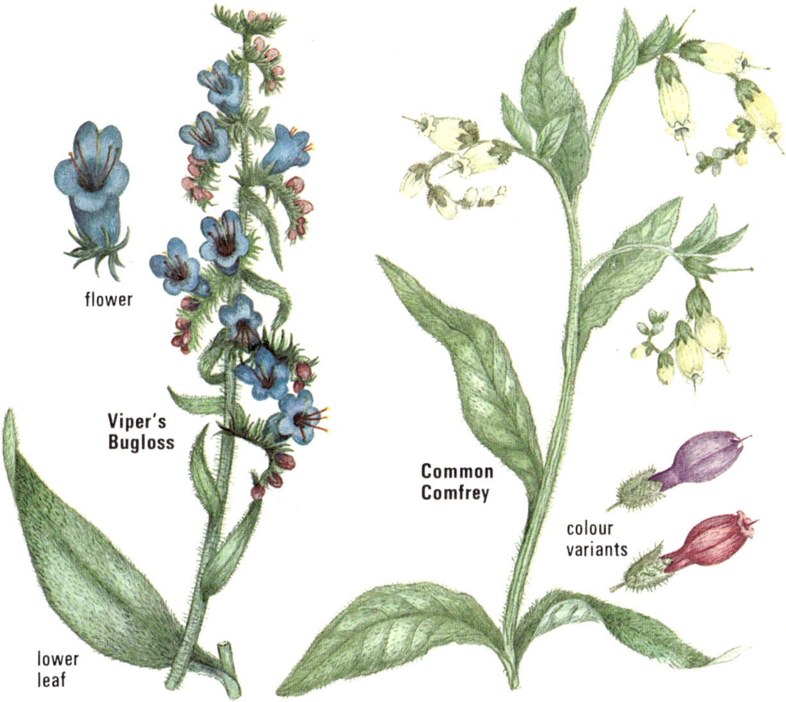

VIPER'S BUGLOSS

Echium vulgare

An erect, stout plant, 20-90 cm tall and densely covered in stiff, whitish hairs with swollen bases, Viper's Bugloss has bright blue flowers, pink in bud, forming an exciting colour combination. It grows in dry places.

Flower: bright blue, 1-2 cm; petals joined into tube at base; 5-lobed; calyx 5-toothed; stamens 5, 4 protruding.

Flower arrangement: a spike of short, curved or coiled cymes.

Flowering time: June-September.

Leaf: lanceolate, tapering gradually to base, up to 15 cm long, stalkless, lowest shortly stalked.

Fruit: 4 nutlets, enclosed by calyx.

Uses: this plant was linked from ancient Greek times with snakes. The nutlet, supposed to resemble a snake's head, was consequently used to treat snake bite.

COMMON COMFREY

Symphytum officinale

Common Comfrey is a branched, stout, stiffly hairy plant of 30-120 cm. The stem has thin prominent ridges, and the plant grows in damp places.

Flower: cream, white, pink or purple, 15-17 mm long; petals joined into tube with 5 short lobes at rim; calyx 5-toothed; style protruding from petal-tube.

Flower arrangement: in nodding cymes, uncoiling as flowers open.

Flowering time: May-June.

Leaf: ovate to lanceolate, tip pointed, bases running down stem in thin, often wavy ridges.

Fruit: 4 nutlets, black, shiny, enclosed by calyx, style persistent.

Uses: in Bavaria the young leaves are fried in batter. Manure water to feed tomato or marrow crops can also be made by soaking Comfrey plants in water for a week. The resulting water is rich in potassium.

BINDWEED FAMILY
Convolvulaceae

The flowers in this family are bell- or trumpet-shaped on stems which often climb by twining. The sap is quite often milky.

HEDGE BINDWEED
Calystegia sepium

This climbing Bindweed covers such supports as railings and hedges with a blanket of arrow-shaped leaves and large, white trumpet-shaped flowers. These are visited at dusk by hawk moths. The stems grow 1-3 m long, twisting anti-clockwise, and contain milky sap.

Flower: white, trumpet-shaped, 3-7 cm across, scentless; sepals 5, enclosed by 2 slightly longer bracts.
Flower arrangement: solitary, on long stalks.
Flowering time: July-September.
Leaf: arrow-shaped, up to 15 cm long, stalked, shortly hairy or not.
Fruit: capsule, enclosed by bracts.

SEA BINDWEED
Calystegia soldanella

The stems of this small plant creep along the sand or pebbles of the beach. It grows 10-60 cm long and is hairless.

Flower: pink or mauve, trumpet-shaped, 5 paler stripes within, 2·5-4 cm across; sepals 5, almost enclosed by 2 large bracts.
Flower arrangement: solitary, on long, 4-angled stalks.
Flowering time: June-August.
Leaf: kidney-shaped, rather thick.
Fruit: capsule, enclosed by bracts.

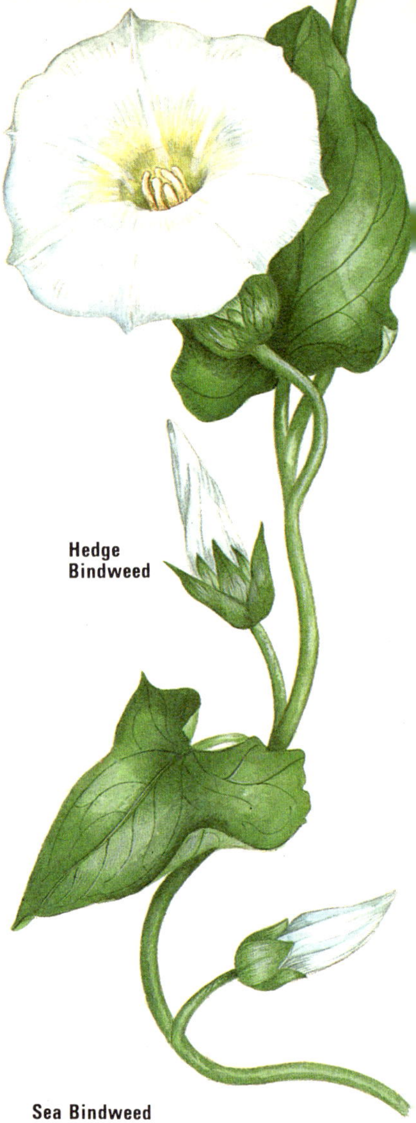

Hedge Bindweed

Sea Bindweed

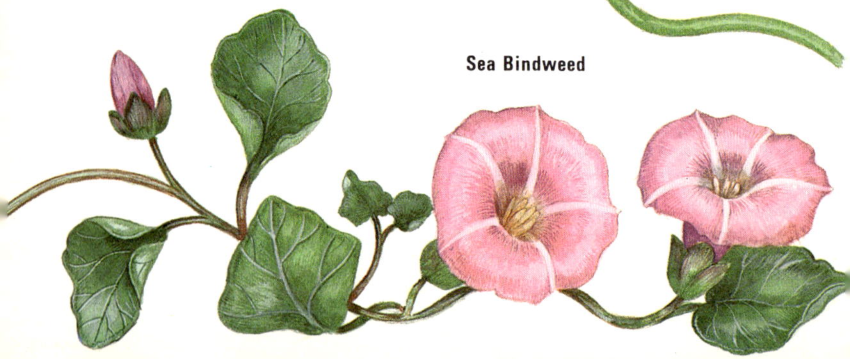

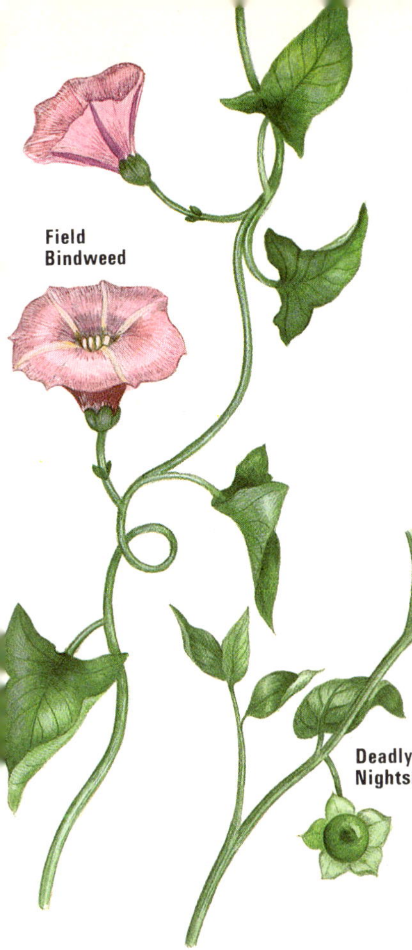

POTATO FAMILY
Solanaceae

The very important economic crop plants, tomato, potato and tobacco all come from this family, as well as chillies and green and red peppers. Two of the more poisonous species are Mandrake and Henbane. The flowers in the family often have a central cone of yellow anthers and the fruits are usually berries.

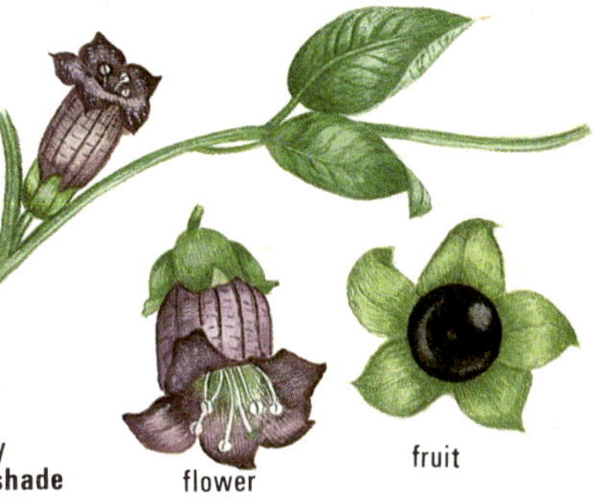

FIELD BINDWEED
Convolvulus arvensis

The invasive roots make this little creeping or climbing plant a stubborn weed of farm and garden. The stem coils anti-clockwise around other plants.
Flower: pink or white, striped darker outside, trumpet-shaped, 1·5-3 cm across, scented; sepals 5, rounded.
Flower arrangement: 1-3 flowers on long stalk with 2 small bracts half-way up.
Flowering time: June-September.
Leaf: arrow-shaped, 2-5 cm long, stalked, shortly hairy or not.
Fruit: capsule, spherical.

DEADLY NIGHTSHADE
Atropa bella-donna

This uncommon, highly poisonous, narcotic plant grows in dry places on chalk or limestone. It is stout, branched and grows up to 150 cm high. It is missing from the greater part of Scandinavia.
Flower: lurid violet or greenish, 2·5-3 cm, nodding, bell-shaped, lobes pointed; sepals pointed.
Flower arrangement: solitary.
Flowering time: June-August.
Leaf: alternate, ovate, up to 20 cm.
Fruit: berry, 1·5-2 cm across, shiny, black, surrounded by persistent calyx.
Uses: the poisonous and medicinal properties of this plant have long been known. An infusion of plant juice was formerly dropped in womens' eyes causing dilation of the pupils to produce a 'wide-eyed' look, hence the name *bella-donna* (beautiful lady).

THORN-APPLE

Datura stramonium

Thorn-apple is another very poisonous plant of the potato family, with large, spiny fruits. Originally from America it is more or less naturalized on rubbish tips and waste ground in southern parts of N. Europe. It is branched, hairless and grows 50-200 cm high.

Flower: white, sometimes purple, 5-10 cm, trumpet-shaped, erect; calyx 5-angled.

Flower arrangement: solitary, short-stalked.

Flowering time: July-October.

Leaf: ovate, irregularly toothed, tip pointed, up to 20 cm long.

Fruit: capsule, spiny, 4-7 cm.

Uses: an extract of the leaves known as stramonium is still used medicinally by asthma sufferers.

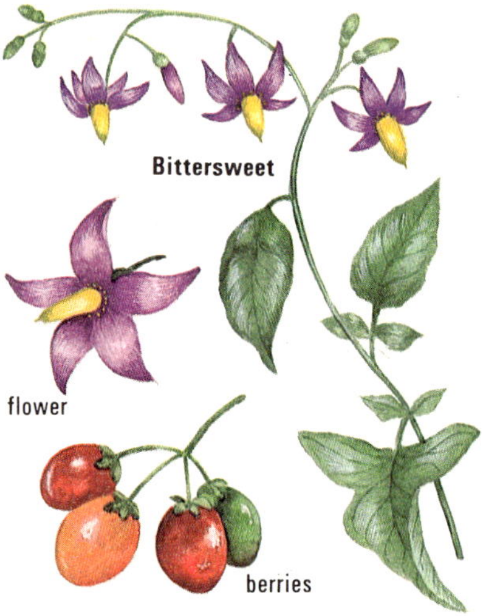

BITTERSWEET

Solanum dulcamara

The small, purple flowers, each with a cone of yellow anthers, are unmistakeable. The plant is mildly poisonous and climbs 30-200 cm high in hedges, woods or waste places. The common name refers to the taste of the leaves – bitter at first but with a sweet aftertaste.

Flower: purple, with central cone of yellow anthers, 1-1·5 cm across; petals 5, pointed; calyx of 5 rounded lobes.

Flower arrangement: cyme.

Flowering time: June-September.

Leaf: ovate, pointed, stalked, with or without 1-4 lobes at base.

Fruit: berry, poisonous, shiny, ovoid, green when unripe, becoming yellow, then red.

Uses: collars of Bittersweet were worn by people and their animals to avert witchcraft.

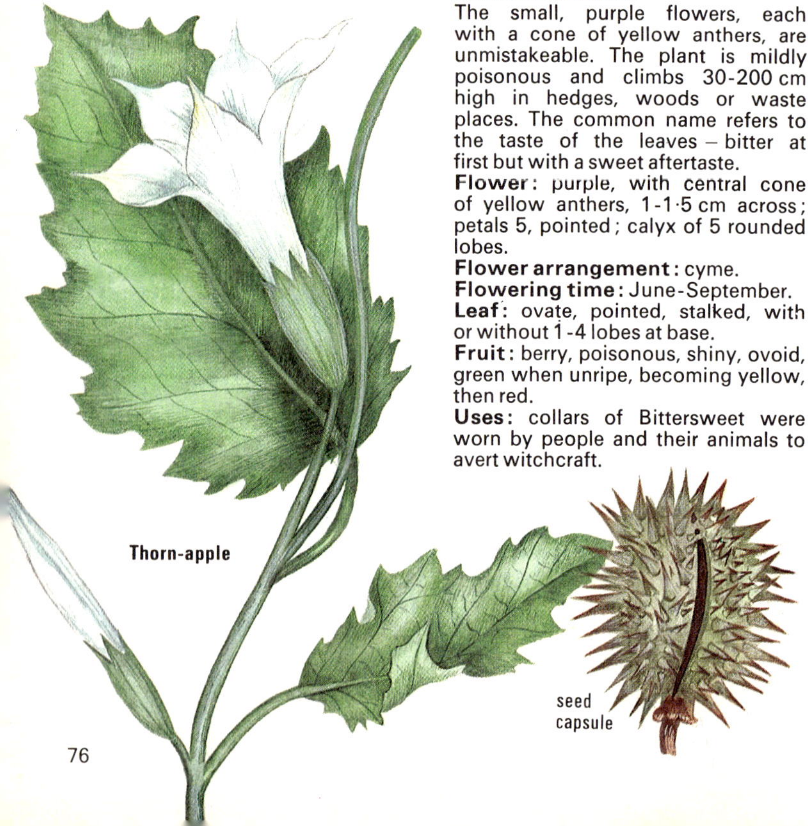

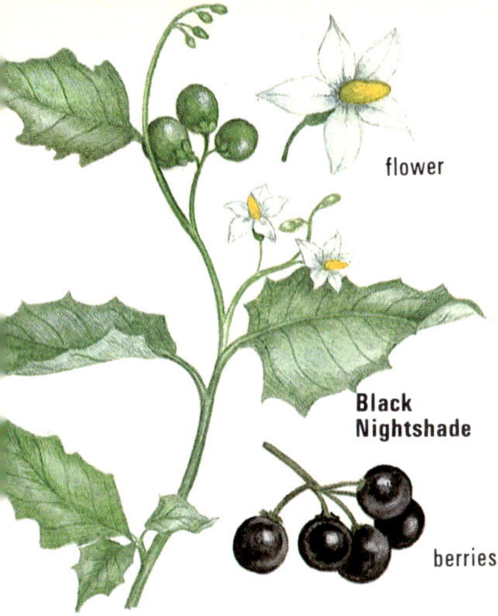

BLACK NIGHTSHADE

Solanum nigrum

This species, like many others of the same family, is poisonous. The plant is hairless or with short hairs and grows up to 60 cm high on waste and cultivated land.

Flower: white, with central cone of yellow anthers, about 5 mm across; petals 5, pointed; calyx of 5 rounded lobes.

Flower arrangement: cyme.

Flowering time: July-September.

Leaf: ovate or diamond-shaped, pointed, stalked, toothed or not.

Fruit: berry, poisonous, black.

FOXGLOVE FAMILY
Scrophulariaceae

Members of this large family come mainly from northern temperate regions. Some species are semi-parasitic, largely on grasses. The flowers are usually tubular, with 2 lips, and attract specialized insect pollinators. The Mint family has similar flowers, but 4-angled stems. Many species, such as Snapdragons, are grown in gardens.

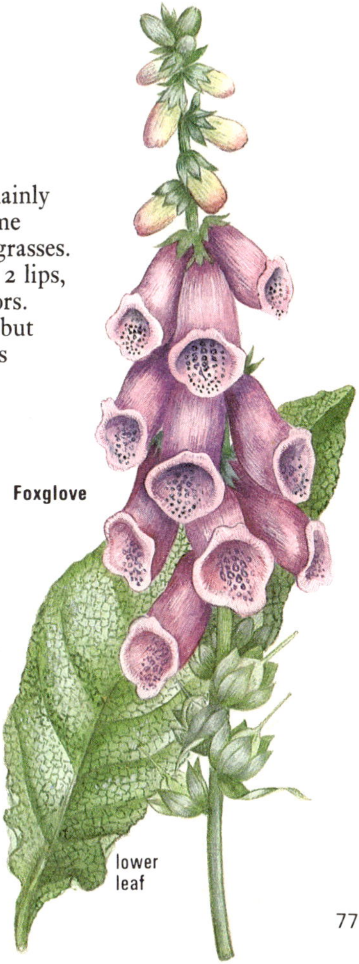

FOXGLOVE

Digitalis purpurea

The upright, softly hairy Foxglove plants with their spikes of purple bells are easy to recognize. They prefer acid soils and grow in open woodland, heaths and field borders. Children poke their fingers in the flowers to make a wish.

Flower: pinkish purple, sometimes white, 4-5 cm long, bell-shaped, shallowly 5-lobed, spotted and whiskery within; sepals 5.

Flower arrangement: long spike.

Flowering time: June-September.

Leaf: ovate, blunt-toothed, softly hairy above, woolly beneath; narrow border on each side of leaf-stalk.

Fruit: capsule, ovoid, with long, persistent style.

Uses: Foxgloves are still cultivated for the heart drug containing digitalin.

EYEBRIGHT

Euphrasia officinalis

The Eyebrights are extremely difficult to tell apart. The following description covers a group of species. All are semi-parasites on grasses and grow 1-40 cm high in grassy places. The stems are hairy and branched.

Flower: white or mauve, with yellow and purple marks; 2-lipped, lower lip of 3 notched lobes; calyx 4-toothed; bracts leaf-like.

Flower arrangement: in leaf-axils.

Flowering time: May-September.

Leaf: circular or oval, deeply toothed.

Fruit: capsule, fringed with hairs.

Uses: this little plant was used in the past to treat eye disorders.

YELLOW RATTLE

Rhinanthus minor

Yellow Rattle is semi-parasitic on grasses, amongst which it grows. The stem may be branched, 10-50 cm high and marked with black.

Flower: yellow, 1-1·5 cm long, tubular, 2-lipped, teeth of upper lip purple; calyx 4-toothed, inflated; bracts leaf-like.

Flower arrangement: crowded with bracts at top of stems.

Flowering time: May-August.

Leaf: oblong to lanceolate, toothed, opposite, stalkless, rough to touch.

Fruit: formed from enlarged calyx in which ripe seeds rattle.

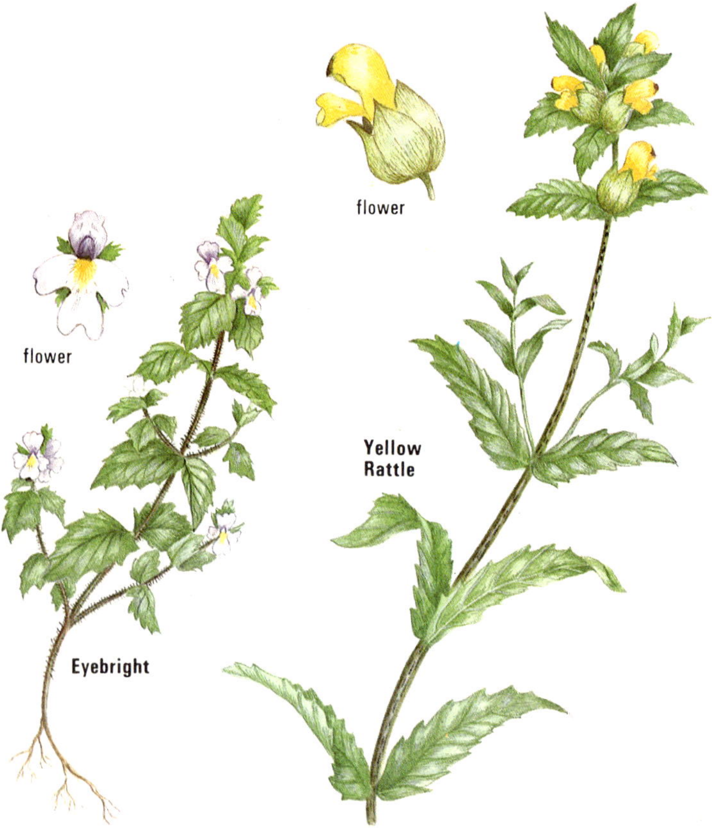

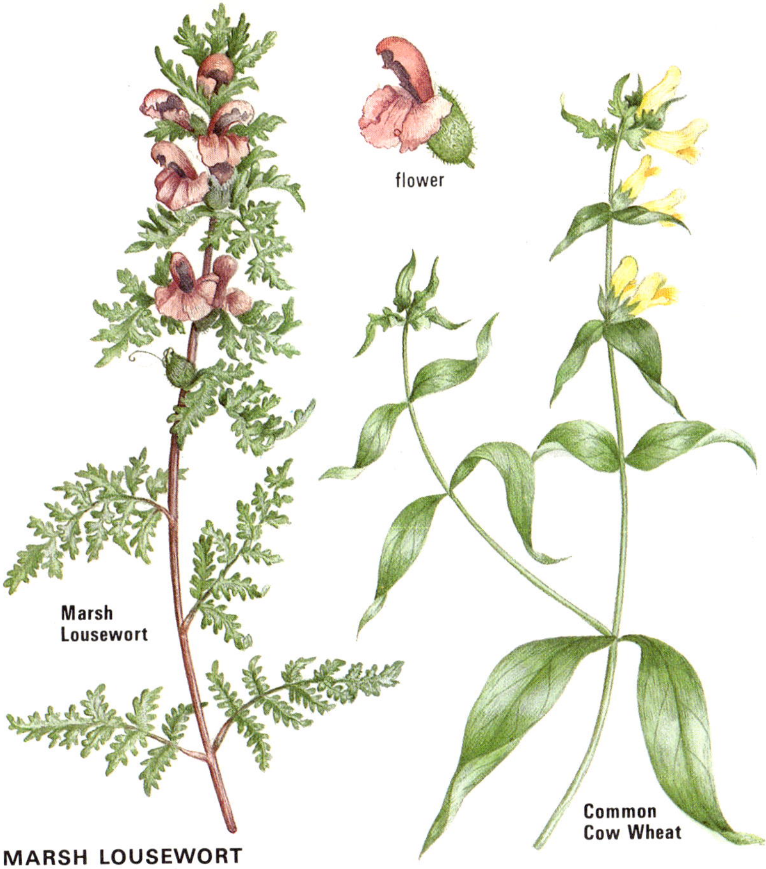

MARSH LOUSEWORT

Pedicularis palustris

This is a small, pretty plant with fern-like leaves and bright mauve-pink flowers. It is found only in damp grass or heathland. The common similar species of Lousewort (*P. sylvatica*) differs in having 3 teeth instead of 5 on the upper lip of the flower.

Flower: mauve-pink, 1·5-2·5 cm long, tubular; 2-lipped, upper lip with 5 small teeth; calyx hairy, blunt-toothed.

Flower arrangement: leafy spikes.

Flowering time: May-September.

Leaf: oblong, finely dissected, 2-4 cm.

Fruit: capsule, curved, calyx becoming inflated.

COMMON COW WHEAT

Melampyrum pratense

This small, slender plant is semi-parasitic on grasses. It grows 8-60 cm high in shady places and grassland and is branched in the upper part.

Flower: pale yellow, 1-1·5 cm long, tubular; 2-lipped, lower lip orange, calyx of 4 narrow teeth, about half as long as flower tube; upper bracts toothed.

Flower arrangement: in pairs in leaf-axils, each pair facing same way.

Flowering time: May-October.

Leaf: lanceolate or ovate, tapering to point, opposite, stalkless.

Fruit: capsule; seeds 4.

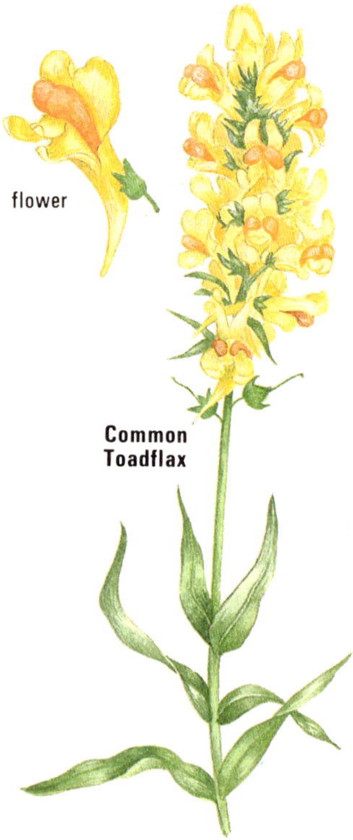

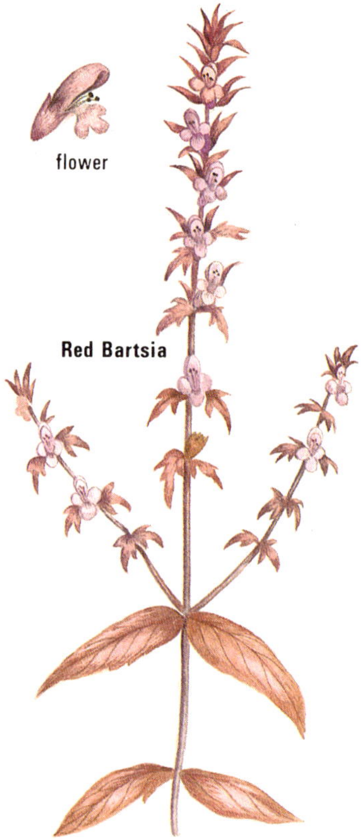

COMMON TOADFLAX

Linaria vulgaris

The flowers look like miniature yellow garden Snapdragons, to which Toadflax is related. Nectar is stored in the long spur behind the flower, accessible only to long-tongued bees. The plant is almost hairless, 30-80 cm high and grows along hedges and in grassy places.

Flower: yellow, top part of lower lip orange; 1·5-2·5 cm long; 2-lipped; spur almost straight; sepals 5, pointed.

Flower arrangement: dense raceme.

Flowering time: June-October.

Leaf: narrow, strap-shaped, pointed, alternate, 3-8 cm long, grey-green beneath.

Fruit: capsule, ovoid; seeds winged.

Uses: the plant is said to make a good fly poison if boiled in milk, the milk serving as an attractant.

RED BARTSIA

Odontites verna

Red Bartsia is very often tinged maroon, much branched and shortly hairy. It grows up to 50 cm high in grassland and waste ground, but is absent from much of Norway and N. Sweden. Curiously, there appears to be no old common name for this plant.

Flower: purple-pink, about 1 cm, tubular; 2-lipped, lower lip 3-lobed; calyx of 4 teeth; bracts leaf-like.

Flower arrangement: in spikes, flowers pointing one way.

Flowering time: June-August.

Leaf: lanceolate, toothed, opposite, stalkless.

Fruit: capsule, seeds ridged.

COMMON FIGWORT

Scrophularia nodosa

This is a rather tall, hairless plant growing in wet woods and ditches. The stem is 4-angled. The dull maroon flowers smelling of decay attract wasps by mimicking carrion.

Flower: upper part maroon, lower green, 1 cm long; 5-lobed, upper 2 slightly longer; sepals 5, rounded.

Flower arrangement: branched clusters.

Flowering time: June-September.

Leaf: ovate, pointed, toothed, opposite, 6-13 cm long.

Fruit: capsule, ovoid, pointed.

Uses: the knobs on the roots were taken as signs that this plant cured both piles and goitre.

GREAT MULLEIN

Verbascum thapsus

The leaves and stem of this tall plant are thickly covered in white wool. It grows in dry, waste places and chalk grassland.

Flower: yellow, 1·5-3 cm across; petals 5, rounded, joined at base; sepals 5, pointed; 3 stamens covered with pale hairs, 2 hairless.

Flower arrangement: tall, dense spike.

Flowering time: June-August.

Leaf: oblong, pointed or rounded at tip; base running down stem as narrow border; basal leaves in rosette.

Fruit: capsule, enclosed by sepals; seeds tiny.

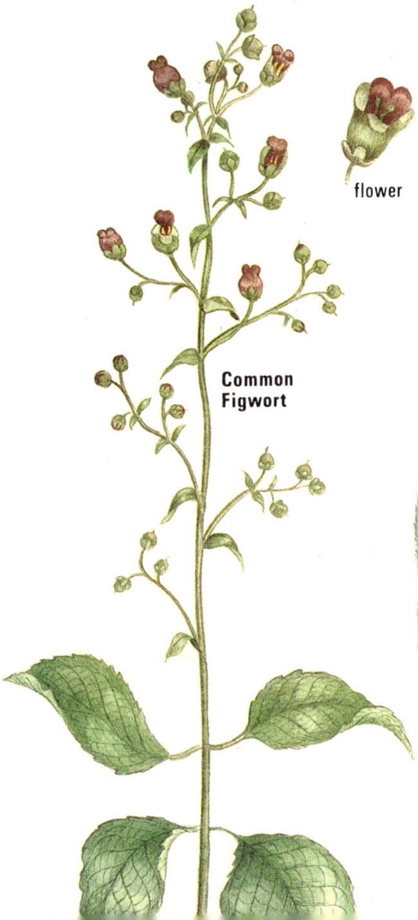

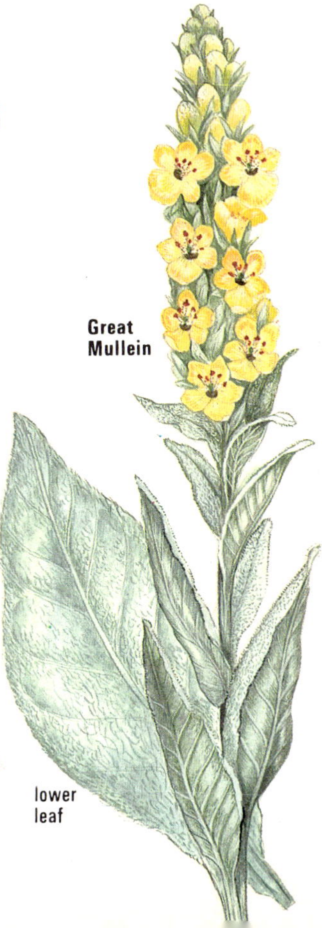

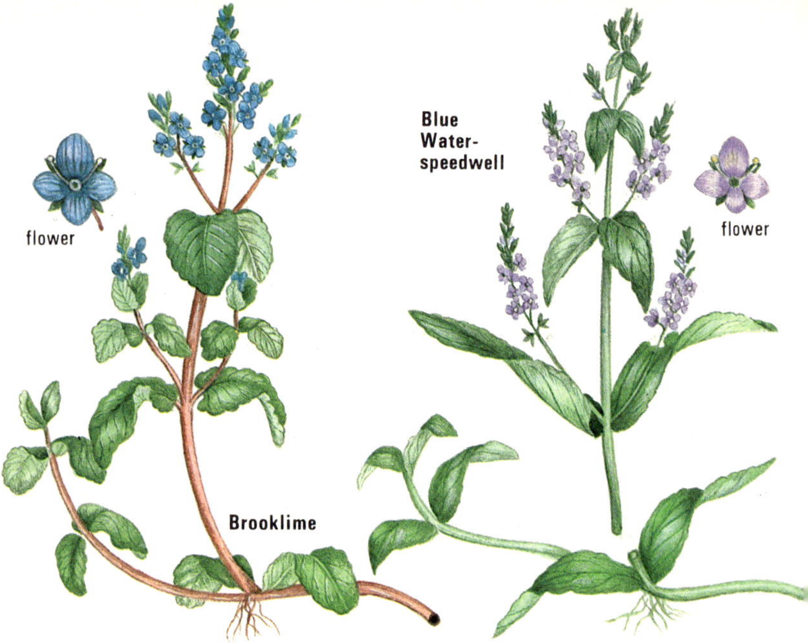

BROOKLIME

Veronica beccabunga

Both stem and leaves of this water-loving plant are hairless and rather fleshy. The bases of the hollow stems creep and root in wet mud or shallow fresh water.

Flower: blue, 5-8 mm across; petals 4, upper petal larger than lower 3; sepals 4; stamens 2.

Flower arrangement: racemes in leaf-axils.

Flowering time: May-September.

Leaf: circular to oval, opposite, slightly fleshy, shiny, blunt-toothed, short-stalked.

Fruit: capsule, spherical, slightly notched.

Uses: the sharp-tasting leaves have been eaten as a substitute for Water-cress.

BLUE WATER-SPEEDWELL

Veronica anagallis-aquatica

This is one of the larger Speedwells and grows in or near fresh water. The rather thick, branching stems are green and hairless. growing 20-30 cm high.

Flower: pale blue, 5-6 mm across; petals 4; sepals 4; stamens 2.

Flower arrangement: racemes in upper leaf-axils.

Flowering time: June-August.

Leaf: lanceolate, pointed, blunt-toothed, opposite, stalkless.

Fruit: capsule, slightly notched, stalk curving up, not at right-angle to stem.

GERMANDER SPEEDWELL

Veronica chamaedrys

Common in grassy places, hedges and woods, this small Speedwell grows 7-25 cm high. The stem, with its 2 lines of hairs, lies along the ground, rooting at intervals and turning up at the tip. Speedwell flowers characteristically drop from the calyx at the lightest touch.

Flower: bright blue, white circle at centre, 1 cm across; petals 4, upper largest; sepals 4; bracts shorter than or equalling individual flower stalks; stamens 2.

Flower arrangement: raceme springing from leaf-axil.

Flowering time: March-July.

Leaf: oval, blunt-toothed, hairy, shortly stalked or stalkless.

Fruit: capsule, heart-shaped, hairy, shorter than sepals.

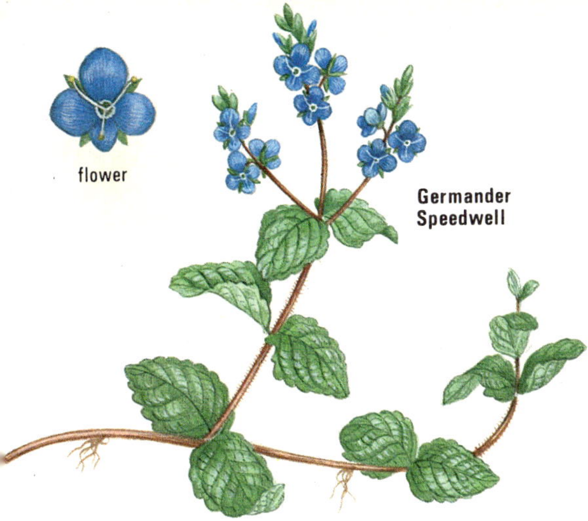

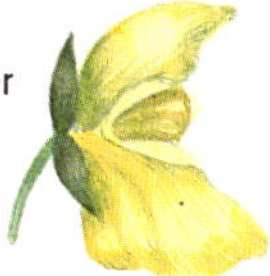

BLADDERWORT FAMILY
Lentibulariaceae

Plants in this small family are insectivorous and live in wet or damp places. They trap and digest insects by rolling up sticky leaves (Butterworts) or by means of small, underwater sacs or bladders (Bladderworts).

GREATER BLADDERWORT
Utricularia vulgaris

This strange, underwater plant has no roots and grows suspended in still water. Small sacs on the finely divided leaves trap mainly water fleas, which are digested by the plant. If touched by a passing flea, sensitive hairs at the mouth of the sac trigger the opening of a trap-door. Water, together with the flea, are sucked into the previously air-filled sac.
Flower: bright yellow, 12-18 mm across; 2-lipped, short spur behind.
Flower arrangement: 2-10 flowers on long stalk, above water surface.
Flowering time: July-August.
Leaf: finely divided, each thread-like segment minutely toothed, with bristles; all leaves green (other species with some colourless leaves), bearing small sacs.
Fruit: capsule, spherical.

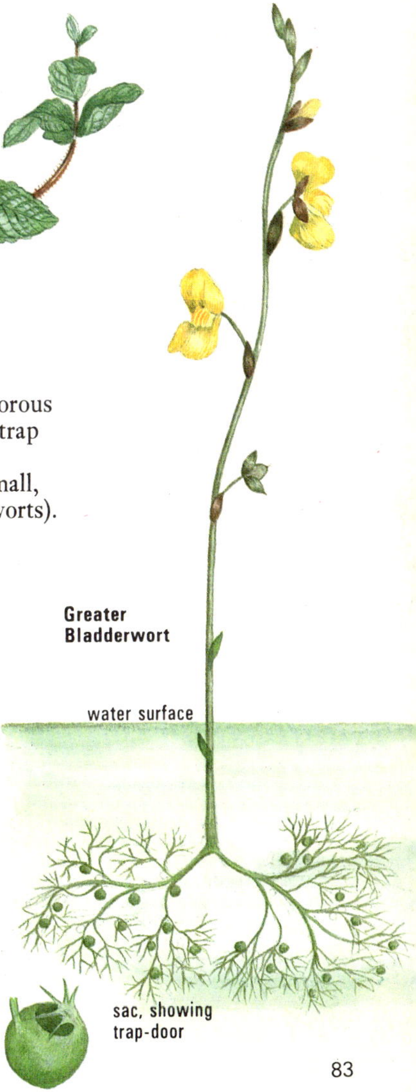

MINT FAMILY
Labiatae

Plants in this large family are often aromatic and include many kitchen herbs, such as Sage and Marjoram. Plant stems are square in cross-section, and the flowers are 2-lipped, often in whorls. Chemicals called *terpenes* are found in the family, and can act as growth inhibitors on surrounding plants. A Californian species exudes terpenes as 'weedkiller' to prevent growth of competing grasses.

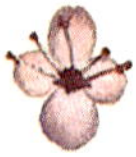

flower

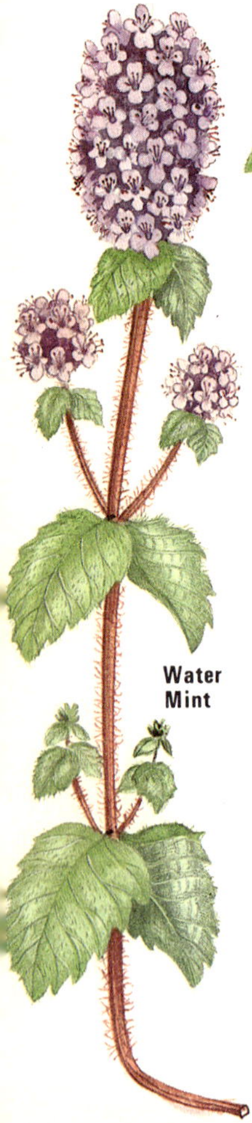

Water Mint

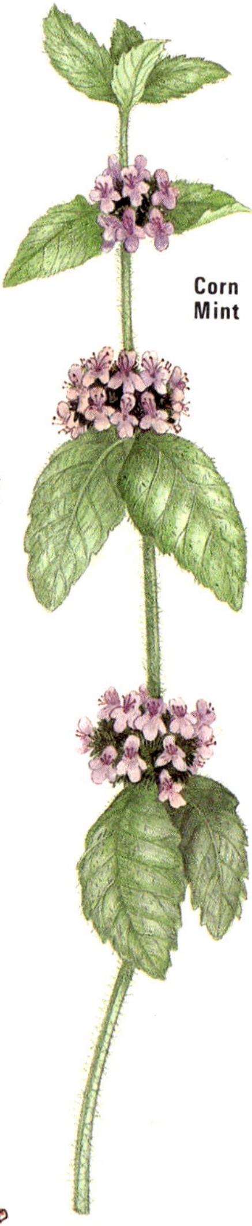

Corn Mint

WATER MINT
Mentha aquatica

The often reddish stems of Water Mint are erect, rising from a creeping underground stem, and 15-90 cm tall. Water Mint grows in wet places. It breeds with escaped garden Spear Mint (*M. spicata*) to give the hybrid Peppermint (*M. piperita*).
Flower: mauve; petals 4; calyx 5-toothed, hairy; stamens long with red anthers.
Flower arrangement: shoots ending in dense, rounded heads of 1-3 whorls.
Flowering time: July-October.
Leaf: ovate, teeth blunt or pointed, opposite, more or less hairy, stalked; if growing in water, the submerged leaves are rounded, toothless.
Fruit: 4 nutlets, smooth.
Uses: as with many other Mints, Water Mint has been used as a stomach medicine and as a herb for strewing on floors of houses.

CORN MINT
Mentha arvensis

Corn Mint grows up to 60 cm high in damp rather than wet places. It is not one of the useful Mints owing to its rather unpleasant smell. The stem is 4-angled and hairy.
Flower: mauve, 4-lobed; calyx with 5 short teeth, hairy; stamens 4, protruding.
Flower arrangement: in dense whorls, shoots not ending in flowers.
Flowering time: May-October.
Leaf: shape variable, usually elliptic and rounded at tip; toothed, stalked, opposite, more or less hairy.
Fruit: 4 nutlets, each ovoid.

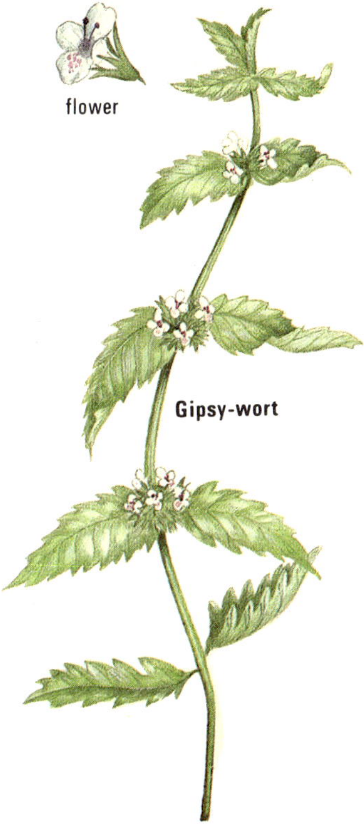

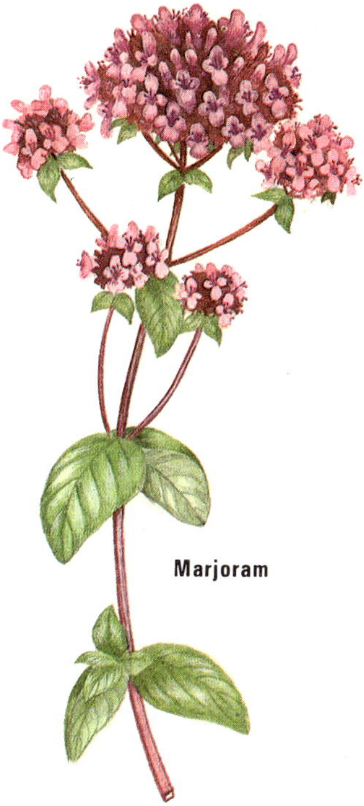

GIPSY-WORT
Lycopus europaeus
Gipsy-wort is tall (20-120 cm) and unbranched, growing in wet places. Unlike many other Labiates this one has no smell when crushed.
Flower: white with purple marks, 3-4 mm; 4-lobed; stamens 2; calyx with spiny teeth.
Flower arrangement: in dense whorls.
Flowering time: June-September.
Leaf: ovate to lanceolate; tip pointed; deeply lobed and toothed, opposite, short-stalked.
Fruit: 4 nutlets, each 5-sided.
Uses: gipsies stained their skin with a black dye from this plant. Another name for the plant is Egyptian's Herb because gipsies, on arrival in Europe were first called Egyptians. It is thought they came from Egypt, though probably before that from India.

MARJORAM
Origanum vulgare
This is a plant of dry places on chalk or limestone, smelling aromatic when crushed, due to tiny translucent oil-filled glands on the leaves, seen if held to the light. The 4-angled stems, 30-80 cm long, are erect and branched in the upper parts.
Flower: mauve, 6-8 mm across; 4-lobed; calyx 5-toothed; stamens 4; bracts often purple.
Flower arrangement: in flat-topped or rounded clusters at top of stems.
Flowering time: July-September.
Leaf: ovate, opposite, slightly toothed or not, short-stalked.
Fruit: 4 nutlets, each ovoid.
Uses: this native species is more pungent than the cultivated, frost-tender species from the Mediterranean used in cooking. Tea can be made from the dried leaves.

GROUND IVY

Glechoma hederacea

Many species in the Mint family have purplish, 2-lipped flowers, all looking rather similar. Ground Ivy is distinguished by having only 2-5 flowers in each whorl and the top petal-lobe being flat, not hooded. Creeping and rooting, it grows in woods and waste places.

Flower: pale violet, 1·5-2 cm long; 2-lipped, upper lip flat, not hooded, lower purple-spotted; calyx 5-toothed.

Flower arrangement: in loose whorls, directed to one side.

Flowering time: March-May.

Leaf: kidney-shaped to almost circular, blunt-toothed, often tinged purple, opposite, long-stalked.

Fruit: 4 nutlets, smooth.

SELFHEAL

Prunella vulgaris

Selfheal is a low-growing, slightly hairy plant of grassland, often tinged purple. The stem is 4-angled, creeping in the lower part and ending in an oblong head of flowers. The plant has no smell when crushed.

Flower: violet, 1-1·5 cm long; 2-lipped, upper lip hooded, lower 3-lobed; calyx of 5 teeth in 2 lips; bract beneath each flower almost circular.

Flower arrangement: in oblong or squat head at top of stem, pair of leaves immediately beneath.

Flowering time: June-September.

Leaf: ovate, tip pointed, 2-5 cm long, shallowly toothed or not, opposite, stalked.

Fruit: 4 nutlets, each oblong.

RED DEAD-NETTLE

Lamium purpureum

Red Dead-nettle is a softly hairy weed of cultivated ground. It has a 4-angled stem and grows 10-45 cm high. Dead-nettles, as the name implies, have no stinging hairs.

Flower: mauve-purple, 1-1·5 cm long; 2-lipped, upper hooded, lower spotted; ring of hairs near flower base; calyx 5-toothed.

Flower arrangement: in whorls in leaf-axils.

Flowering time: March-October.

Leaf: ovate to almost circular, blunt-toothed, often tinged purple, surface puckered, opposite, stalked.

Fruit: 4 nutlets, 3-angled.

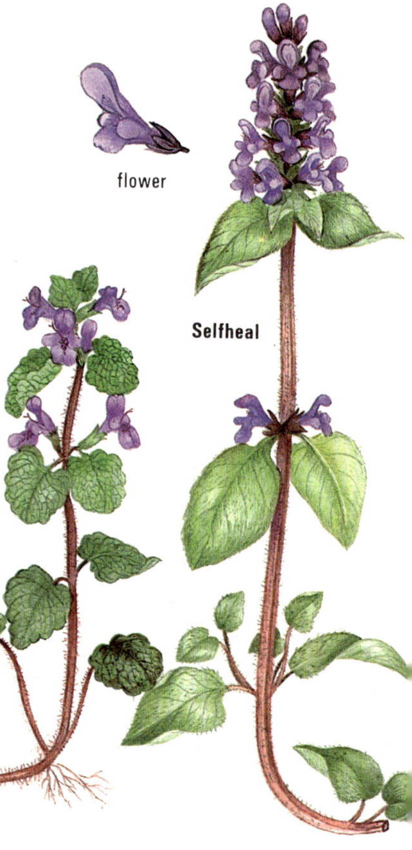

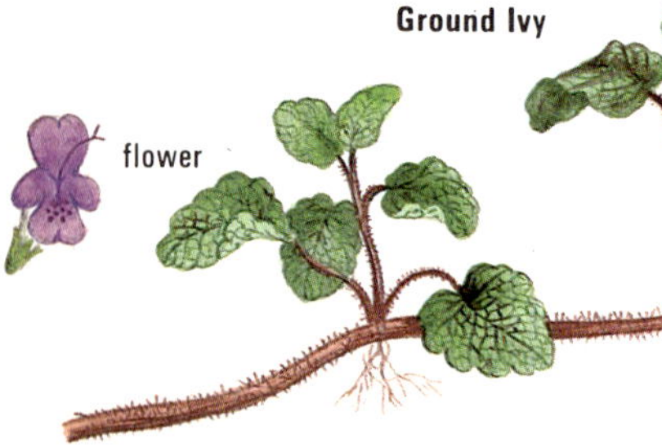

WHITE DEAD-NETTLE

Lamium album

Although a very common plant of waste places and roadsides, the tight whorls of plump-looking, pure white flowers make this an attractive plant. The 4-angled stem is unbranched, hairy and 20-80 cm high. This Dead-nettle is not related to the Common Nettle and does not sting, although the leaves are similar.

Flower: white, 2-2·5 cm long; 2-lipped, upper lip pronouncedly hooded, hairy, lower lip with 2 or 3 short teeth each side; calyx with 5 narrow, pointed teeth.

Flower arrangement: in compact whorls.

Flowering time: May-December.

Leaf: ovate, tapering to point, coarsely toothed, opposite, stalked.

Fruit: 4 nutlets, 3-angled.

Uses: country children have made whistles out of the hollow stems.

COMMON HEMP-NETTLE

Galeopsis tetrahit

The branched, roughly hairy stem has red or yellow glandular hairs and is swollen where the leaf stalks join. The swellings contain special cells to enable the plant to make slight movements. This plant is 10-100 cm tall and found on cultivated land, less often in damp places.

Flower: mauve with darker markings, occasionally white or pale yellow, 1·5-2 cm long; 2-lipped, upper lip hooded, lower 3-lobed, middle lobe notched or not; calyx with 5 narrow teeth.

Flower arrangement: in whorls.

Flowering time: July-September.

Leaf: ovate, tapering to point, blunt-toothed, stalked, blue-green.

Fruit: 4 nutlets, 3-angled.

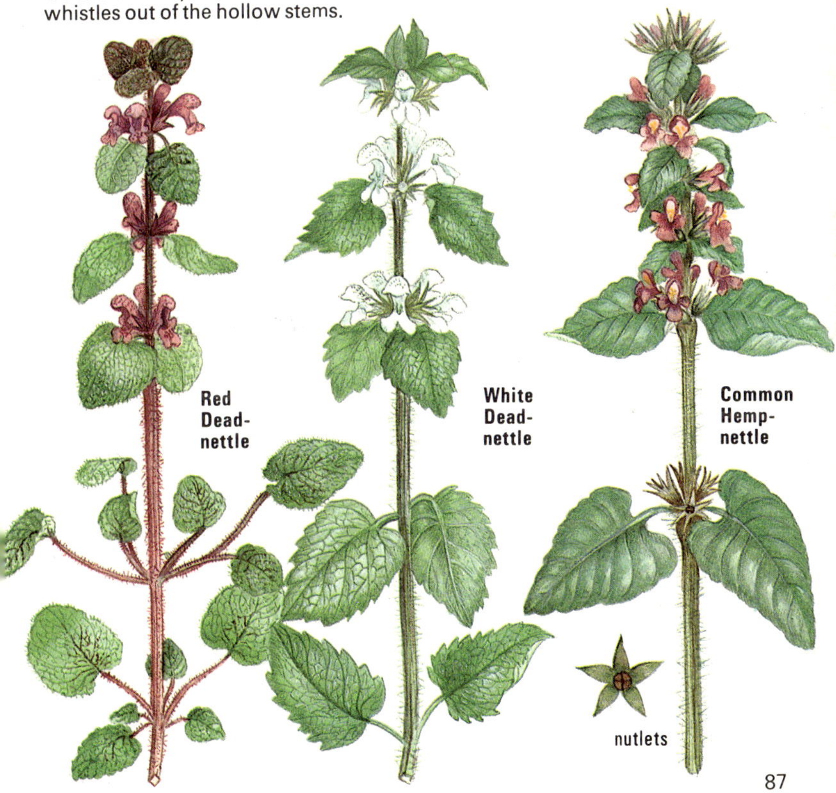

HEDGE WOUNDWORT

Stachys sylvatica

The tough stems of this rather tall plant are roughly hairy and 4-angled. The plant grows 30-120 cm high in the shadier parts of hedgerows. If crushed the whole plant, in particular the creeping, underground stem, gives off a foul smell.

Flower: light maroon with white marks, 1-1·5 cm; 2-lipped; calyx with 5, narrow teeth and glandular hairs.

Flower arrangement: spike of whorls.

Flowering time: July-August.

Leaf: ovate, tip pointed, toothed, stalked, opposite, sparsely hairy.

Fruit: 4 nutlets.

Uses: the common name refers to the old use of this plant in staunching bleeding wounds. The plant also contains antiseptic properties.

SKULL-CAP

Scutellaria galericulata

This is a slender plant of 7-50 cm, found in damp, grassy places, often by streams. The stem is 4-angled.

Flower: blue-violet, whitish toward base, 1-2 cm long; 2-lipped; tube long, slightly curved; calyx 2-lipped.

Flower arrangement: in pairs in leaf-axils.

Flowering time: June-September.

Leaf: lanceolate, tips rounded or bluntly pointed, blunt teeth widely spaced; short-stalked.

Fruit: 4 nutlets, rounded.

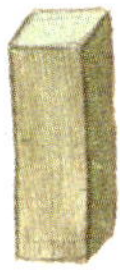

stem section

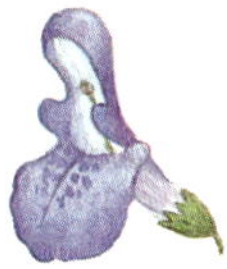

flower

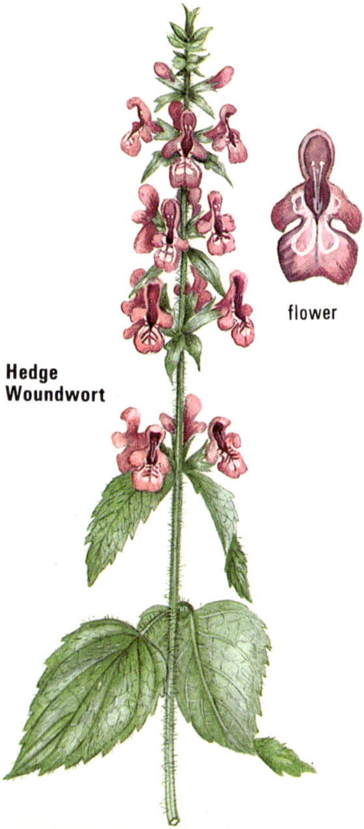

flower

Hedge Woundwort

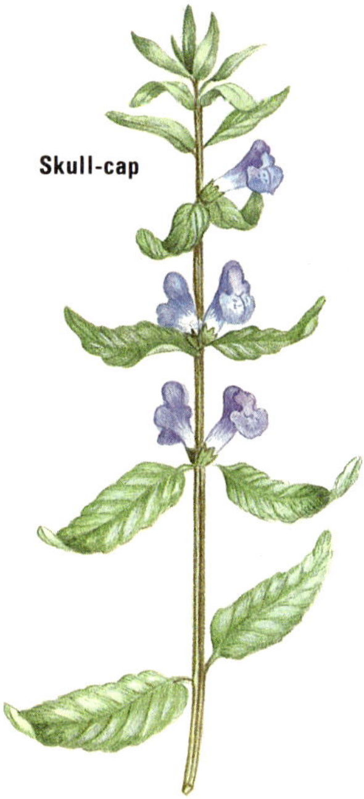

Skull-cap

PLANTAIN FAMILY
Plantaginaceae

This is a family of temperate areas and tropical mountains. The small flowers, clustered into tight spikes, are mainly wind-pollinated, producing large amounts of powdery pollen. Several species of Plantain are stubborn weeds.

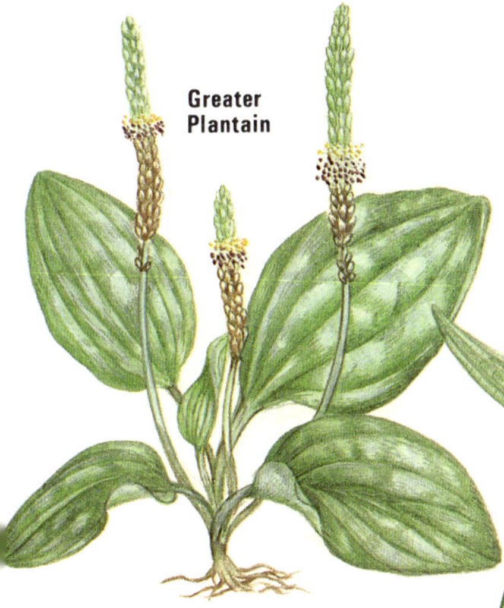

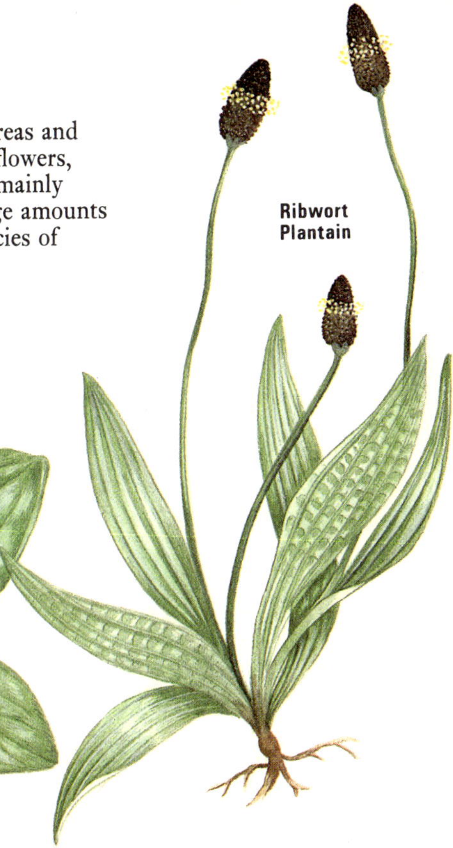

GREATER PLANTAIN
Plantago major

The rosettes of tough, ribbed leaves, often flattened by, but very resistant to trampling, are seen at the sides of almost every path and piece of trodden ground.
Flower: greenish yellow, tiny; anthers mauve, becoming yellow, protruding, wind-pollinated.
Flower arrangement: in long, dense, stalked spike, 10-15 cm, encircled by whorl of anthers.
Flowering time: May-September.
Leaf: broadly elliptic, in rosette; 10-15 cm long, usually without teeth, strongly ribbed, abruptly narrowed into broad stalk.
Fruit: capsule, 2-5 mm.
Uses: when in seed the flower spikes may be hung up for cage-birds to feed on.

RIBWORT PLANTAIN
Plantago lanceolata

The ribbed leaves of this Plantain are long and narrow, forming rosettes. The plant grows in grassy places.
Flower: browny-black, tiny; anthers cream, protruding, wind-pollinated.
Flower arrangement: in dense, short spike of 1-2 cm, on grooved, tough stalk, much longer than leaves.
Flowering time: April-August.
Leaf: lanceolate, in rosette; 10-15 cm long, usually without teeth, strongly ribbed.
Fruit: capsule, about 5 mm.
Uses: the seeds become slimy-coated when wet. In France the coating was used as a fabric stiffener, especially of muslin.

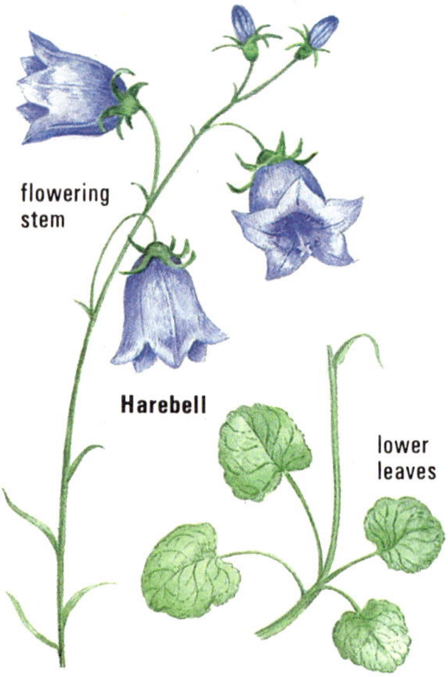

BELLFLOWER FAMILY
Campanulaceae

Many of the flowers in this family are blue and bell-shaped and are grown as garden ornamentals. A sugar (*inulin*) occurs in the sap that is identical to that found in plants of the Daisy family. The two families are thought to be closely related.

HAREBELL
Campanula rotundifolia

Called Bluebell in Scotland, the Harebell is unrelated to the English Bluebell of woods. It is a very slender, hairless plant of dry, grassy places and grows 15-40 cm.
Flower: pale blue, 1-2 cm, bell-shaped with 5 pointed lobes, nodding; calyx with 5 narrow, pointed teeth; stigmas 3.
Flower arrangement: solitary or in loose cluster, on thread-like stalk.
Flowering time: July-September.
Leaf: very narrow, pointed, unstalked on stem; basal leaves ovate or circular, blunt-toothed, stalked.
Fruit: capsule, papery, 3-5 mm.

BEDSTRAW FAMILY
Rubiaceae

As well as the Bedstraws, plants yielding coffee and the drug quinine are included in this very large family. Bedstraw seeds apparently taste of coffee if roasted.

LADY'S BEDSTRAW
Galium verum

The stems of this yellow-flowered Bedstraw are more or less erect, 15-100 cm high, with 4 raised lines and without the minute, hooked bristles used by other Bedstraw species for climbing. The plant becomes black when dried and grows in dry grassland.
Flower: golden yellow, 2-4 mm across; petals 4.
Flower arrangement: in many-flowered clusters at ends of branches.
Flowering time: July-August.
Leaf: in whorls of 8-12, grass-like, 6-25 mm long, bristle-tipped; margins rolled under; dark green and shiny above, paler beneath.
Fruit: of 2 joined lobes, 1·5 mm, hairless, black when ripe.
Uses: this Bedstraw in particular was used to turn and colour the milk in cheese-making.

COMMON MARSH-BEDSTRAW
Galium palustre

Wet places are the habitat of this Bedstraw. The leaf tips are blunt and have no bristle – an important characteristic. The 4-angled stem straggles over other vegetation by means of minute, hooked bristles. It is up to 120 cm long and slightly rough to the touch.
Flower: white, 3-4·5 mm across; petals 4.
Flower arrangement: in clusters, on long stalks, with whorl of leaf-like bracts.
Flowering time: June-July.
Leaf: in whorls of 4-6, narrow, tip blunt, single-veined.
Fruit: of 2 joined lobes, 1 mm, without bristles, black when ripe.

fruit

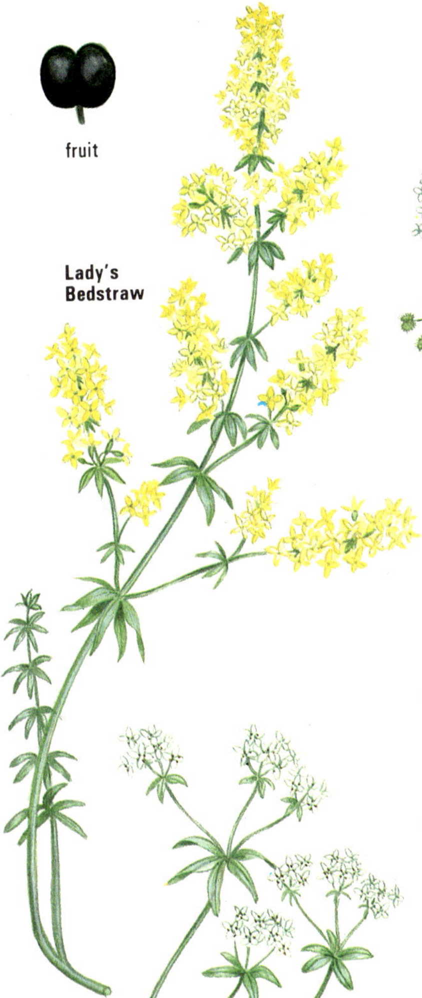

Lady's Bedstraw

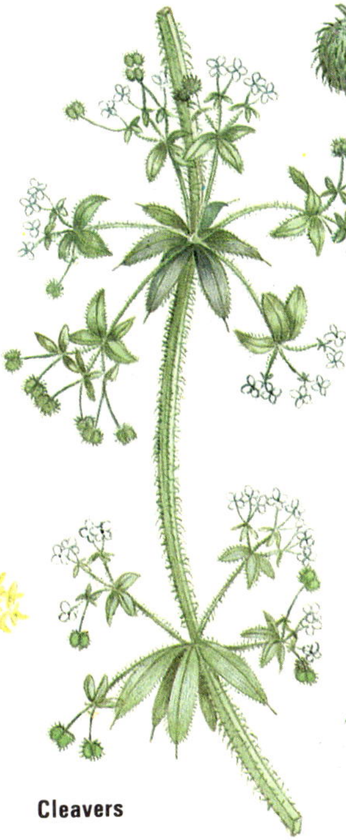

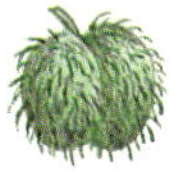

fruit

Cleavers

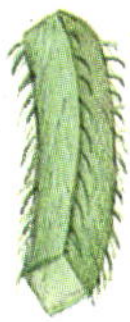

stem section, showing hooks

CLEAVERS

Galium aparine

This scrambling plant of 15-180 cm clings to other vegetation, often in dense masses, with minute hooked bristles, rough and tacky to the touch. A characteristic to look for is the bristle at the leaf tip. The stem is 4-angled and branched. The plant grows in hedges and woods and is a weed of cultivation.

Flower: white, 2 mm across; petals 4.

Flower arrangement: in clusters of 2-5, on long stalks, with whorl of leaf-like bracts.

Flowering time: June-August.

Leaf: in whorls of 6-9, narrow, tip ending in bristle, single-veined.

Fruit: of 2 joined lobes, 3-6 mm, covered with tiny, white, hooked bristles; purplish when ripe.

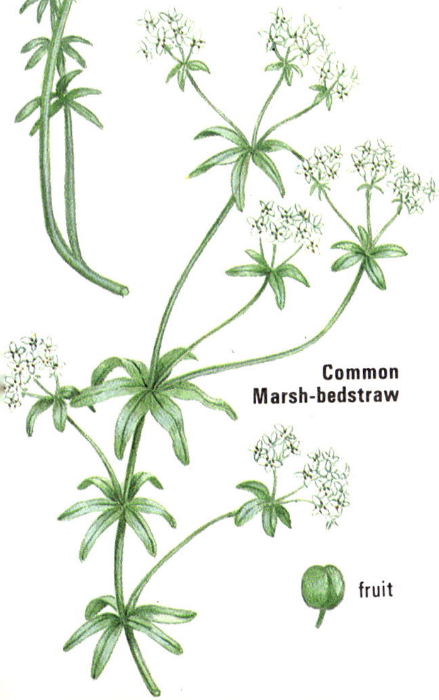

Common Marsh-bedstraw

fruit

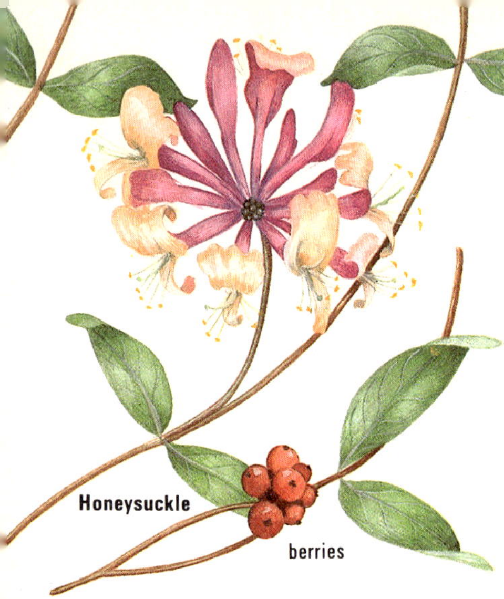

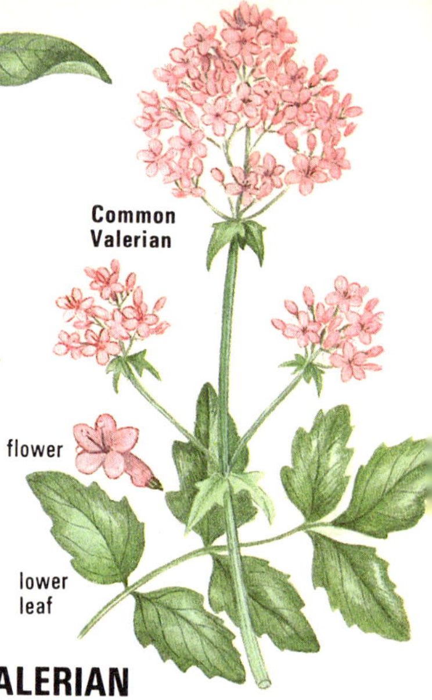

HONEYSUCKLE FAMILY Caprifoliaceae

Most of the species in this family are shrubs, some of them climbing. The flowers are often tubular, and the fruits are usually berries. There are many garden ornamentals, including Honeysuckles, Snowberries and Viburnums.

HONEYSUCKLE

Lonicera periclymenum

A climbing shrub of up to 6 m, Honeysuckle may also be found sprawling over the ground. It grows in hedges and woods and is planted in gardens for the scented flowers.

Flower: cream, tinged with pinky red; trumpet-shaped with 4 upper lobes, 1 lower; 4-5 cm long, stamens and style protruding.

Flower arrangement: in head, flowers directed outwards.

Flowering time: June-October.

Leaf: elliptic or oblong, tip usually pointed, opposite, no teeth, stalkless, 3-9 cm long, dark green above, paler beneath.

Fruit: tight head of red berries.

VALERIAN FAMILY Valerianaceae

Plants in this family give off an unpleasant smell. Cats are often drawn to the smell, and appear to become intoxicated. The small, clustered flowers each have a tiny pouch near the base. In many species there is a plume of hairs on the fruit for wind dispersal.

COMMON VALERIAN

Valeriana officinalis

Often tall and erect, Valerian is usually hairless and not much branched. It differs from other Valerian species in having all the leaves divided into leaflets. The plant has a sickly smell when crushed. It is mostly found in damp places.

Flower: pale pink, about 5 mm across, 5-lobed, tubular at base; pouch at base of tube; stamens 3.

Flower arrangement: clustered.

Flowering time: June-August.

Leaf: divided into pairs of broad or narrow leaflets, toothed or not, lower leaves stalked.

Fruit: 2-5 mm with plume of hairs.

Uses: the roots contain medicinal properties used as a sedative.

TEASEL FAMILY
Dipsacaceae

This is a small family which includes Teasels and Scabious. The tight heads of tiny flowers look like those of the Daisy family, except for the stamens which stand out from each flower.

FIELD SCABIOUS
Knautia arvensis

The beautiful mauve flower-heads, made up of many tiny flowers, are often larger than the other Scabious species. The erect plants grow 25-100 cm high on dry banks and fields, and the stem has rough bristles, at least at the base.

Flower: mauve, 4-lobed; outer flowers larger than inner; stamens protruding.

Flower arrangement: in flattish head, 3-4 cm across, on long stalk; bracts directly below head ovate, in 2 overlapping layers, not reaching edge of head.

Flowering time: July-September.

Leaf: variable, deeply lobed, opposite, hairy; basal leaves often forming rosette, some unlobed.

Fruit: 5-6 mm, crowned by 8 bristles; dispersed by ants, which find them attractive.

DEVIL'S BIT SCABIOUS
Succisa pratensis

This Scabious has undivided leaves and an erect, slightly hairy stem 15-100 cm high. It grows in damp places, including woods. The curious root gives the plant its name. After the first year's growth the tip of the thick root falls away leaving an abrupt end, as if bitten off.

Flower: mauve, 4-lobed; outer flowers not much larger than inner; stamens protruding.

Flower arrangement: in domed head, 1·5-2·5 cm across, on long stalk; sepal-like bracts lanceolate, in 2 overlapping layers, reaching edge of head.

Flowering time: June-October.

Leaf: elliptic, tip pointed or rounded, opposite, untoothed or with a few teeth; basal leaves stalked, forming rosette.

Fruit: 5 mm, crowned by 5 bristles.

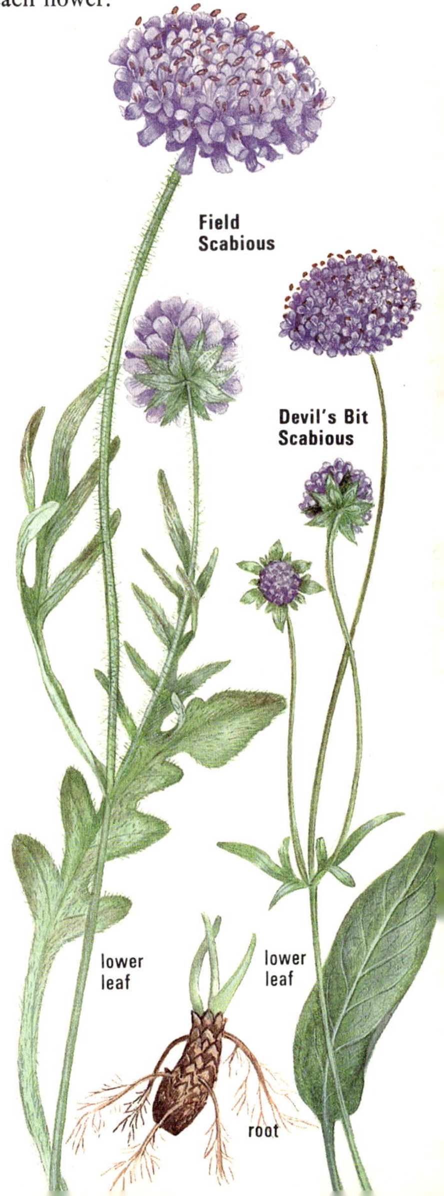

DAISY FAMILY
Compositae

This enormous family of 25,000 species includes many cosmopolitan weeds. The family is characterized by tiny flowers (*florets*) grouped in tight heads. The florets are of 2 kinds, a simple tube (*disc floret*) and a tube elongated on one side into a strap shape (*ray floret*). The heads may consist of all disc florets (Groundsel-like), all ray florets (Dandelion-like) or both (Daisy-like). The heads often look like single flowers, the bracts directly underneath simulating sepals. The fruits (*achenes*) often have a parachute of hairs (*pappus*) for wind dispersal. Cultivated Composites include lettuce, artichokes and Chrysanthemums.

DAISY
Bellis perennis

Familiar in the short grass of meadow, lawn and verge, the Daisy is known to all who have ever made a daisy chain. The flower stalks rise straight from a rosette of leaves and the flowers close at night and in wet weather.

Flower: ray florets white, tinged pink beneath, many; disc florets yellow; head 1·5-3 cm across.

Flower arrangement: head solitary, on long stalk.

Flowering time: March-October.

Leaf: spoon-shaped, with or without a few teeth.

Fruit: achene, 1·5-2 mm, downy.

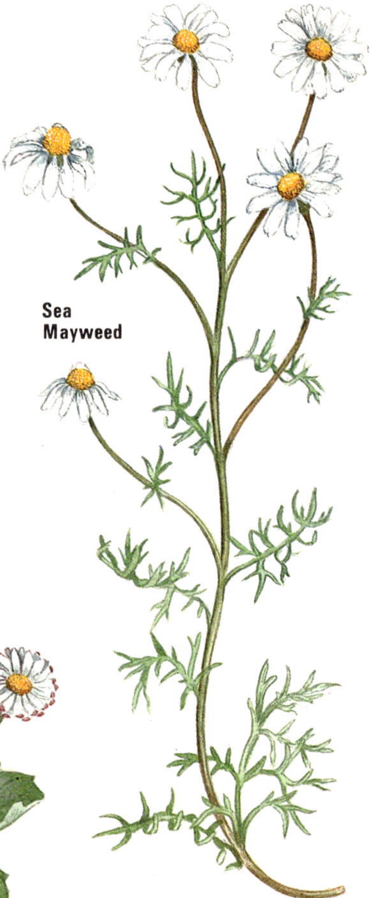

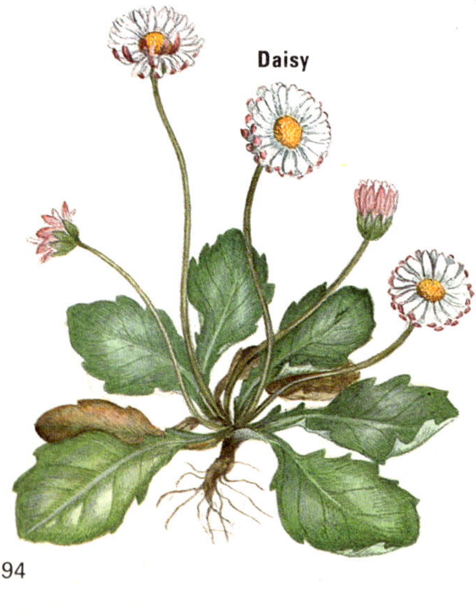

SEA MAYWEED

Matricaria maritima

This Mayweed has Daisy-like flower-heads and ferny leaves. It has no smell when crushed. The branched stem is 10-30 cm high, usually prostrate. The whole plant is hairless, and is found near the sea.

Flower: ray florets white; disc florets yellow; heads 1·5-5 cm across; sepal-like bracts with narrow, papery margins.

Flower arrangement: heads solitary, on long stalks.

Flowering time: July-September.

Leaf: ferny, very finely dissected; segments sometimes fleshy.

Fruit: achene, with 2 dark dots near top.

OX-EYE DAISY

Leucanthemum vulgare

The Ox-eye Daisy has large, Daisy-like flower-heads, smaller in exposed places. The almost hairless stems grow 20-70 cm tall in grassy places.

Flower: ray florets white; disc florets yellow; head 2·5-5 cm across; sepal-like bracts with purplish borders.

Flower arrangement: heads solitary, on long stalks.

Flowering time: June-August.

Leaf: Often forming non-flowering rosettes, dark green, toothed; lower stem leaves rounded or spoon-shaped, long-stalked; upper leaves oblong, stalkless.

Fruit: achene, pale grey, ribbed.

PINEAPPLEWEED

Chamomilla suaveolens

Familiar by the warm, aromatic smell when walked on (supposed to resemble a pineapple smell), Pineappleweed is low-growing on trampled ground. It is a weed introduced to Europe, probably from N. E. Asia and has ferny leaves and little greeny-yellow, petal-less flower-heads.

Flower: yellow-green, disc florets only; heads domed, 5-8 mm across; sepal-like bracts rounded, pale-bordered.

Flower arrangement: heads on branched stalks.

Flowering time: June-July.

Leaf: finely dissected, fern-like.

Fruit: achene.

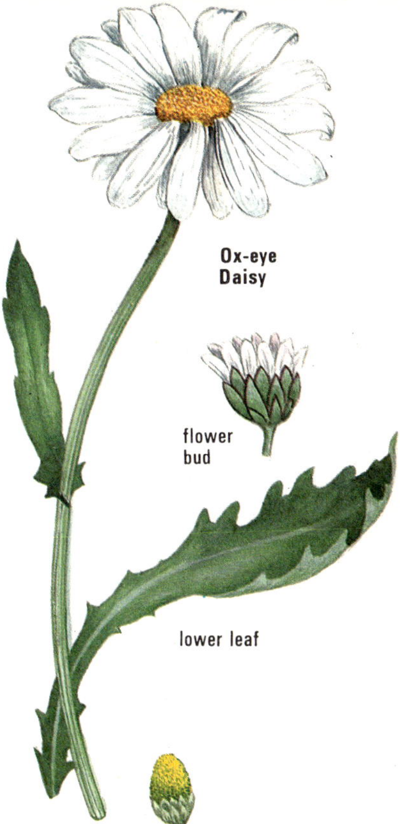

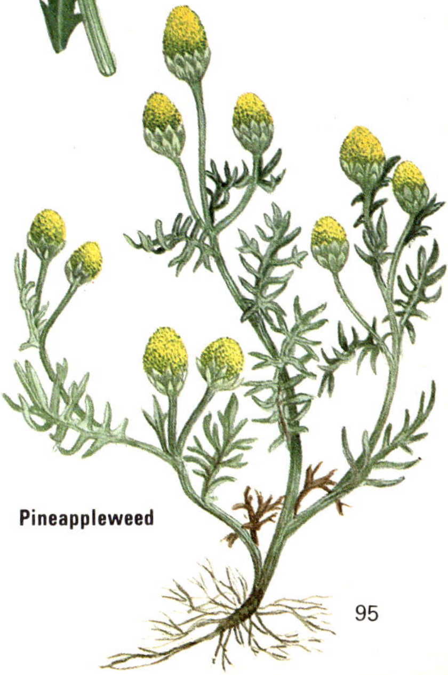

flower without ray florets

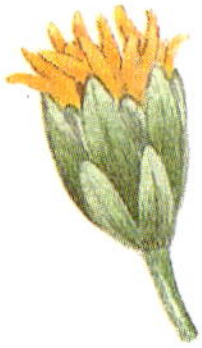

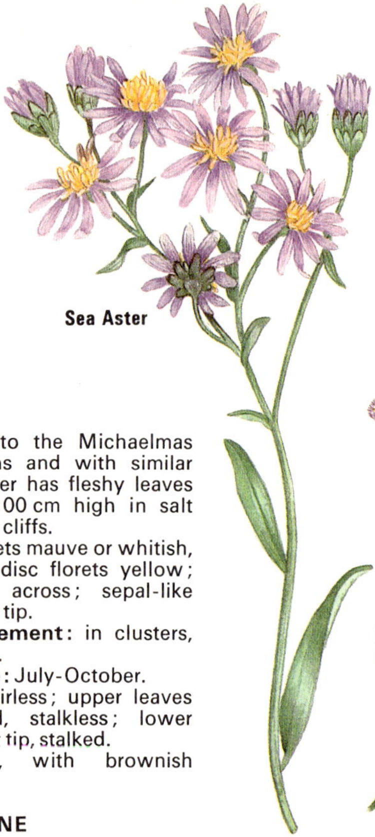

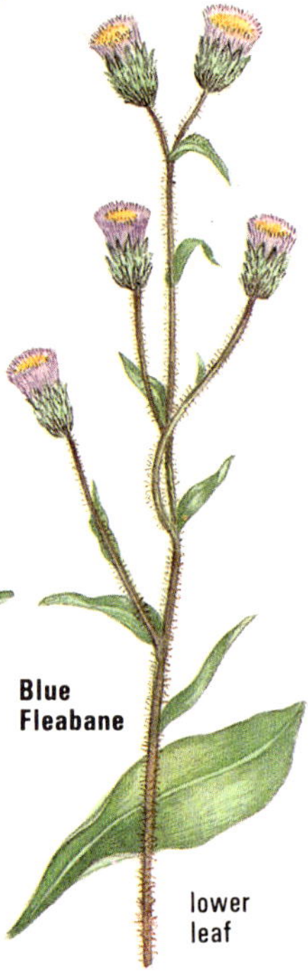

SEA ASTER

Aster tripolium

Closely related to the Michaelmas Daisy of gardens and with similar flowers, Sea Aster has fleshy leaves and grows 15-100 cm high in salt marsh and on sea cliffs.

Flower: ray florets mauve or whitish, many or none; disc florets yellow; head 8-20 mm across; sepal-like bracts rounded at tip.

Flower arrangement: in clusters, often flat-topped.

Flowering time: July-October.

Leaf: fleshy, hairless; upper leaves narrow, pointed, stalkless; lower leaves rounded at tip, stalked.

Fruit: achene, with brownish pappus.

BLUE FLEABANE

Erigeron acer

The flower-heads are of similar colour to those of the Sea Aster but the mauve ray florets are erect, not spread out. The slender, roughly hairy stems are 8-60 cm high, often reddish and branched in the upper part. This Fleabane grows in dry places, especially on chalk.

Flower: ray florets pale mauve, erect, in 2 or more rows; disc florets yellow; head 12-18 mm across; sepal-like bracts narrow, pointed, red-tinged.

Flower arrangement: in long-stalked cluster, less often solitary.

Flowering time: July-August.

Leaf: lanceolate, untoothed, stalkless, leaf base clasping stem; basal leaves stalked.

Fruit: achene, with pinkish pappus.

TRIFID BUR-MARIGOLD

Bidens tripartita

The branched stem of this rather dull-looking plant is 10-60 cm high. The plants grow near fresh water, and the fruits are dispersed by catching on the fur of passing animals or on clothing.

Flower: brownish-yellow; disc florets only; head 1-2·5 cm across; inner sepal-like bracts brownish-green; outer collar of 5-8 leaf-like bracts spreading beyond head.

Flower arrangement: solitary, nodding slightly.

Flowering time: July-September.

Leaf: of 3 toothed segments or undivided, stalked, opposite.

Fruit: achene, each barbed with 2-4 bristles.

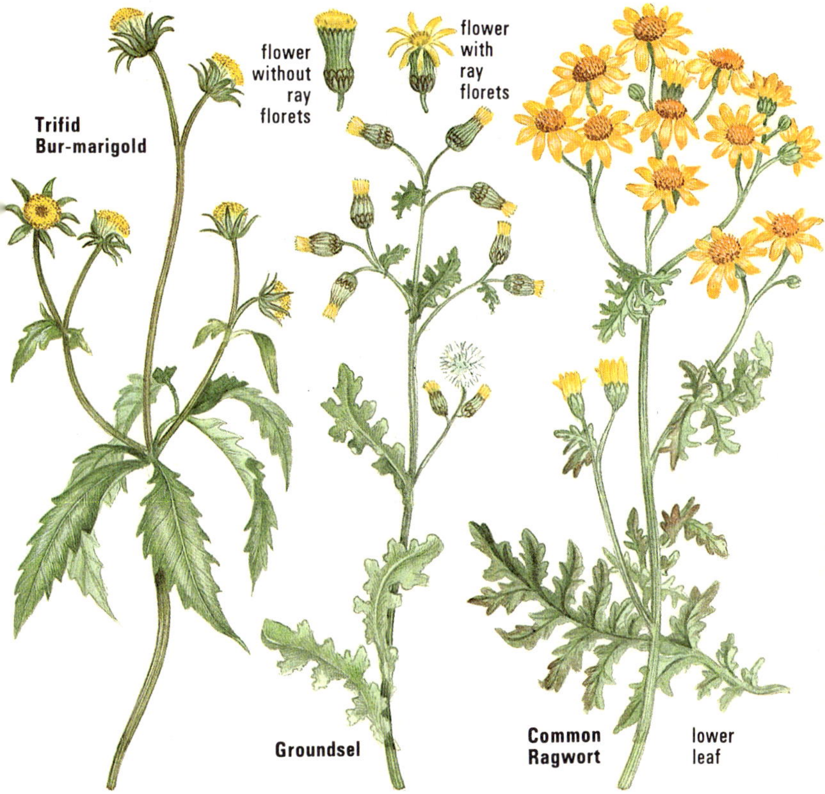

GROUNDSEL

Senecio vulgaris

Groundsel grows on waste and cultivated ground. The branched stem is 8-45 cm high. The common name is very old, coming from an Anglo-Saxon word meaning 'ground swallower', from the way this weed spreads.

Flower: yellow; disc florets only, occasionally rayed; heads about 4 mm across; sepal-like bracts dark-tipped, outer short.

Flower arrangement: heads in loose clusters.

Flowering time: all year.

Leaf: lobed, the lobes irregularly toothed; upper leaf bases clasping stem; hairless or slightly hairy.

Fruit: achene, with pappus forming clocks.

COMMON RAGWORT

Senecio jacobaea

Neglected fields are often overgrown with this species of Ragwort. It is also found on waste ground. The grooved stem branches above the middle and grows 30-150 cm high.

Flower: ray florets yellow, 12-15; disc florets orange; heads 1·5-2·5 cm across; sepal-like bracts black-tipped.

Flower arrangement: heads in flat-topped clusters.

Flowering time: June-October.

Leaf: deeply lobed, lobes blunt-toothed, end lobe rounded; dark green, hairless or with sparse hairs beneath.

Fruit: achene, ribbed, with pappus.

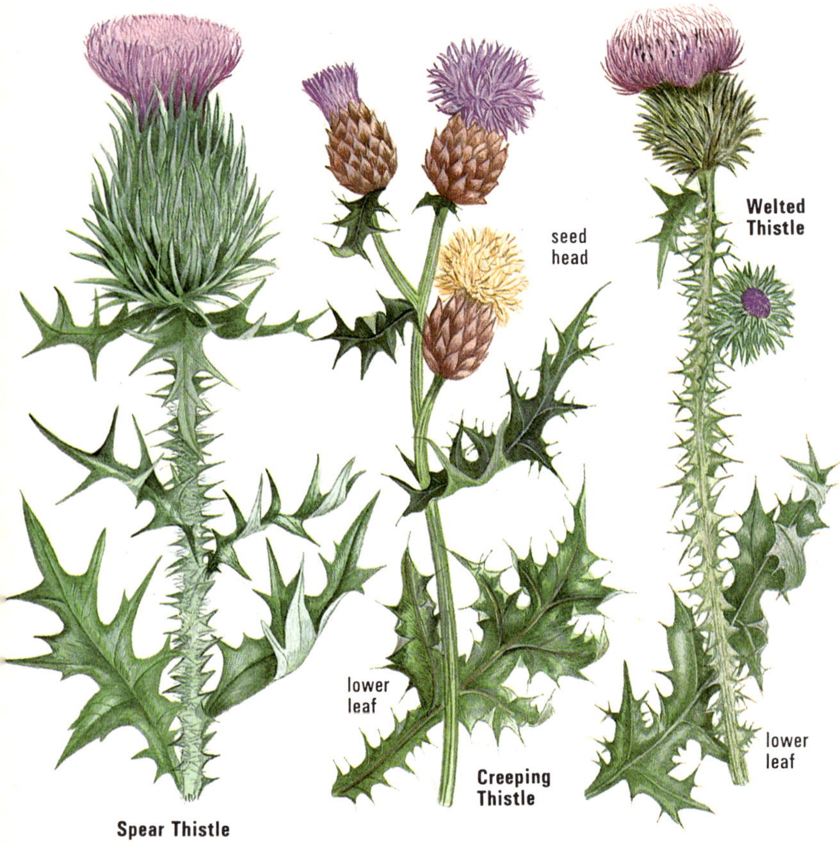

SPEAR THISTLE
Cirsium vulgare
Thin, spiny ridges run down the stems of this common thistle. The stems have white, woolly hairs and grow 30-150 cm tall in fields and waste places, and by roadsides.
Flower: mauve; disc florets only; head 3-5 cm across; sepal-like bracts spiny, hairy.
Flower arrangement: solitary, or cluster of 2-3.
Flowering time: July-October.
Leaf: lanceolate, margins wavy, very spiny; end segment sword-shaped; white-hairy or rough beneath.
Fruit: achene, yellow with black streaks; pappus long, white.

CREEPING THISTLE
Cirsium arvense
Creeping Thistle is a stubborn weed on cultivated and waste land. The creeping roots send up new plants. The grooved stem is not continuously spiny-ridged, as in the common Spear Thistle, and grows 30-120 cm high.
Flower: mauve; disc florets only; head 1·5-2·5 cm across; sepal-like bracts sharply pointed but not spiny, purple-tinged.
Flower arrangement: solitary, or in clusters.
Flowering time: July-September.
Leaf: lanceolate, margin undulating, very spiny, hairless above, white-hairy or not beneath.
Fruit: achene; pappus long, fawn.

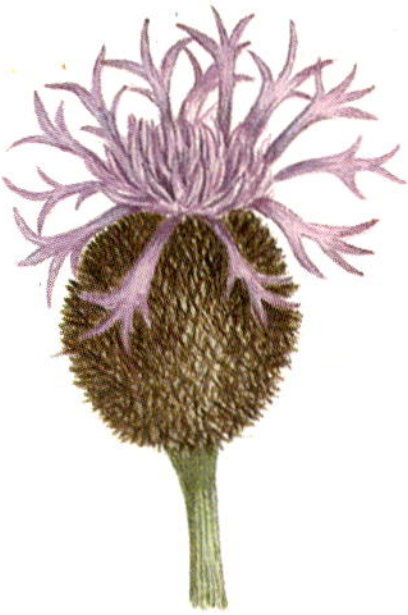

other type
of flower

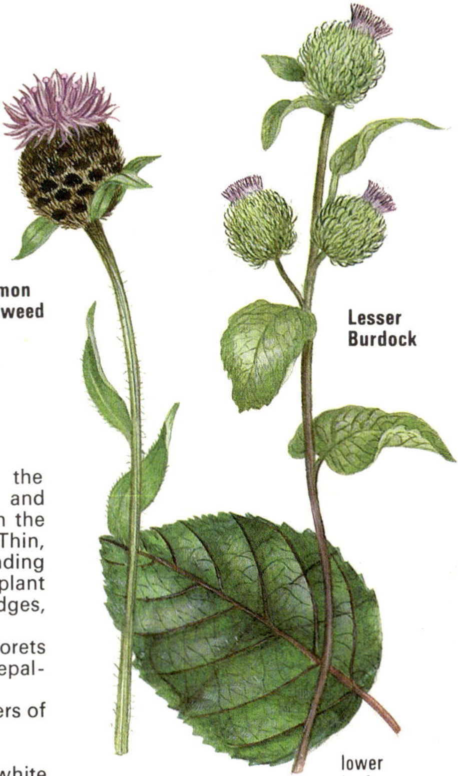

WELTED THISTLE

Carduus acanthoides

The common name refers to the matted white hairs on the stem and undersides of the leaves, though the degree of hairiness varies. Thin, spiny ridges run up the stem, ending short of the flower head. The plant grows 30-150 cm tall in hedges, verges and stream-sides.

Flower: reddish purple; disc florets only; head 2-2·5 cm across; sepal-like bracts many, sharply pointed.

Flower arrangement: in clusters of 3-5.

Flowering time: June-August.

Leaf: margins spiny, wavy, white hairs beneath; upper leaves narrow, lower deeply lobed.

Fruit: achene, with long pappus.

COMMON KNAPWEED

Centaurea nigra

The Thistle-like flower-heads of this Knapweed may be shaped either like a shaving brush or with the outer florets enlarged and dissected. The unspined plants grow 15-100 cm tall in grassland and along roadsides.

Flower: reddish purple; disc florets only or outer florets enlarged, dissected; head 2-4 cm across; sepal-like bracts browny-black, each edged by dark fringe.

Flower arrangement: solitary.

Flowering time: June-September.

Leaf: lanceolate, with or without a few teeth, hairy; lower leaves stalked.

Fruit: achene, fawn; pappus short.

LESSER BURDOCK

Arctium minus

Stout, sometimes bushy, Lesser Burdock grows 50-150 cm high in waste places and on roadsides. After flowering the hooked bracts of the seed-heads attach themselves as burs to clothing and animal fur, so transporting the seeds.

Flower: red-purple; disc florets only, in thistle-like, ovoid heads, 1·5-4 cm; bracts hooked.

Flower arrangement: in leaf-axils below; upper heads clustered.

Flowering time: July-September.

Leaf: ovate, tip pointed, toothed, up to 30 cm long; hairless above, sparse hairs beneath; stalk hollow.

Fruit: achene, with short pappus; whole seed-head forming bur.

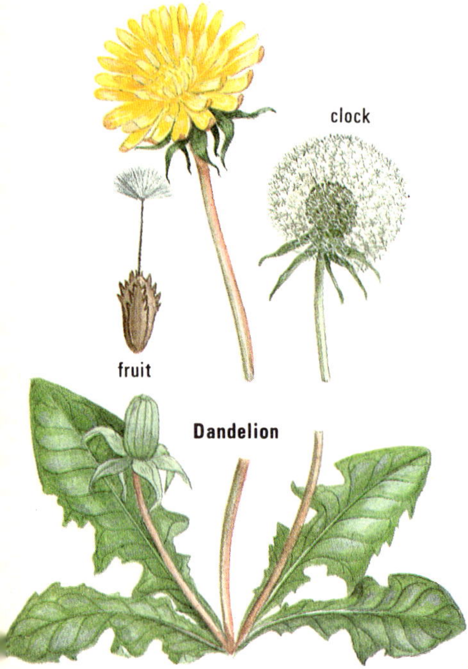

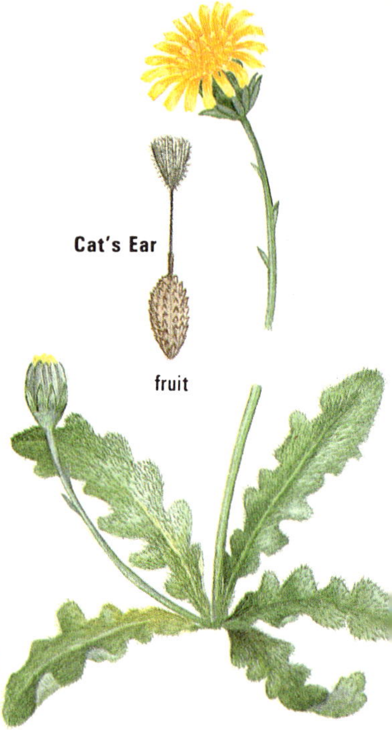

DANDELION

Taraxacum officinale

There are many species of Dandelion, all very variable and difficult to identify. This description covers a group of species. Dandelions grow in grassy and waste places. The pappus forms the familiar 'clocks' of children's games.

Flower: yellow; ray florets only, outer brown or mauve beneath; heads 3-7·5 cm across; outer sepal-like bracts turned down or spread out.

Flower arrangement: heads solitary, stalk unbranched, stout, hollow, exuding milky sap if broken.

Flowering time: March-October.

Leaf: in basal rosette, lobes deep, toothed, pointing down, hairless.

Fruit: achene, with stalked pappus.

CAT'S EAR

Hypochaeris radicata

Important features are the rosette of rough, lobed leaves and tiny bracts on the upper parts of the branched, hairless stem. The stem bears Dandelion-like flower-heads and exudes milky sap if broken. The plant grows 20-60 cm high in grassy places.

Flower: yellow; ray florets only, outer green or grey beneath; heads 2·5-4 cm across.

Flower arrangement: heads on hairless, few-branched stalks with tiny bracts.

Flowering time: June-September.

Leaf: in basal rosette, roughly hairy, lobed, end lobe rounded.

Fruit: achene, pappus fawn, stalked.

AUTUMNAL HAWKBIT

Leontodon autumnalis

The outer petals of the Dandelion-like flower-heads are often striped red beneath. The stems are branched, usually hairless, with tiny bracts towards the top. If broken, the stem exudes milky sap. The plants grow 5-60 cm high in grassy places.

Flower: yellow; ray florets only, striped red beneath; heads 1-3·5 cm across; buds erect; sepal-like bracts

hairless (with dark hairs on mountain plants).
Flower arrangement: heads on branched, usually hairless stalks.
Flowering time: June-October.
Leaf: in rosette, lobed or with widely spaced teeth, tip pointed, hairless or slightly hairy.
Fruit: achene, with pappus.

SMOOTH HAWK'S-BEARD
Crepis capillaris
The branched stems of this rather slender, Dandelion-like plant are 20-100 cm high. It grows in grassland and waste places.
Flower: bright yellow; ray florets only, outer often reddish beneath; heads 1-2·5 cm across; sepal-like bracts lanceolate, with black bristles or not, in 2 layers, outer bracts pressed close to inner.
Flower arrangement: loose clusters.
Flowering time: June-September.
Leaf: variable; lower leaves with many narrow lobes or toothed; upper leaves narrow, stalkless, with base having 2 pointed lobes which clasp stem.
Fruit: achene, fawn, 10-ribbed; pappus white.

GOAT'S-BEARD
Tragopogon pratensis
The Dandelion-like flower-head of this curious-looking plant is over-topped by long bracts and closes around noon. The stem bears grass-like leaves and grows 30-70 cm high in grass- and waste land.
Flower: yellow; ray florets only; heads broad; sepal-like bracts longer than head, narrow.
Flower arrangement: head solitary.
Flowering time: June-July.
Leaf: grass-like, often clasping stem at base, white-veined, hairless.
Fruit: achene, with stalked pappus, forming large clock.

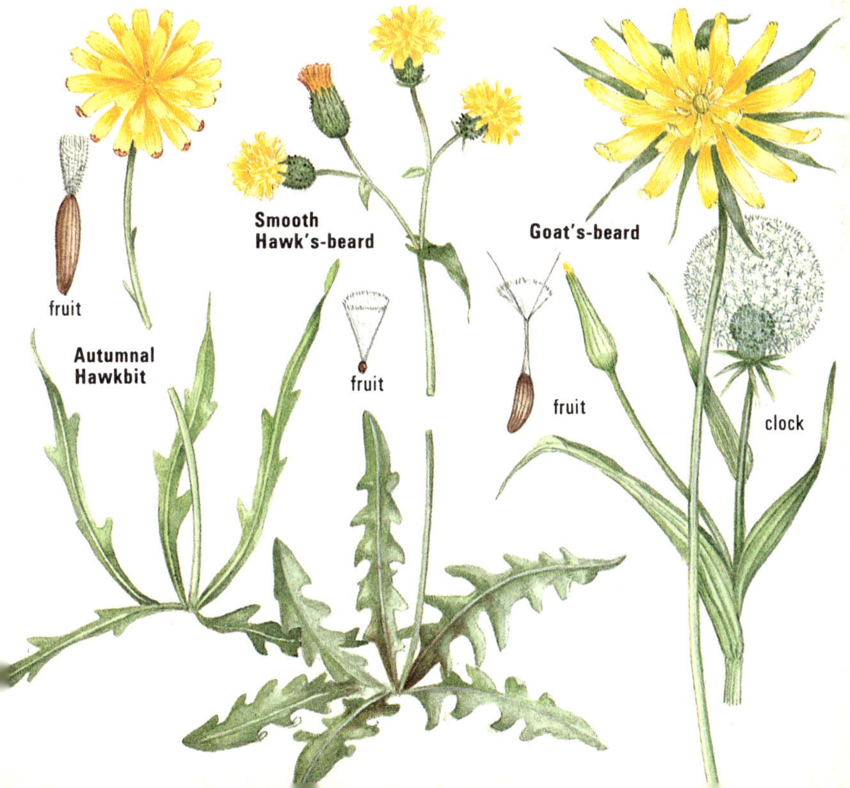

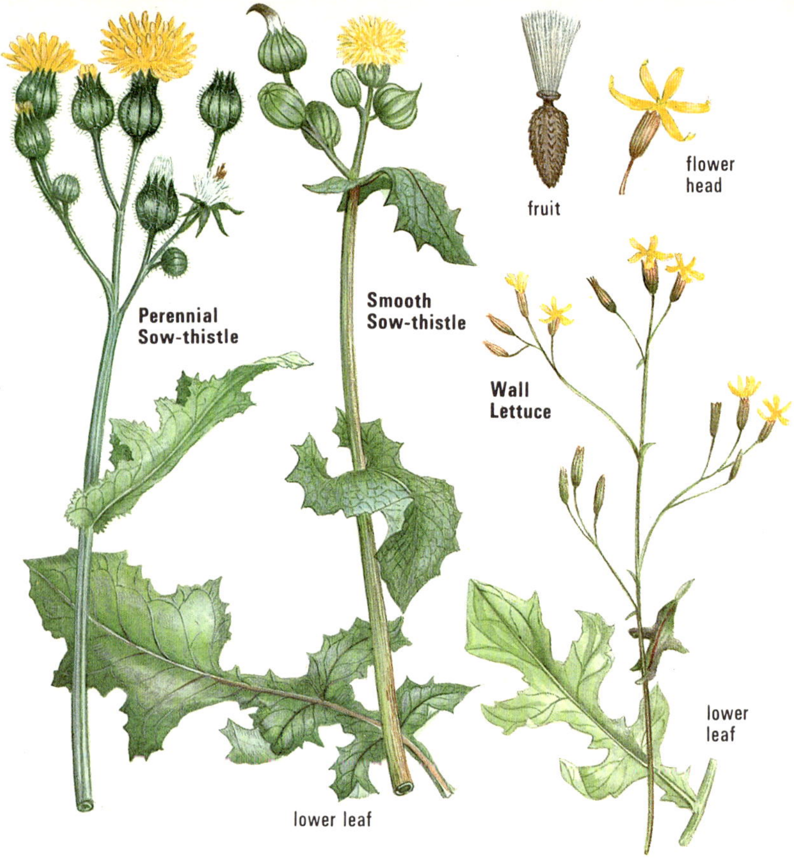

PERENNIAL SOW-THISTLE

Sonchus arvensis

The plant has Dandelion-like flowerheads, and leaves with rounded basal lobes. The hollow stem is 30-150 cm tall with sticky hairs on the upper parts. If cut, the stem oozes milky sap. The plant grows in waste places, by streams and on the coast.

Flower: golden yellow; ray florets only; heads 4-5 cm across; sepal-like bracts with yellow-tipped, sticky hairs.

Flower arrangement: heads in loose, flat-topped clusters.

Flowering time: July-October.

Leaf: oblong, lobed, margins weakly spiny; leaf bases clasping stem with 2 rounded lobes.

Fruit: achene, with white pappus.

SMOOTH SOW-THISTLE

Sonchus oleraceus

This plant has Dandelion-like flowerheads and pointed basal lobes to the leaves. The stem is hollow, 20-150 cm high and usually lacks sticky hairs. If cut, it oozes milky sap. The plants grow in waste places and as a weed of cultivation.

Flower: pale yellow; ray florets only; heads 2-2·5 cm across; sepal-like bracts usually without sticky hairs.

Flower arrangement: heads clustered.

Flowering time: June-August.

Leaf: variable in shape, often deeply lobed, margins weakly spiny; leaf bases clasping stem with 2 pointed lobes; blue-green.

Fruit: achene, with white pappus.

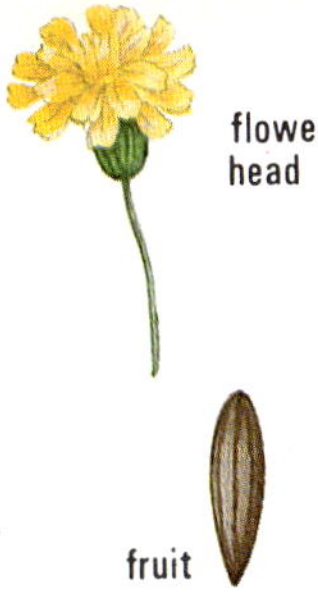

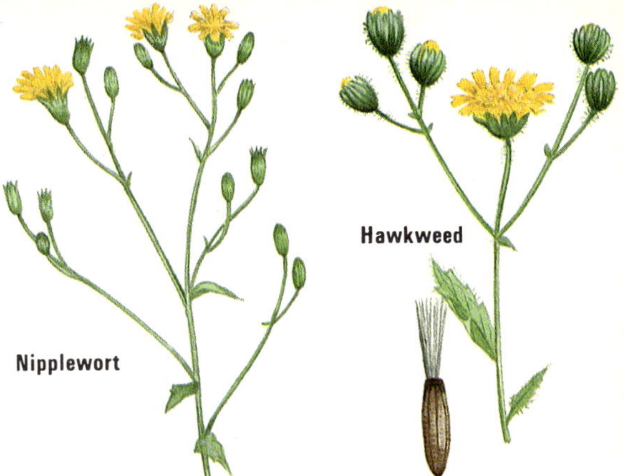

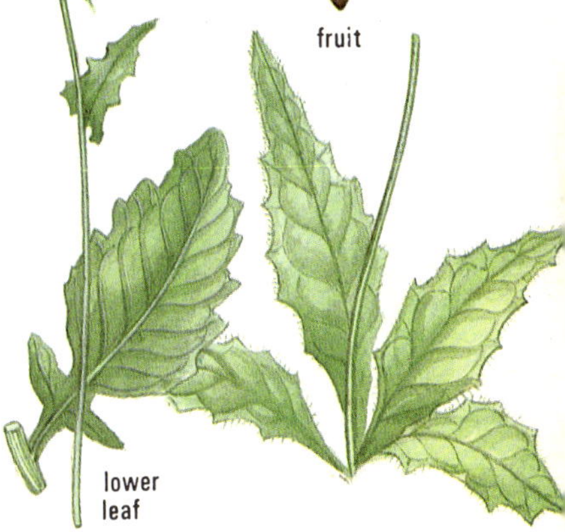

WALL LETTUCE

Mycelis muralis

The flower-heads, on branched stalks, each have only 5 pale yellow florets. The stem bears leaves, often purple-tinged, with red veins. Wall Lettuce is hairless and grows 20-100 cm high on walls, and in rocky places and woods.

Flower: pale yellow; 5 ray florets only; heads about 1 cm across; sepal-like bracts in cylinder shape.

Flower arrangement: heads on branched stalks.

Flowering time: July-September.

Leaf: alternate, deeply lobed, coarsely toothed; basal lobes of upper leaves clasping stem; often purple-tinged, red-veined.

Fruit: achene, with pappus.

NIPPLEWORT

Lapsana communis

The flower-heads are like small Dandelions on branched stalks, and the leaves grow up the stem. The plant can grow up to 90 cm high in shady, waste places. The common name is said to come from the shape of the flower buds.

Flower: yellow; ray florets only; heads 1·5-2 cm across; sepal-like bracts narrow, tips rounded, dark-striped down centre.

Flower arrangement: heads on branched stalks.

Flowering time: July-September.

Leaf: alternate, toothed; lower leaves with toothed lobes; all often slightly hairy.

Fruit: achene, ribbed, no pappus.

HAWKWEED

Hieracium Sect. Vulgata

Hawkweed species are extremely numerous and difficult to identify. A section containing some of the most common species is described here. The branched, hairy stem grows 15-80 cm tall and exudes milky sap if broken. Hawkweeds are found in shady or rocky places.

Flower: yellow; ray florets only, Dandelion-like; sepal-like bracts dark green, glandular, hairy.

Flower arrangement: heads on branched, glandular hairy stalks.

Flowering time: June-September.

Leaf: elliptic to lanceolate, variably toothed, not lobed, both ends narrowed, hairy in parts; basal leaves in rosette.

Fruit: achene; pappus brownish.

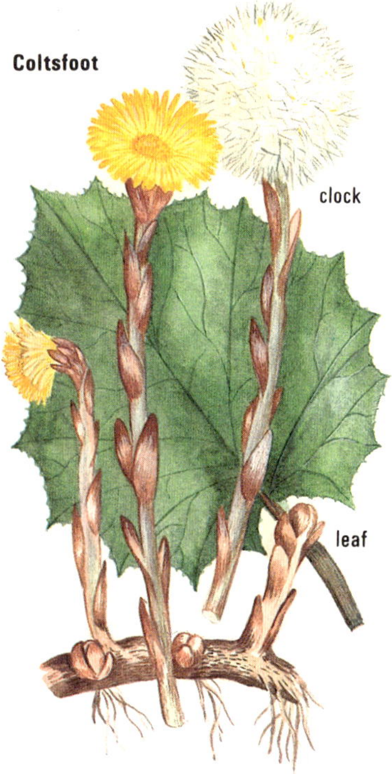

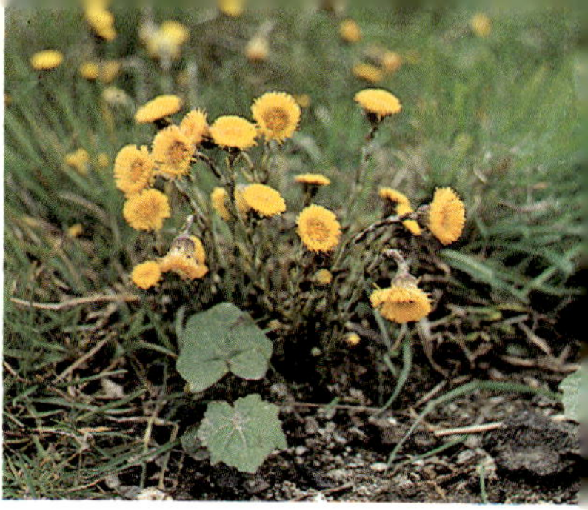

Coltsfoot is often found on waste ground such as railway banks.

COLTSFOOT

Tussilago farfara

Coltsfoot is found on waste and arable land, especially on clay soil. The flowering stems appear before the leaves in early spring, rising from a creeping, underground stem, as do the leaves later on.

Flower: yellow; disc florets surrounded by many narrow ray florets; head 1·5-3·5 cm across, drooping after flowering.

Flower arrangement: head solitary; stalk thick, scaled, 5-15 cm high.

Flowering time: February-April.

Leaf: appearing after flowers, 10-30 cm across, in clumps, heart-shaped, irregularly toothed, stalked, white-woolly beneath.

Fruit: achene, pappus forming clock.

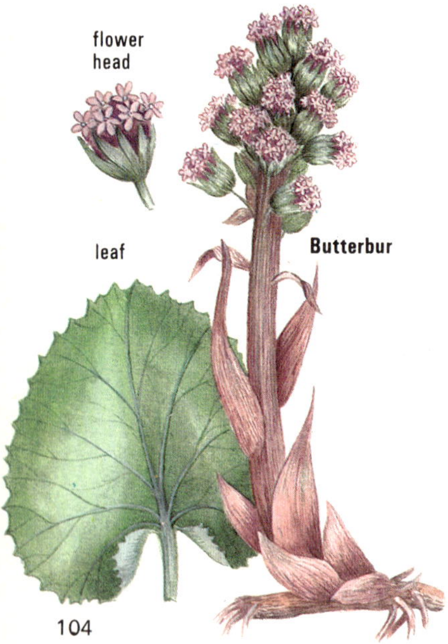

BUTTERBUR

Petasites hybridus

The rather short, large-leaved plants of Butterbur are found in damp places, often growing in masses. Flowering stems with broad bracts appear before the leaves.

Flower: pink or mauve; disc florets only; heads 3-12 mm; sepal-like bracts narrow, purplish.

Flower arrangement: heads in dense racemes.

Flowering time: March-May.

Leaf: 10-90 cm across, kidney-shaped, toothed, grey beneath, stalked.

Fruit: achene, with pappus.

Uses: the large leaves were used to wrap butter, hence the common name.

YARROW

Achillea millefolium

The stem is erect and 8-60 cm hign, with soft hairs. Yarrow grows in grass- and waste land and the narrow, ferny leaves may be found creeping through lawns. The plant looks Umbellifer-like, except that the flower stalks do not all join at one point. If crushed, the plant smells aromatic.

Flower: ray florets white or pink, 5; disc cream; head 4-6 mm across.

Flower arrangement: in flat-topped clusters.

Flowering time: June-August.

Leaf: very finely dissected, fern-like, alternate, 5-15 cm long, narrow; lower leaves stalked.

Fruit: achene, 2 mm, greyish.

MUGWORT

Artemisia vulgaris

The backs of the finely cut leaves are strikingly white, and the plant is faintly aromatic. The stem is 60-120 cm tall, erect and often red. It grows on roadsides and in waste places.

Flower: brownish-yellow; disc florets only in bell-shaped heads, 3-4 mm long; sepal-like bracts hairy.

Flower arrangement: branched raceme.

Flowering time: July-September.

Leaf: deeply dissected, segments toothed, main vein translucent, almost hairless above, densely white-hairy beneath.

Fruit: achene, about 1 mm.

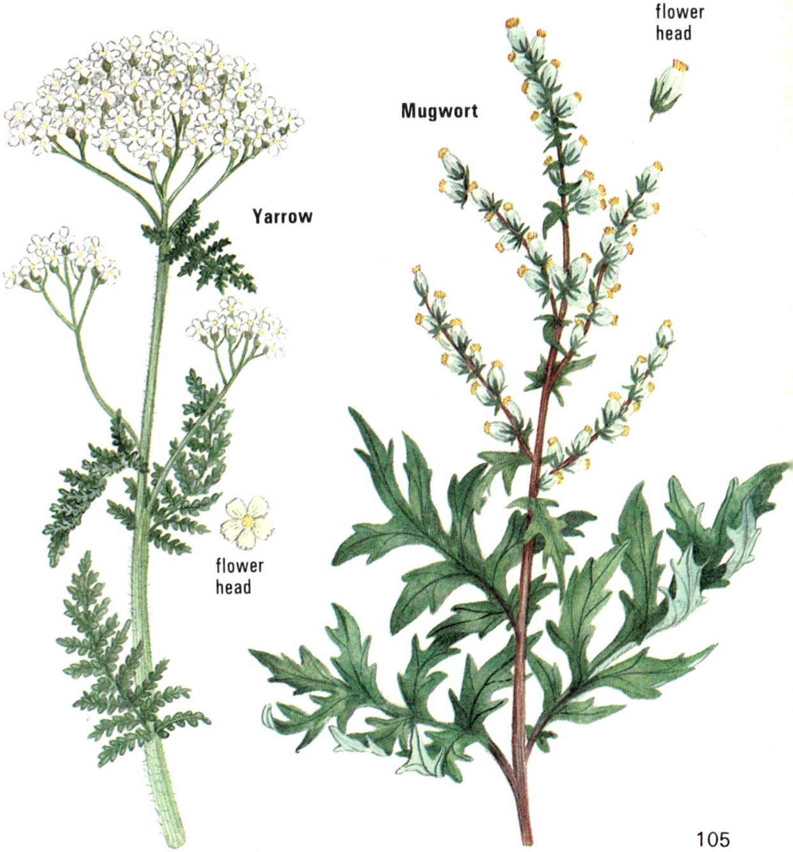

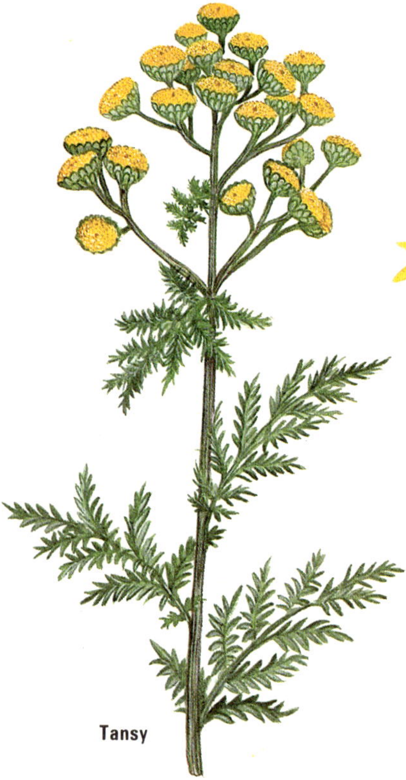

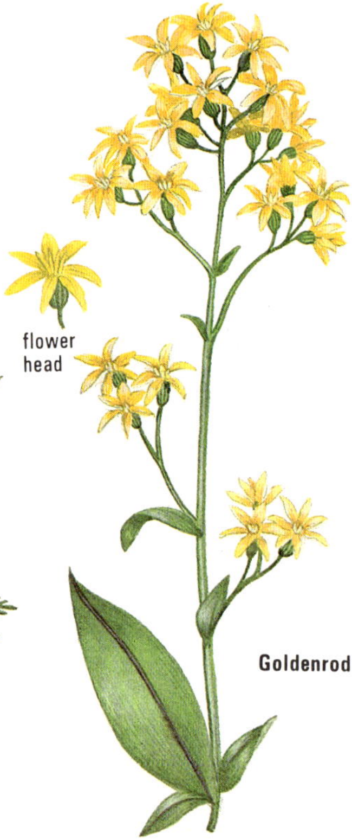

TANSY

Tanacetum vulgare

The flower-heads are like little yellow buttons clustered at the ends of stems 30-100 cm high. The plant is highly aromatic and grows in hedgerows and waste places. It is often found as an escape from gardens, where it has been grown for ornament and medicine.

Flower: orange-yellow; disc florets only; heads 7-12 mm across.

Flower arrangement: heads in flat-topped clusters.

Flowering time: July-September.

Leaf: ferny, divided into narrow, toothed segments, alternate, dark green, hairless, gland-dotted, 15-25 cm long.

Fruit: achene, 5-ribbed.

GOLDENROD

Solidago virgaurea

Goldenrod grows in woods, on heaths and in grassy places. The height of this erect plant varies widely, up to 100 cm in lowland areas and 5-20 cm in mountain forms. The garden Goldenrod (*S. canadensis*), which often escapes, has leaves with 3 main veins.

Flower: yellow; ray florets 6-12 surrounding disc florets; heads 6-10 mm across; sepal-like bracts with pale margins.

Flower arrangement: heads in branched clusters.

Flowering time: July-September.

Leaf: ovate or lanceolate, short-stalked, toothed, with 1 main vein.

Fruit: achene; pappus whitish.

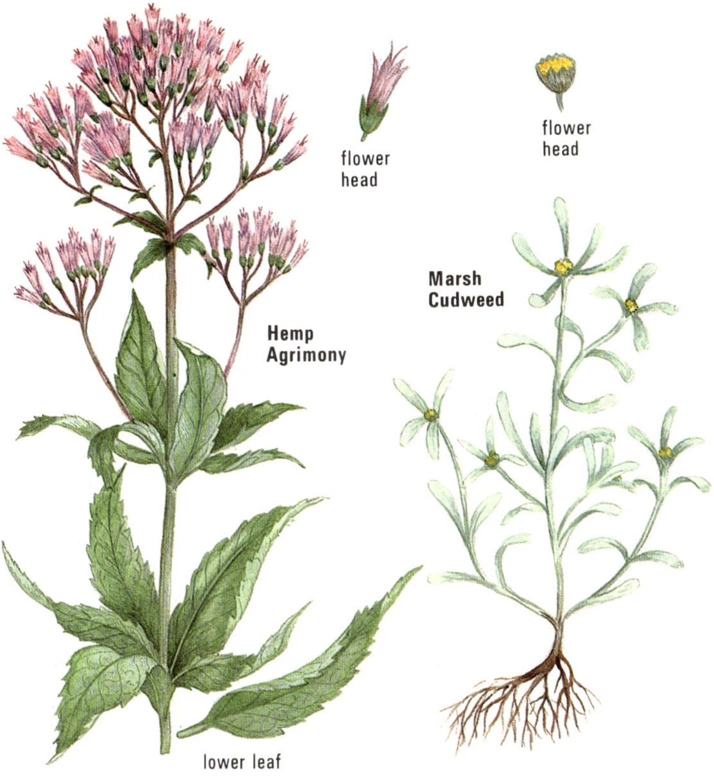

HEMP AGRIMONY

Eupatorium cannabinum

The tall plants grow 30-170 cm high in masses in damp places. The tiny pink flower-heads are gathered in fairly loose clusters.

Flower: pinkish; disc florets only; styles protruding; head of 5-6 florets, 2-5 mm across; sepal-like bracts purple-tipped.

Flower arrangement: heads in rather loose, domed clusters.

Flowering time: July-September.

Leaf: divided to base into 3-5 toothed segments, almost stalkless, opposite; upper leaves undivided.

Fruit: achene, black, with pappus.

Uses: tea made from the leaves was taken at the onset of influenza; also used as a purge.

MARSH CUDWEED

Gnaphalium uliginosum

The leaves and branched stems of this small plant are covered in white wool. It grows 4-20 cm high in damp places.

Flower: yellow; disc florets only; heads 3-4 mm across; sepal-like bracts brown, papery, pointed.

Flower arrangement: in dense, rounded clusters at the branch-tips, shorter than surrounding leaves.

Flowering time: July-August.

Leaf: white-woolly, narrow, tip rounded or pointed.

Fruit: achene, usually hairless, with pappus.

Uses: Cudweed boiled in water makes a gargle for sore throats.

MONOCOTYLEDONS

The following families are all *monocotyledons* – that is, they differ from the preceding dicotyledon families in their usually narrow leaves with parallel veins. The flower-parts are usually in threes, and there is a single rather than double seed leaf.

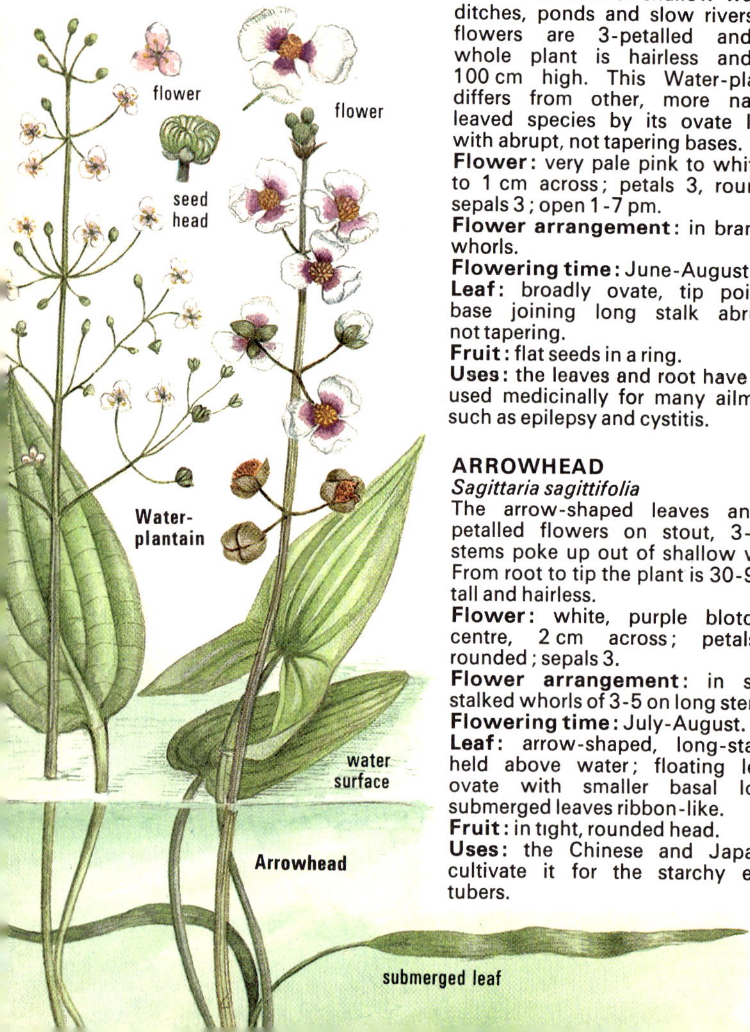

WATER-PLANTAIN FAMILY
Alismataceae

All the plants in this small family grow near or standing in fresh water. The flowers have 3 white or pink petals rarely lasting more than a day.

WATER-PLANTAIN
Alisma plantago-aquatica

This is a pretty plant which grows in the wet mud or shallow water of ditches, ponds and slow rivers. The flowers are 3-petalled and the whole plant is hairless and 20-100 cm high. This Water-plantain differs from other, more narrow-leaved species by its ovate leaves with abrupt, not tapering bases.

Flower: very pale pink to white, up to 1 cm across; petals 3, rounded; sepals 3; open 1-7 pm.
Flower arrangement: in branched whorls.
Flowering time: June-August.
Leaf: broadly ovate, tip pointed; base joining long stalk abruptly, not tapering.
Fruit: flat seeds in a ring.
Uses: the leaves and root have been used medicinally for many ailments, such as epilepsy and cystitis.

ARROWHEAD
Sagittaria sagittifolia

The arrow-shaped leaves and 3-petalled flowers on stout, 3-sided stems poke up out of shallow water. From root to tip the plant is 30-90 cm tall and hairless.

Flower: white, purple blotch at centre, 2 cm across; petals 3, rounded; sepals 3.
Flower arrangement: in short-stalked whorls of 3-5 on long stems.
Flowering time: July-August.
Leaf: arrow-shaped, long-stalked, held above water; floating leaves ovate with smaller basal lobes; submerged leaves ribbon-like.
Fruit: in tight, rounded head.
Uses: the Chinese and Japanese cultivate it for the starchy edible tubers.

FROG-BIT FAMILY
Hydrocharitaceae

Some members of this family grow partly or wholly submerged in fresh water, and some grow in the sea (rare in flowering plants). There are several unusual methods of pollination in the family. In the Tape-grasses (*Vallisneria*) the male flowers break off the submerged plant and float about on the water-surface until they meet and pollinate the long-stalked female flowers.

CANADIAN PONDWEED
Elodea canadensis

This waterweed has many little dark green leaves closely spaced up the long stems. It grows submerged in slow-moving fresh water. Male and female flowers are on separate plants, females flowering occasionally, males very rarely.
Flower: white, tinged pink, 5 mm across; petals 5.
Flower arrangement: solitary, floating, on long stalk.
Flowering time: May-October.
Leaf: dark green, translucent, lanceolate, tip pointed or rounded, in overlapping whorls of 3.
Uses: this plant is widely grown in aquaria for the large amounts of oxygen it produces and for the shelter it provides.

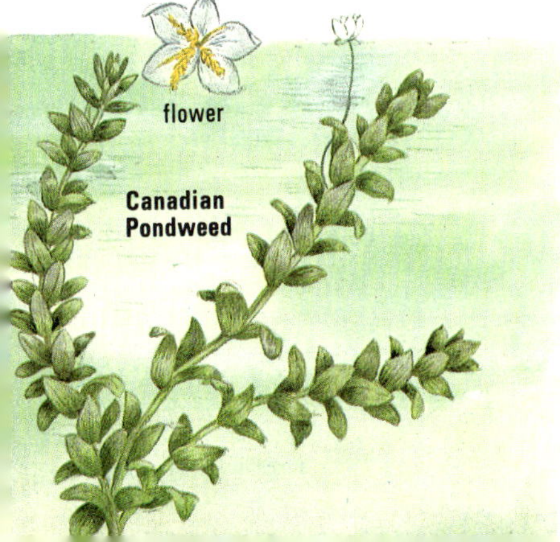

ARROW-GRASS FAMILY
Juncaginaceae

The small Arrow-grass family is made up of marsh plants. They are not grasses, but look grass-like, and grow in cold and temperate, often coastal, areas. The flowers are inconspicuous and wind-pollinated.

MARSH ARROW-GRASS
Triglochin palustris

This plant is not a grass despite the common name and grass-like leaves. It grows 15-50 cm high in marshes, often hidden among tall grasses. Marsh Arrow-grass is most common in Scandinavia, Scotland and N. England. A similar species of Arrow-grass (*T. maritima*) grows in salt-marsh at the coast.
Flower: green, edged with purple, tiny.
Flower arrangement: on long spike.
Flowering time: June-August.
Leaf: long, narrow, grass-like, fleshy, channelled towards base.
Fruit: narrow, opening from below by 3 valves.

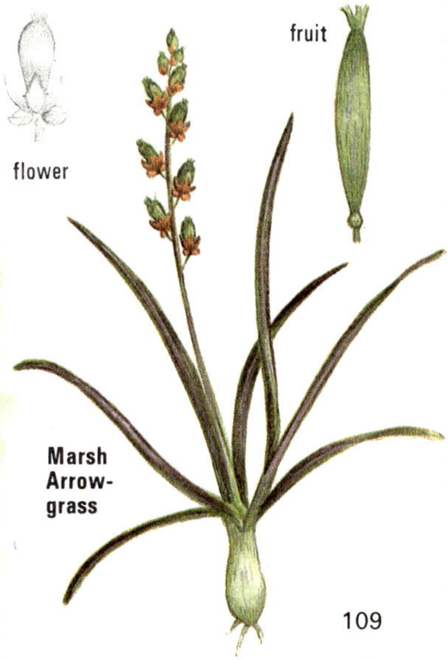

PONDWEED FAMILY
Potamogetonaceae

Most plants included in this world-wide family grow in fresh, some in brackish, water. Some species have broad, floating leaves while others are narrow-leaved and submerged.

BROAD-LEAVED PONDWEED
Potamogeton natans

Rooting in the mud of ponds and rivers, the stems of this Pondweed are up to 100 cm long and bear both broad, floating leaves and narrow, submerged ones. Although many of the Pondweed species are difficult to identify this one can be recognized by the bend, often with 2 tiny flaps, which occurs between the floating leaf-blade and its stalk.

Flower: green, inconspicuous, wind-pollinated.
Flower arrangement: in dense spike above water surface.
Flowering time: May-September.
Leaf: alternate; floating leaves elliptic, tip more or less pointed, stalked, slightly leathery; base of young leaves inrolled; submerged leaves narrow; stipules long.
Fruit: dark green, slightly flattened, dispersed by floating on water surface and eventually sinking.

LILY FAMILY
Liliaceae

This is one of the largest of the flowering plant families. Many members have bulbs as storage organs. Included in the family are onions, leeks and very many garden plants such as the many hybrid Tulips, and the Lilies. The flowers appear 6-petalled, having 3 true petals and 3 petal-like sepals.

LILY-OF-THE-VALLEY
Convallaria majalis

This little plant may sometimes be found escaped from gardens, where it is commonly grown. It is also native to Europe in woods, mostly on chalk or limestome. There is a pair of broad leaves at the base of the flowering stem.

Flower: white, sweet-scented, bell-shaped, nodding, 8 mm.
Flower arrangement: in raceme of 6-12 flowers, all directed one way.
Flowering time: May-June.
Leaf: broad, elliptic, stalked, hairless, in a pair; scales sheathing base of leaf-stalks and flowering stem.
Fruit: red berries.
Uses: the plant contains a heart drug close to that found in Foxgloves. It was used to revive gassed soldiers in World War I.

Broad-leaved Pondweed

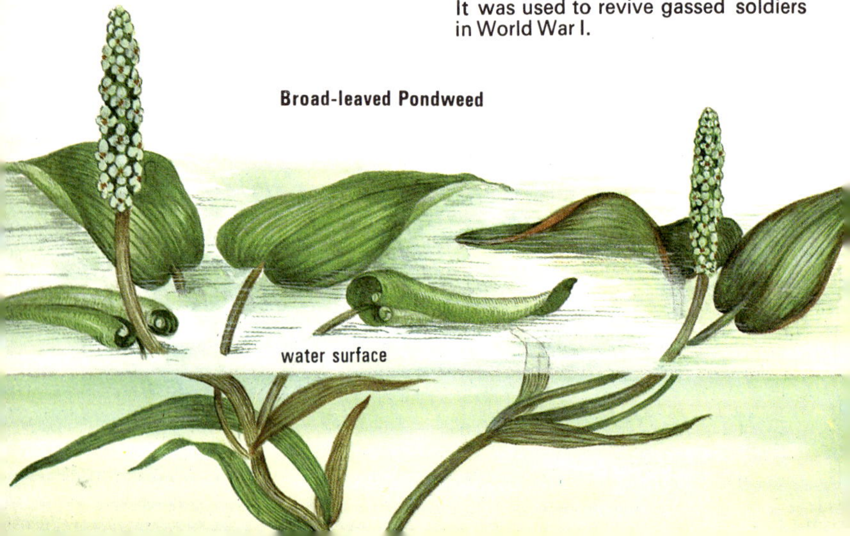

RAMSONS

Allium ursinum

Walkers through woods may notice the strong garlic smell before the plants themselves. Ramsons also grow in hedges. There is a small, narrow bulb at the base of the 3-angled stem. The leaves are broad and spring from the bulb.

Flower: white; petals 6, pointed; stamens 6.

Flower arrangement: 6-20 flowers in rounded umbel on unbranched, 3-angled stem 10-45 cm high.

Flowering time: April-June.

Leaf: broad-elliptic, tip pointed, stalked, hairless.

Fruit: 3-lobed, containing black seeds.

HERB PARIS

Paris quadrifolia

This strange-looking little plant can hardly be mistaken for any other, with its ring of 4 leaves near the top of the stem, just below the greeny-yellow flower. It grows 15-40 cm high in damp woods on chalk or limestone. *Paris* is a Latin word meaning equality and refers to the balance between the number of leaves and flower parts.

Flower: green-yellow; sepals petal-like, 4-6; petals thread-like, 4-6; stamens 8.

Flower arrangement: solitary, stalked.

Flowering time: May-August.

Leaf: in whorl of 4 or more, broadly ovate, tip pointed, short-stalked, hairless.

Fruit: black berry.

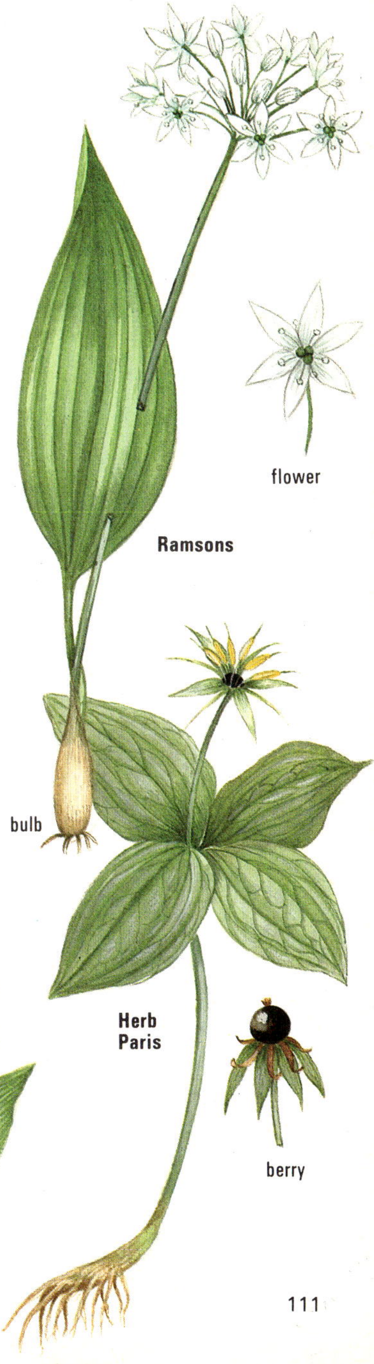

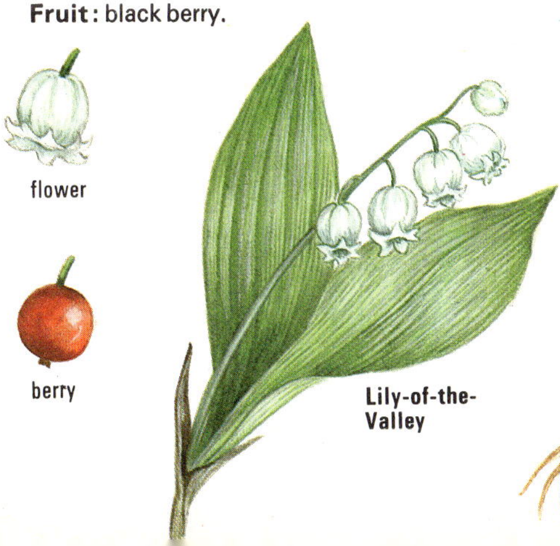

DAFFODIL FAMILY
Amaryllidaceae

This is an important family for garden plants, in particular the Narcissus and Daffodil, many of which are hybrids. The species are mainly from warm-temperate areas and the tropics.

SNOWDROP
Galanthus nivalis

Snowdrops are native to Central and S. Europe. In N. Europe they are commonly planted in gardens and widely naturalized in damp woods and hedges. There is a small bulb at the base of the plant, from which spring the leaves and flower stem.
Flower: white and green, bell-shaped, 14-17 mm long; outer petals 3, white; inner petals 3, shorter than outer, deeply notched, green-tipped and striped, forming tube; flower-sheath green.
Flower arrangement: solitary, nodding, on long stem.
Flowering time: January-March.
Leaf: linear, grey-green, keeled.
Fruit: capsule.

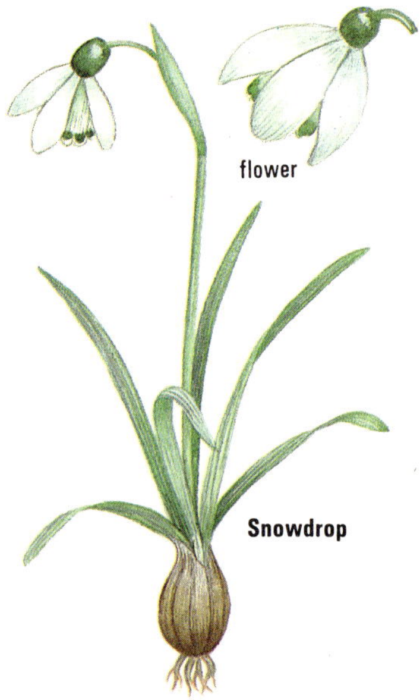

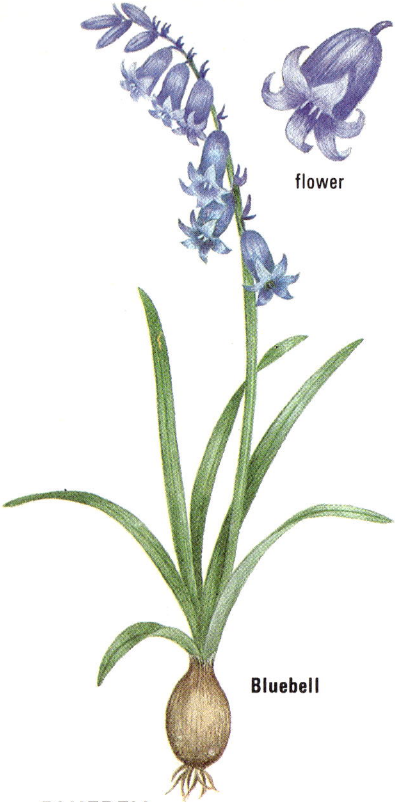

BLUEBELL
Hyacinthoides non-scripta

This species of Bluebell is native to the western, Atlantic part of Europe. It was not known to the ancient Greek recorders of plants, hence the species name of *non-scripta,* meaning 'not written upon'. The plant grows 20-50 cm high, often carpeting woods.
Flower: purplish blue, 1·5-2 cm long, bell-shaped; rim with 6 curled-back teeth; anthers cream; bracts paired, bluish.
Flower arrangement: raceme, drooping at tip; buds erect; open flowers nodding, all directed to one side of long stem.
Flowering time: April-June.
Leaf: long, narrow, all rising directly from bulb, keeled, shiny.
Fruit: about 15 mm.
Uses: a slimy glue can be obtained by scraping the bulbs.

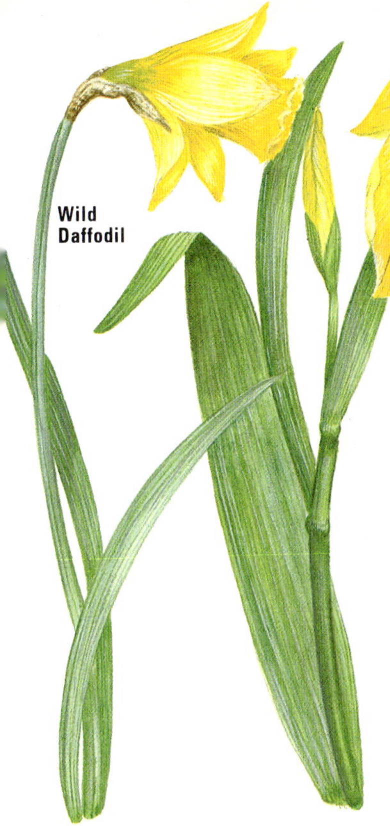

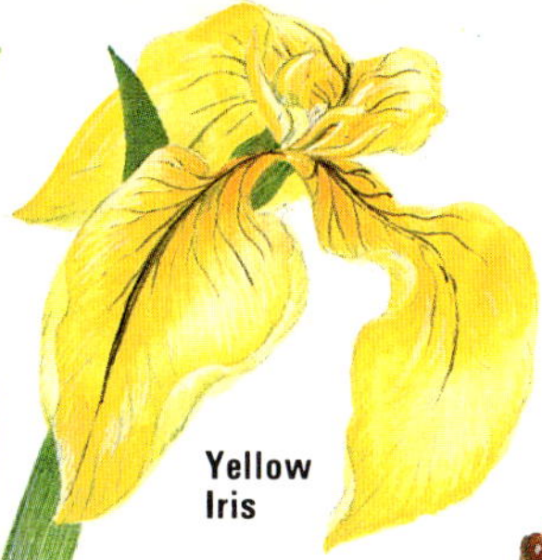

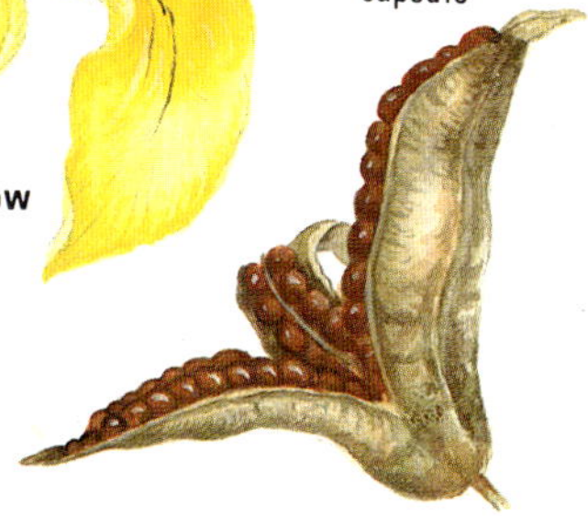

IRIS FAMILY
Iridaceae

Many of the plants in the Iris family are widely grown in gardens, such as Crocus, Gladiolus and Iris, of which there are many hybrids. The flowers appear 6-petalled, and the leaves often form a flattened fan-shape at the base. Storage organs mostly take the form of swollen underground stems.

WILD DAFFODIL
Narcissus pseudonarcissus

The Wild Daffodil is native in woods and grassland in N. Europe and naturalized in Scandinavia, Scotland and Ireland. The flower stem and leaves end in a bulb of 2-3 cm. The bulbs are poisonous and have been eaten in mistake for onions.
Flower: trumpet golden yellow, as long as or slightly shorter than surrounding 6 paler yellow petals, 3·5-6 cm long; flower-sheath brown, papery.
Flower arrangement: solitary, drooping, on flattened stalk 20-35 cm high.
Flowering time: February-April.
Leaf: linear, 12-35 cm long, grey-green.
Fruit: capsule.

YELLOW IRIS
Iris pseudacorus

The leaves and flower-stem are tall and stiff, growing 40-150 cm high in river or ditch margins, marshes or marshy woods. The thick rhizomes often arch up above the soil surface.
Flower: yellow, 8-10 cm across; outer petals 3, broad, drooping, often dark-veined; inner petals 3, erect; stigmas 3, petal-like, forked at tip.
Flower arrangement: 2-3 on long, flattened stem.
Flowering time: May-July.
Leaf: very long, narrow, blue-green, 1·5-2·5 cm across, midrib raised; together, leaves form a flattened fan-shape at base.
Fruit: capsule; seeds brown.
Uses: the rhizomes give a black dye and black ink.

ORCHID FAMILY
Orchidaceae

The beautiful flowers of this large family are cultivated commercially. They have 6 petal-like segments, the lowest, called the *lip*, often projecting as a nectar-filled spur behind. Pollen is often amassed into stalked pellets (*pollinia*) which stick to the insect visitor's body for transference to the next flower. The tiny seeds have no food store and need a fungus partner to start growth, the fungus often continuing to live in the root of the mature plant. Orchids, in particular, are not for picking, often being rare or sporadic.

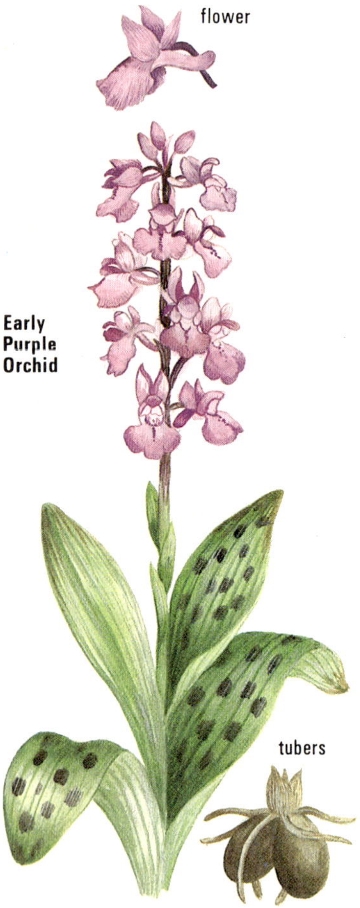

EARLY PURPLE ORCHID
Orchis mascula

These spring-flowering Orchids are found growing 15-60 cm high in woods and grassland. They often grow among Bluebells and Dog's Mercury. The lovely purple or mauve flowers have the unlovely smell of tom cats.

Flower: purple or mauve; lip pale with dark spots at top-centre, broad, 3-lobed; spur thick, blunt; bracts purple.

Flower arrangement: spike.

Flowering time: April-June.

Leaf: usually dark-spotted, alternate, slightly fleshy, oblong, tip shortly pointed or rounded; bases sheathing stem.

Fruit: capsule.

Uses: because of the twin tubers, looking like testicles, this orchid was used as an aphrodisiac. The name Orchid comes from the Greek for testicle.

COMMON SPOTTED ORCHID
Dactylorhiza fuchsii

This conspicuous Orchid is also one of the more common, and grows 15-50 cm high in damp or dry grassy places and open woods. Like many other Orchids, this one hybridizes readily with other species.

Flower: pale pink or whitish with dark red marks; segments each side of hood pointing up; lip broad, 3-lobed; middle lobe pointed, slightly longer than broader side lobes; spur 5·5-8·5 mm long; bracts equalling or longer than flowers.

Flower arrangement: dense spike.

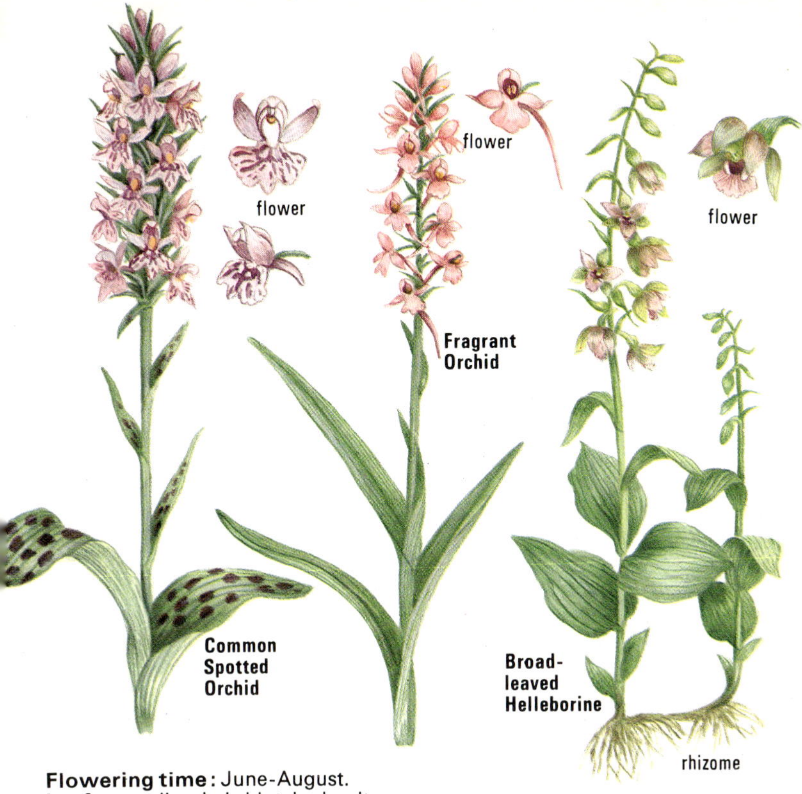

Flowering time: June-August.
Leaf: usually dark-blotched, alternate, slightly fleshy, bases sheathing stem; lower leaves broad-elliptic, tip rounded; upper leaves narrower.
Fruit: capsule.

FRAGRANT ORCHID

Gymnadenia conopsea

The scent of this Orchid is strongest in the evening, when it attracts pollinating moths. The spurs on the flowers are very narrow and long, as are the leaves. The stems grow 15-40 cm high in grassland and marshy ground, particularly on chalk or limestone.
Flower: pink-lilac; lip of 3 rounded lobes; spur 11-13 mm long, slender; bracts equalling flowers.
Flower arrangement: dense spike.
Flowering time: June-August.
Leaf: long, narrow, folded down midrib, tip more or less rounded, slightly fleshy; bases sheathing stem.
Fruit: capsule.

BROAD-LEAVED HELLEBORINE

Epipactis helleborine

There are up to 3, often tall stems, short-hairy at the top, to this Helleborine. They rise from a short length of underground stem and grow up to 80 cm high in hedge-banks and woods. This Orchid is rare in Scotland and N. Scandinavia. The cup-shaped lip of the flower holds nectar for visiting bees and wasps.
Flower: green to dull purplish, scentless; lip cup-shaped with narrow, turned-back tip; no spur; bracts almost equalling flowers.
Flower arrangement: loose spike of drooping flowers turned to one side.
Flowering time: July-October.
Leaf: alternate, broadly ovate, tip pointed, middle leaves longest, margins rough.
Fruit: capsule.

COMMON TWAYBLADE

Listera ovata

The common name refers to the 2 broad leaf-blades just below the middle of the stem. The stem is 20-60 cm high and hairy above the leaves. The plant grows in damp woods and grassland, particularly on limestone or chalk. A smaller species of Twayblade (*L. cordata*) can be found in pine woods and moorland.

Flower: yellow-green; lip oblong, furrowed down centre, forked at tip; no spur; bracts tiny.

Flower arrangement: long spike.

Flowering time: June-July.

Leaf: pair of very broad, ovate leaves, slightly fleshy; bases sheathing stem.

Fruit: capsule.

FROG ORCHID

Coeloglossum viride

This unassuming little green-flowered Orchid is often hard to spot in the grass of high land, where it usually grows. The stem is 6-25 cm high and often reddish above.

Flower: yellow-green, tinged with red-brown; upper segments in round hood; lip oblong, 3-toothed at tip; spur 2 mm long; bracts long.

Flower arrangement: spike.

Flowering time: June-August.

Leaf: alternate, slightly fleshy; bases sheathing stem; lower leaves broad, tip rounded; upper leaves narrow, tip pointed.

Fruit: capsule.

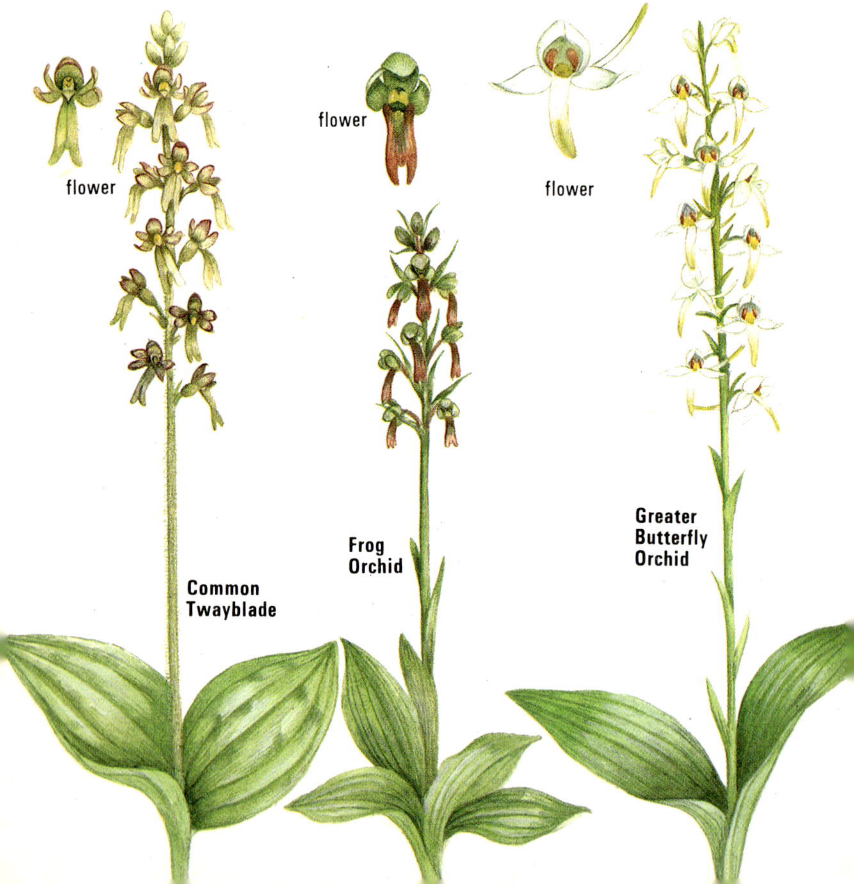

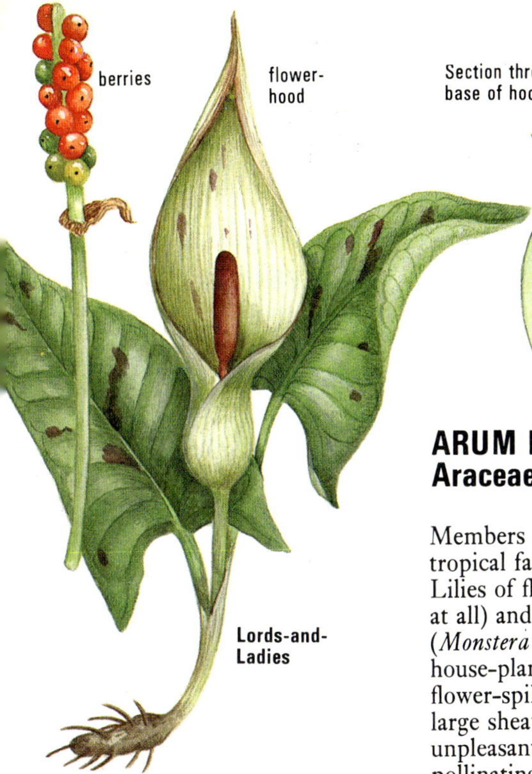

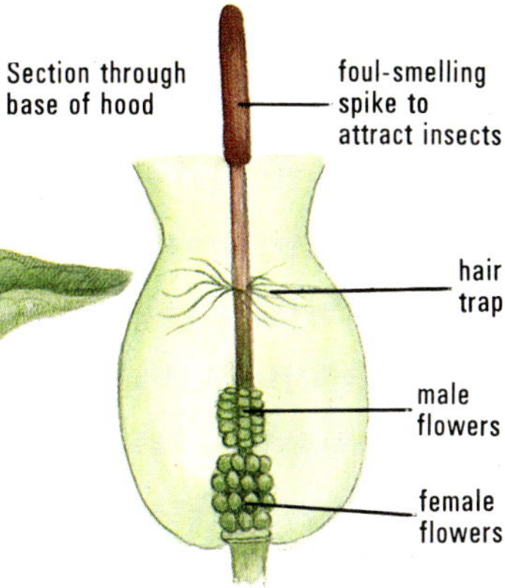

ARUM FAMILY
Araceae

Members of this large, mainly tropical family include Arum Lilies of florists' shops (not Lilies at all) and the Swiss Cheese Plant (*Monstera deliciosa*), a common house-plant. The poker-like flower-spike is surrounded by a large sheath; many exude unpleasant smells to attract pollinating flies.

GREATER BUTTERFLY ORCHID
Platanthera chlorantha

The pale, rather widely spaced flowers of this Orchid attract moths as pollinators by their clove-like evening scent. The plant grows 20-40 cm high in grassy and wooded areas, particularly on chalk. The less common Lesser Butterfly Orchid (*P. bifolia*) has smaller flowers.
Flowers: greeny white, 18-23 mm across; side segments long, narrow, spread out; lip long, narrow; unlobed; spur long, narrow, curved; bracts almost equalling flower stalks.
Flower arrangement: loose spike.
Flowering time: May-July.
Leaf: pair of elliptic leaves at stem-base; upper leaves much smaller, narrower, alternate, tips short-pointed, bases sheathing stem, slightly fleshy.
Fruit: capsule.

LORDS-AND-LADIES
Arum maculatum

The tiny flowers are hidden at the base of a purple, poker-shaped stalk, half-enclosed by a yellow-green hood. Midges are trapped in the base of the hood and pollinate the flowers. They later escape and effect cross-pollination by becoming trapped in other flower-hoods. The plants grow in shady hedges and woods.
Flower: tiny.
Flower arrangement: inside hood.
Flowering time: April-May.
Leaf: arrow-shaped, usually dark-blotched, shiny; stalks rising directly from roots.
Fruit: spike of orange berries.
Uses: the roots were a source of laundry starch, especially for ruffs in the 16-17th centuries. They were also thought to be aphrodisiac.

DUCKWEED FAMILY
Lemnaceae

The plants in this family are very small and made up of simple, leaf-like lobes which float on fresh water. Included in the family are species of Wolffia – the smallest known flowering plants.

DUCKWEED
Lemna minor

The tiny, round, leaf-like lobes of this plant spread on the surface of still water, often covering large areas. A single thread-like root hangs in the water from each plant. The plants normally reproduce by the budding of new lobes, and over-winter in the mud of pond- or ditch-bottoms.
Flower: minute (flowers fairly uncommon).
Flower arrangement: in pouch on lobe-surface.
Flowering time: June-July.
Leaf: leaf-like, rounded lobe, 1·5-4 mm across, almost flat, not swollen below.
Uses: eaten by water-fowl.

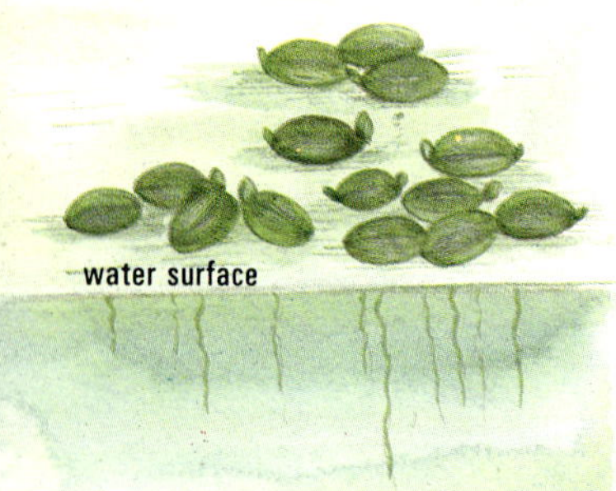

BUR-REED FAMILY
Sparganiaceae

Some plants in this small family float in fresh water, while others grow erect at the water-side. The tiny flowers are gathered into round heads on the same stem, male separate from female. Most species are found in temperate regions.

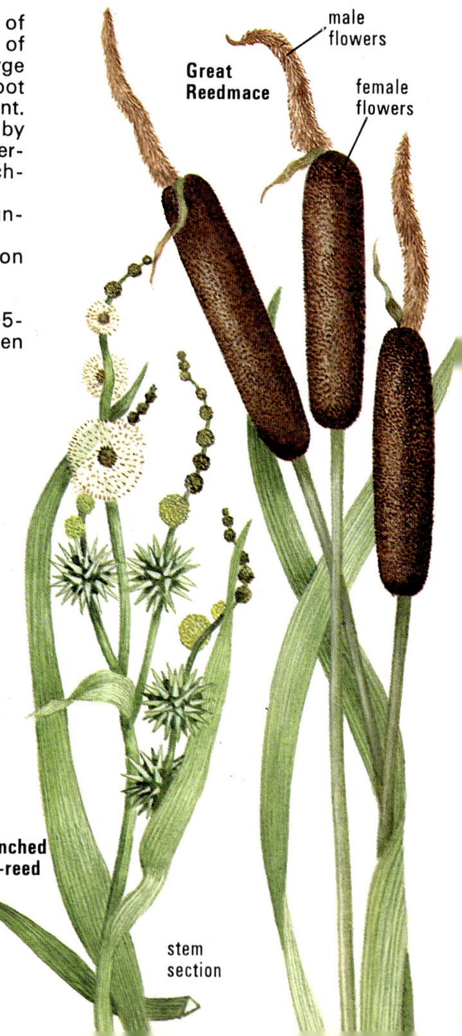

BRANCHED BUR-REED
Sparganium erectum
This is a stout, erect, hairless plant of 50-150 cm, growing at the edge of still or slow-moving fresh water. The long, stiff leaves look like Iris leaves except for the 3-angled bases. The less common Unbranched Bur-reed (*S. emersum*) has a single stem of flower-heads.
Flower: tiny, greenish, black-edged.
Flower arrangement: males and females in separate, round heads on branched, leafy stem (male above female).
Flowering time: June-August.
Leaf: long, narrow, 3-angled and sheathing stem at base.
Fruit: in bur-like head, each bearing spike.
Uses: stands of Bur-reed shelter wild-fowl, and the fruits provide food for them in winter.

REEDMACE FAMILY
Typhaceae

Most species in this small family are very tall and grow in shallow, fresh water. The tiny flowers form a long, dense club-shape. The plants are commonly known as 'Bulrushes'.

GREAT REEDMACE ('BULRUSH')
Typha latifolia
Great Reedmace is very tall (1·5-2·5 m), and grows in large stands in the shallows of still or slow-moving fresh water. It is often found growing with Reed (*Phragmites communis*), a tall water-side grass.
Flower: tiny, dark brown.
Flower arrangement: females in large, dense club-shape, continuous with thinner, paler male spike above (Lesser Reedmace, *T. angustifolia*, has a gap between).
Flowering time: June-July.
Leaf: very long, narrow, 10-18 mm wide, grey-green, rather leathery.
Fruit: wind-borne.
Uses: the leaves can be used for weaving and basketry.

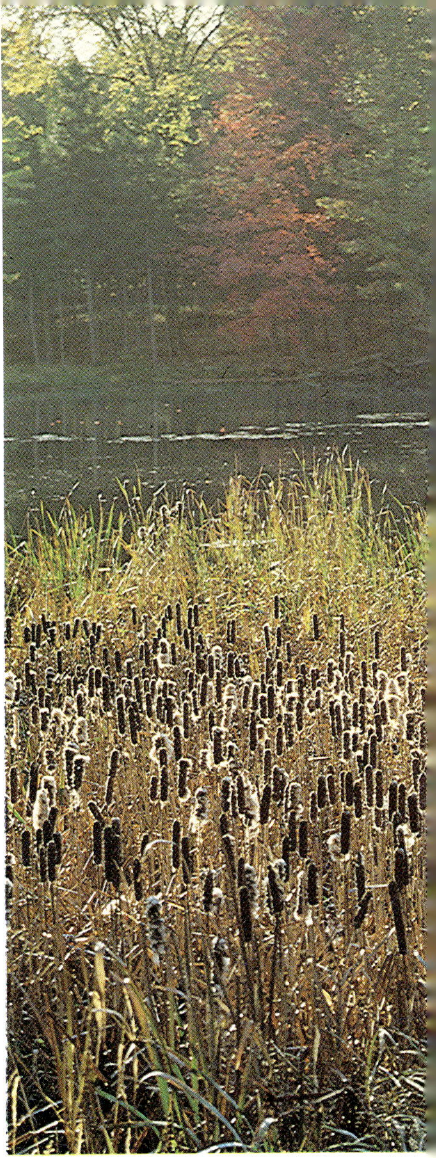

The Great Reedmace disperses its tiny seeds on the wind by means of a parachute of soft hairs. It stands erect, sometimes up to a height of 2·5 metres, at the margins of lakes. The imposing brown heads are popular with flower arrangers.

Glossary

achene: small, dry, 1-seeded fruit, not splitting when ripe.
aggregate: group of very closely related species.
anther: top part of stamen containing pollen.
axil: upper angle formed where leaf joins stem.
bract: small, leaf-like structure on, or at base of, flower stalk.
bracteole: minute bract.
calyx: the sepals as a whole.
capsule: dry fruit, splitting open to shed seeds.
carpel: a single female organ of flower.
compound leaf: leaf made up of several leaflets.
compound umbel: umbel, itself made up of umbels.
cyme: flower cluster in which each growing point ends in a flower, the oldest flowers being at the top or centre of the cluster.
elliptic: oval with narrowed ends.

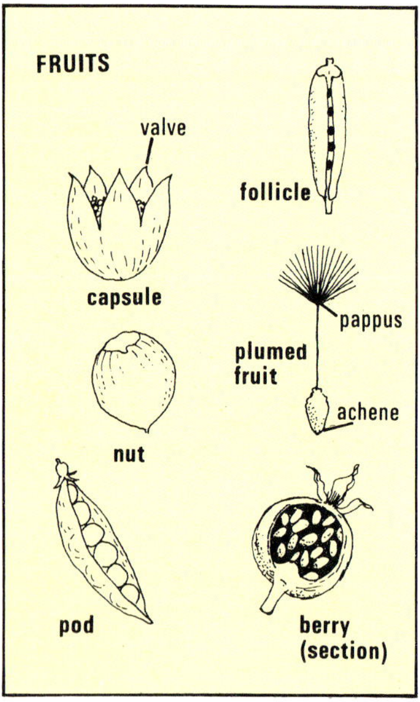

entire: untoothed (leaf margin).
fertilization: joining of male and female sex cells resulting in seed formation.
floret: small flower making up flower-head in Daisy family; *ray florets* have a strap-shaped petal, *disc florets* do not.
follicle: dry fruit, splitting down one side when ripe.
glands: tiny, disc-shaped structures on plant containing oil or resin; they may be stalked and called *glandular hairs*.
glaucous: with pale bloom, as on grapes.
habitat: surroundings in which a plant grows.
herb: any flowering plant without a woody stem.
hybrid: plant produced by one species interbreeding with another.
insectivorous: trapping and digesting insects.
keel: boat-shaped fold in leaf or petal.
lanceolate: narrowly ovate.
latex: milky sap.
linear: strap-shaped.
lip: group of petals divided from rest and more or less joined.
lobed: describing leaves or other plant parts that are deeply indented.
mealy: pale-powdery.
naturalized: describing a foreign plant that has been introduced and established.
nectary: gland in a flower which produces sugary fluid (*nectar*) to attract insect visitors.
nut: woody, 1-seeded fruit, not opening when ripe; a *nutlet* is a tiny nut.
ochrea: papery sheath surrounding stem and base of leaf stalk.
ovate: egg-shaped in outline.
ovoid: egg-shaped (3-D).
palmate: describing a leaf made up of lobes radiating from central point.
pappus: tuft of hairs on fruits in Daisy family.
pinnate: describing a leaf made up of leaflets in 2 rows along common stalk; *double-pinnate* etc describes leaflets that are themselves pinnate.
pollination: process by which pollen is carried from male to female part of flower.

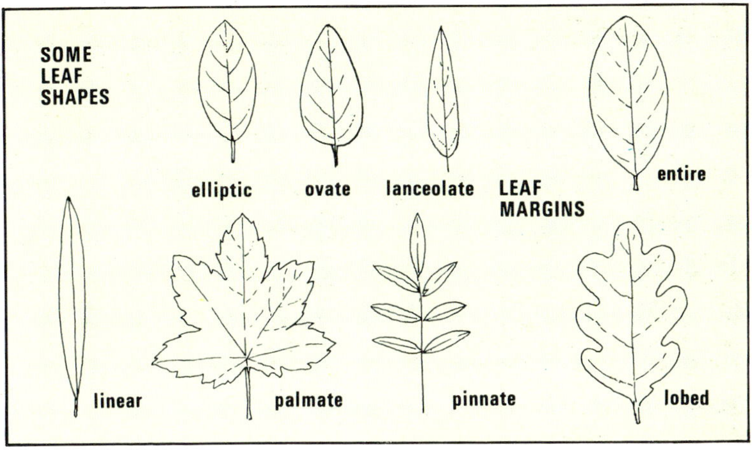

prostrate: lying along ground.
raceme: cylindrical head of stalked flowers.
ray: spoke-like stalks within umbels.
rosette: ring of leaves at stem-base.
runner: long, creeping stem, rooting and forming new plants.
scrub: area covered mainly by shrubs.
sepal: usually green, leaf-like part of flower, in ring beneath petals, enclosing flower in bud.
simple: undivided.
spike: cylindrical head of unstalked flowers.
spur: hollow, usually cone-shaped projection at base of a petal.
stamen: male part of flower made up of pollen-producing anther on stalk.
stigma: tip of female part of flower which receives the pollen.
stipule: small, scale-like structure at base of leaf-stalk.
style: stalk of stigma leading to ovary.
tendril: spiral, thread-like structure on stem or leaf for climbing.
tuber: part of stem or root used for food storage, lasting 1 year.
umbel: umbrella-shaped flower-head in which equal flower-stalks arise from same point on stem.
umbellifier: plant in the Carrot family.
valve: one of the pieces a capsule breaks into on ripening.
whorl: leaves or flowers arranged around stem in a ring.

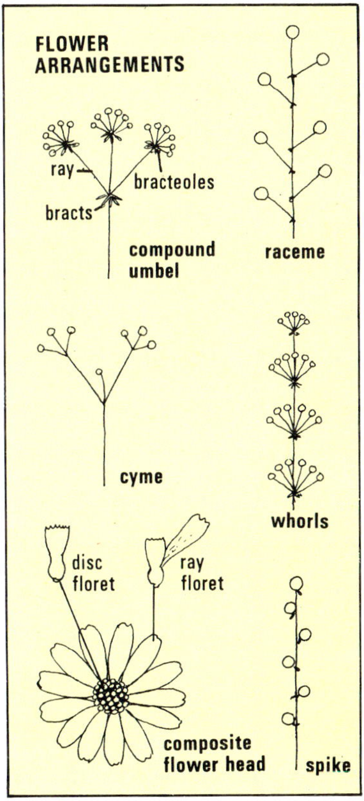

Index

Wild Flowers (English Names)

Wild Flowers (Scientific Names)

ACKNOWLEDGMENTS

The author and publishers wish to thank the following for their kind help in supplying photographs for this book:

A-Z Collection 19, 25, 61, 66; Heather Angel 8, 10 centre and bottom, 28, 39, 45, 69, 119; P. Morris 39 left, 53; NHPA 10 top (Hugh Newman), 12 (Stephen Dalton), 8 inset (R. G. Argent), 16 (G. M. Bain) 44, 104 (E. A. Janes), 67 (M. Savonius).

Picture research by Tracy Rawlings.